P9-EDQ-681

African Literature,
African Critics

Recent Titles in
Contributions in Afro-American and African Studies
Series Advisers: John W. Blassingame and Henry Louis Gates, Jr.

African Literature, African Critics

THE FORMING OF CRITICAL STANDARDS, 1947-1966

Rand Bishop

CONTRIBUTIONS IN AFRO-AMERICAN AND
AFRICAN STUDIES,
NUMBER 115

Greenwood Press
NEW YORK • WESTPORT, CONNECTICUT • LONDON

Library of Congress Cataloging-in-Publication Data

Bishop, Rand.
  African literature, African critics : the forming of critical
  standards, 1947-1966 / Rand Bishop.
      p. cm. -- (Contributions in Afro-American and African
  studies, ISSN 0069-9624 ; no. 115)
  Bibliography: p.
  Includes index.
  ISBN 0-313-25918-6 (lib. bdg. : alk. paper)
  1. African literature (English)--History and criticism--Theory,
etc. 2. African literature (French)--History and criticism--Theory,
etc. 3. Criticism--Africa--History--20th century. 4. Literature
and society--Africa--History--20th century. 5. Canon (Literature)
I. Title. II. Series.
  PR9340.B5 1988   7/978   87-36091
  820'.9'96--dc19

British Library Cataloguing in Publication Data is available.

Library of Congress Catalog Card Number: 87-36091
ISBN: 0-313-25918-6
ISSN: 0069-9624

First published in 1988

Greenwood Press, Inc.
88 Post Road West, Westport, Connecticut 06881

Printed in the United States of America

The paper used in this book complies with the
Permanent Paper Standard issued by the National
Information Standards Organization (Z39.48-1984).

10 9 8 7 6 5 4 3 2 1

Copyright Acknowledgments

A part of Chapter 3 appeared originally as "African Literature for Whom? The Janus-like Function of African Literary Criticism" in *Présence africaine* 101-102 (1977), 57-80. A section of Chapter 4 appeared originally as "African Critics and the Western Literary Tradition" in *Ba Shiru* 8.1 (1977), 65-75. I am grateful to the editors of *Présence africaine* (Paris) and *Ba Shiru*, respectively, for permission to use these materials here.

I am also grateful to the following parties for permission to quote as follows:

Présence africaine (Paris), for quotations from Mohamadou Kane, "The African Writer and His Public," *Présence africaine* 58 (Eng. ed. vol. 30) (1966), 10-32; and for lines from Birago Diop's poem, "Souffles," in *Leurres et lueurs* (Paris: Présence africaine, 1960, pp. 64-66;

Ibadan University Press, for quotations from Ezekiel Mphahlele, "A Reply," in *African Literature and the Universities*, ed. Gerald Moore (Ibadan: Ibadan University Press, 1965), pp. 22-26; and for quotations from Ben Obumselu, "The Background of Modern African Literature," *Ibadan* 22 (June 1966), 46-59;

Longman, for quotations from Lewis Nkosi, *Home and Exile* (London: Longman, 1965);

The Organisers of the Report on the Proceedings of the First International Congress of Africanists, and Northwestern University Press, for quotations from Ezekiel Mphahlele, "African Literature" in *The Proceedings of the First International Congress of Africanists*, eds. Lalage Bown and Michael Crowder (London: Longman; and Evanston: Northwestern University Press, 1964), pp. 220-232;

Optima, for quotations from Leopold Sedar Senghor, "Negritude: A Humanism of the 20th Century," trans. Clive Wake, *Optima* 16.1 (March 1966), 1-8;

Literature East & West, for quotations from Austin J. Shelton, "Critical Criteria for the Study of African Literature," *Literature East & West* 12 (1968), 1-21;

Macmillan Publishing Co., and Routledge & Kegan Paul, for quotations from Paul Bohannon, "Artist and Critic in an African Society," in *The Artist in Tribal Society*, ed. Marian W. Smith (Glencoe, Ill.: Free Press, 1961), pp. 85-94;

African Forum, for quotations from Wole Soyinka, "And After the Narcissist?" *African Forum* 1.4 (Spring 1966), 53-64;

Editions du Seuil, for quotations from Leopold Sedar Senghor, *Liberté I: Négritude et Humanisme* (Paris: Editions du Seuil, 1964). © Editions du Seuil, 1964.

Every reasonable effort has been made to trace the owners of copyright materials in this book, but in some instances this has proven impossible. The publishers will be glad to receive information leading to more complete acknowledgments in subsequent printings of the book, and in the meantime extend their apologies for any omissions.

For Myra Lu and David, with love

Contents

Preface

This study is the outgrowth of a lifelong interest in literature, coupled with a longstanding interest in Africa as a result of traveling and having lived and taught for three years in that continent. More specifically it is an outgrowth of the volatile, ongoing dialogue between African and non-African critics concerning the evaluation of modern African literature during the two decades following World War II. Wherever scholars have gathered to discuss modern African literature, the question of critical standards invariably has been raised: By what standards is African literature to be judged?

For a long time, this debate was academic, acrimonious, and for me unsatisfying. Then one day, in one of those lucid moments that come all too seldom, it occurred to me that there was no need to approach the question academically, for Africans had in fact been evaluating their literature for years. And if they had been doing so, it would perhaps be more productive—and surely less contentious—to analyze the nature of the criticism already written rather than theorize about what the criticism should be. In other words, Africans had for several years been answering the question of how their literature should be evaluated—by virtue of evaluating it. And therefore the means of answering the question was not theoretical; it was *empirical*.

This, then, is the study of how Africans in black, Sub-Saharan Africa came to evaluate African literature in English and French during its extraordinary growth from the close of World War II to the opening of the First World Festival of Negro Arts in Dakar in 1966. It is a study of the critical standards that emerged in those exuberant years.

It should be noted that no judgment is offered of the standards that were formed in this first generation, nor of any of the individual evaluations cited. The purpose here has been to discover what was being said; judgment is left to those more certain of what the critics should have said.

I should also emphasize that my concern here has been with the first generation of African critics; a study of the criticism after 1966—which has increased geometrically—will require a much more ambitious undertaking.

During the researching and writing of this study I received generous, un-
flagging support from many people—notably Alfred Opubor, Georges Joyaux,
Eugene deBenko, and the late Irvine Richardson, all of Michigan State University; the members of my family, my parents, my son, Andrew; Teresa
Wilkes, for tireless typing and insightful criticism; and Henry Louis Gates,
Jr., of Cornell University, who so kindly encouraged the work in its later
stages. I appreciate also the time and wherewithal afforded by a sabbatical
leave from the State University of New York to complete this study.

Without such generous assistance from so many sources, this material
might still be scattered in hundreds of separate places, and we might still be
arguing over how Africans *should* evaluate their literature. I hope this study
lays that question peacefully to rest.

Many of the sources I have cited appeared originally in French. This will
be apparent from the titles in the Bibliography, but they are also indicated
by an asterisk after the page references in the text. The translations are mine.

The shortcomings of the study—and the translations—and any errors of
commission or omission are, of course, my own responsibility—the result
of those less lucid times that, alas, are too much with us.

R. B.

Oswego, New York

African Literature,
African Critics

1 Introduction

BACKGROUND

When modern African literature began to mushroom in the years between World War II and the First World Festival of Negro Arts in 1966, it led critics the world over—African and non-African alike—to raise questions seldom asked, for the growth of African literature brought an entirely new and unique entity into the already existing world family of literatures. How and where did this new phenomenon fit into the literary scheme of things? How—by what standards—was it to be judged?

One of the first Western critics to address this question was Robert P. Armstrong, then of Northwestern University, in a paper entitled "African Literature and European Critics" given at the seventh annual meeting of the African Studies Association in Chicago in 1964. Professor Armstrong noted at the outset of his paper that one's critical approach to this literature would in part be determined by whether the critic thought of African literature as an entity in itself or as an extension of European literature. He quoted Jean-Paul Sartre's essay, "Black Orpheus," in defense of his belief in an African literature and also disagreed with the position that African literature was European by virtue of its being written in European languages. He said:

> It makes considerable sense to assert, as Sartre suggests, that a literature exists when the unique perceptions and experiences of a people begin to take literary shape, to demand their own modifications of form, to assert themselves in their own metaphor, regardless of what language they may or may not share in common. Metaphor, symbol, situation—these, not words, are the items in the lexicon of literature. (3)

Professor Armstrong said further that the definition of a literature would depend upon "domicile, perception and experience—but subject matter not at all" (3). He concluded his paper saying,

> What is required is a frank admission on the part of the critics that we are here working with a new literature that will shape its own forms, dictate its own diction, express its own values. What is needed, both from here [the West] and from Africa is a determined exploration, by the most highly trained people, of the nature of this new literature. (11)

This call by Professor Armstrong for more knowledge of "the nature of this new literature" is part of the rationale behind this study.

Another European critic, Lilyan Lagneau-Kesteloot, also took up the question of critical evaluation in 1964. At a conference of African poets held in Berlin, she is reported to have chided the Africans for being too imitative of European writers and for not being African enough. Richard Rive, a South African writer, replied:

> To expect a literature that is essentially African, which is unique in its Africanness, is to deny the many differences in the African experience, the many and varied factors at work from which the true poet assimilates the best and fashions it as an instrument of his own. ("African Poets," 67)

In another essay, however, Lagneau-Kesteloot said that whereas she would defer to the African critic entirely in matters concerning traditional literature (41), there is a role the Western critic could play:

> One must never, of course, try to influence the actual ideas of a writer, only to make him feel that he is entitled to put down everything he has in his mind. And his mind is never completely turned against his traditional culture!
>
> In such cases the critic acts as a sort of cultural psycho-analyst. His task is to restore confidence to the victim of the cultural anxiety, brought on by a colonial education. (40)

In the same essay, Lagneau-Kesteloot suggested three criteria "of almost certain value" by which a Western critic might judge African fiction: plot, characterization, and "whether the problems dealt with are genuine ones." As for the third category, Lagneau-Kesteloot said, "But to determine what is genuine one must, of course, be familiar with African society" (38). Unfortunately, she did not explain how she arrived at her three criteria. Were they her own? Were they, supposedly, universal?

At the Conference on African Literature and the University Curriculum held in Dakar in March 1963, Dorothy Blair of South Africa was also concerned with the proper approach to African literature. She took the position that

> obviously I can apply only the canons of aesthetics to which I am ac-
> customed by reason of my philological studies, or indeed of my Euro-
> pean cultural roots. May that not be held against me! Personally, I
> can't see any harm in this provided that one accepts . . . a certain uni-
> versality of aesthetics, based on truth, or rather on certain truths that
> are applicable to *any* culture, those truths that certain writers have de-
> fined here in the recent few days. (76)

One of these "truths," according to Blair, was "the love of suffering humanity." It was this love that she said she appreciated in the work of Aimé
Césaire, "this love that lends the depth of emotion to his work. For the
understanding of suffering is universal" (77).

Blair's "universal aesthetic" failed, however, to come to terms with Lagneau-Kesteloot's insistence on a familiarity with African society. Blair's
concept was laudable enough, yet it seems facile. While she may appreciate
the "love" and the "depth of emotion" in Césaire, it would seem that it is
the "striking expression" of them that brings them to her attention in the
first place. Any "True Romance" magazine would seem to have "love" and
"depth of emotion" in abundance; the "striking expression" of them is
what is missing in inferior literature. Blair did not tell us enough about what
her term meant. She seemed most reasonable when holding to the idea that
her own aesthetic—universal or no—was the only one she could employ.

In the introduction to his *New Approaches to African Literature*, J. A.
Ramsaran, a Caribbean critic, was aware of his shortcomings as a critic of
African literature but took the position that his dual grounding in European
and Oriental literature rendered him somehow neutral in his judgment of
African literature. Speaking of himself in the third person, he said:

> He is therefore aware that although he can satisfy neither the African
> nor the European critic, in this very fact lies his hope that he will be
> saved from the pitfall of trying to impose rigid criteria from any one
> particular culture upon African literature, which is compounded of
> many simples and must evolve its own standards of judgment in fields
> where they are undefined, uncertain or non-existent. (3-4)

Edgar Wright, a Canadian critic, agreed with Ramsaran that Africa must
evolve its own standards of judgment but then retreated from this position,
saying, "Yet it is difficult to avoid the conclusion that a literature in English
must also take its place in the total body of such literature," and further
that "the only point at issue is whether the wave of African writing is in some
way a literature of an essentially different order, not to be subject to the

same standards as, say, American or Jamaican or Indian-English literature, as part of a world literature in English ("African Literature," 108)." However, Wright failed to establish the cohesiveness of a "world literature in English," while implying at the same time that African literature in English would be somehow closer to the tradition of English literature than it would be to African literature in French—a hypothesis African writers and critics would probably be quick to reject, their disagreements over Negritude and other issues notwithstanding. Yet in all fairness Wright planted in the same article one of the seeds that led to this study:

> It is likely that some standards of comparison [evaluation] will emerge from within [Africa] as sufficient books appear to make comparison inevitable. This development will be hastened as the amount of objective, non-racial and non-political *criticism by Africans* (at the moment very small) increases. (107) (my italics)

The analysis of "criticism by Africans" is the purpose of this study.

Wright tended to mitigate this position as well, however, by suggesting that some criticism by Africans would be more valid than others and by positing something resembling Blair's defense of the "universal aesthetic." Wright said, "The two levels [of critical standards], 'local' and 'universal', need not necessarily conflict with each other. What is necessary is that the local standard, while encouraging its own ideas, is at the same time responsive to the basic principles and standards" (108). It is not clear exactly what these "basic principles and standards" were, but one assumes they were those of the traditions of English and Western literature. It is interesting here to note the African response to this Western insistence of Wright that the African aesthetic adjust itself to the "universal."

As might be expected, the Africans argued that it was the "universal" that must adjust itself to Africa. The retort of Malagasay poet Jacques Rabemananjara was that

> in so far as the African is authentically African, he automatically attains the universal. When you [the West] speak of universal one gets the impression of opposition between universal and African because for centuries the notion of "universal" was monopolized by the West. But we say to you, a universal form from which we were absent was truncated and we do not accept it. ("The Negro Theatre," 351)

As for Leopold Senghor, poet and past president of Senegal, the concept of a "Civilization of the Universal" was a cherished ideal, though it was not perhaps the same concept that Western critics had in mind when they spoke of a "basic" or "universal" value. Senghor said:

For if European civilisation were to be imposed, unmodified, on all Peoples and Continents, it could only be by force. That is its first disadvantage. A more serious one is that it would not be *humanistic*, for it would cut itself off from the contemporary values of the greater part of humanity. As I have said elsewhere, it would be a universal civilisation; it would not be the Civilisation of the Universal. ("What Is Negritude?" 1211)

John F. Povey was one of the few Western critics who stated openly his belief that African literature is subject to the canons of Western literary criticism. He gave at least two reasons for his argument. First, the African writer writes primarily for an international, not an African, audience; Povey said, "The question of intended audience seems to me fundamental as a basis for our decision as to the proper quality of our critical judgment" ("Canons," 81). Second, African poets such as J. P. Clark are influenced as much by European as by African tradition: "We are forced to consider the demonstrable fact that Clark is drawing upon the whole tradition of twentieth century poetry in English" (86). Povey added, "It soon becomes clear, I think, as one reads the poems of Clark that the African information is not, at the obvious level, a very significant part of the problem in making a sensitive and just evaluation" (87).

The argument of an international audience seems tenuous, resting as it does on the African reliance upon European publishers, on passing comments by authors, and the undignified approach that would determine critical canons from sales. It will become clear in Chapter 3 that a sizable number of African critics felt that writing for an international audience led not infrequently to—by this standard—bad African literature.

As for the African writer's use of Western literary tradition, this was, I think, Povey's strongest argument. In order to make this argument, however, he had to downplay the African elements of the literature—a spurious, if not dangerous, gutting of its ethnological aspects, to the benefit of its universal elements. For example, Povey said of J. P. Clark's poem "Abiku,"

It is not necessary that we know the precise motivation for his [Clark's] mood nor, though this is more dangerous an assertion, it may not be necessary for us to even know the significance of "Abiku"—"child of the spirits." It is not even required that we learn much of the apparently urgent desire for the child in the African social context—the shame and horror that extends to a barren wife—a theme that Clark has argued dramatically in his play Song of a Goat. Rather in tone and theme this poem is universal. (89)

Povey concluded that "this African poem is humane and familiar and because of this its feeling is available to all who read it sympathetically" (89).

The argument was further weakened in that, while it may apply to the poems of J. P. Clark, Christopher Okigbo, and others, it clearly had to be modified, if not abandoned, when considering authors less influenced by the West. Moreover, it required a prejudgment to be made in each case. It ran the further risk of judging those African works as best that resemble Western literature most.

Donald Stuart was another Western critic who considered the matter. After stating that "it is a blunt reality that African countries are free to choose their circles of influence," he added that the Western critics "are not relieved of the duty to criticize. We have a responsibility to praise those books which seem to us to present Africa intelligibly, even if we can't say how faithfully; and, still more, those books which suddenly show us our common humanity" (114). Again, this is the Western critic's tendency to shun the African dimension, no doubt out of an honest appraisal of his or her own shortcomings, and to take refuge in the "universal." And one may ask, finally, "Why not?" Can the literary critic be expected to double as anthropologist?

In answer to that question, Austin J. Shelton, an American anthropologist, took issue with another opinion on the subject put forth by Anthony Astrachan. Shelton quoted Astrachan as saying:

> If a novel gives me a society and invididuals with manners, good or bad, that is enough. I may be able to provide more profound insights into Nigerian novels as I learn more about the world out of which they were written, but I can still make valid criticisms of the novels—of the world within the novel without knowing too much about Nigeria or Africa. All I have to do is read the book. (7)

Shelton responded,

> One fundamental mistake inherent in this attitude, as well as its basically self-centered injustice, is the failure to distinguish between the casual reader and the serious student of African literature. How does one know if the manners are *good* or *bad*? What is *knowing too much* about Nigeria or Africa? The casual reader might pick up a work of African literature and read it for its effect upon him as he reacts to it according to his own system of values. Any "valid criticism" which he might make certainly cannot be put to an objective test, but rather will depend upon what he construes as the "world within the novel"—that is, his "valid criticism" will depend upon his subjective and uninformed response to the work as he experiences it without reference to any other information. But this is not what the reader does, even casually, in his reading of European literature. As a European, he brings to that other literary experience a whole life of information and awareness of the

values of European culture in general. When he reads the European work, he depends for his understanding not solely upon the so-called "world within the novel," but understands that "world" in terms of all the knowledge and values of the actual world in which it occurs. Thus, such an attitude about the reading of African literature can give only short shrift to that literature. (7)

Along with Lagneau-Kesteloot, then, Shelton advocated more knowledge of Africa, not less, and discouraged a retreat into "universals" or the formalism of the New Criticism. Of the latter he said,

The formal approach of the New Criticism (which no longer is very "new"), emphasizing the search for the unifying principle in the work itself, the study of the text to ascertain the way the parts are interstructured to form a unique organism, supposedly to lead to a total experience of the literary work by its very nature is either ethnocentric (one will exercise value judgments from his own culture) or it requires detailed study of backgrounds of the work. (20)

But Shelton offered an answer to his question, "Does this mean, therefore, that the student of African literature must become an anthropologist, a historian, a political scientist, a sociologist?" (8). He replied, "Not precisely; but to understand events of the literary work other than casually he must understand something of their context beyond what the author can furnish— unless the author resorts to footnotes after the manner of T. S. Eliot in *The Wasteland*" (8). Just where one drew the line, however, between the anthropologist and the "serious student of African literature," was not made clear. But Shelton did provide three "Values and Other General Critical Norms" by which the Western critic might approach African literature: (1) "Much African art and literature tends to be didactic"; (2) "Some African literature tends to reflect the analogical flow of activity rather than the movement according to a Western-type logic or cause-effect system"; and (3) "African literature, indeed, reflects African values" (11-13). It seems that the first two norms could easily be subsumed under the third and that Shelton's main point was to ask for more knowledge of Africa in order to relate African literature properly to its context. His article's title, after all, was "Critical Criteria for the *Study* of African Literature," (my italics), which still leaves us with the search for the criteria by which to *evaluate* African literature.

METHODS

What will perhaps be apparent from these attempts of Westerners to understand and evaluate African literature is that they have been based for the most part on the literary texts themselves, while only some Westerners would recognize also the need to understand the cultural context of the literature. As for the reading of literary texts alone, Nancy Schmidt has said that

> it is hoped that students of comparative literature and literary critics will realize that meaningful cross-cultural literary criticism cannot be conducted on the basis of Western literary standards even if the literature is written in a Western language. By trying to apply Western standards to literature which is not wholly within the Western tradition, judgments become inconsistent and criticisms become naive or wholly incorrect. (47)

She added:

> Until more is learned about aesthetic standards and the histories of both oral and written literatures in non-Western societies, there can be no basis for a valid cross-cultural literary criticism, which must consider literature primarily in the context of the culture in which it is created and secondarily in terms of the critic's own culture. (47-48)

And with her, I am sure, Armstrong, Kesteloot, Wright, and Shelton would agree. But the question of cultural context is complicated.

Paul Bohannon has questioned the efficacy of the past methods by which one has arrived at an understanding of the cultural context of art, which, he suggested, has been caused by only a partial application of a precept of the aesthetician Benedetto Croce, whom he paraphrased as saying that "it is not enough to use art objects to explain an exotic culture, nor yet to subject the objects to aesthetic judgement without a knowledge of that culture. Rather, we must understand the attitude toward art which is a part of the culture in question" (85). Bohannon then described how he thought this dictum might be considered and followed in a broader sense than it had been in the past:

> It has been repeatedly stressed that in order to reach this desired end, we must discover the background, social position, training, motivation and aesthetic principles of the artist. . . . It is, perhaps, the oldest precept now before students of primitive art.
>
> Therefore, heeding Professor Whitehead's advice that we are likely to make most progress if we question the assumption longest unquestioned, it might be well to take a new look at what we mean by "studying the artist" in primitive societies. Will "studying the artist" really provide the information we need in order to evaluate primitive art?
>
> Ask the same question about contemporary art: can "studying the artist" in contemporary society explain contemporary art? By itself, it undoubtedly cannot. It elicits the artist's motivation, it elucidates his personal aesthetics, and it clarifies technical problems. It may even help

to solve some of the many difficult Western problems about "creativity." But it cannot explain the reason that some art is accepted and other is not, nor why some is considered better than others.

It would seem—and again the point is Croce's—that there is a dimension in art evaluation which goes far beyond the artist. It is the dimension which is added by what we today would call contemporary criticism. Surely, we need both the study of the contemporary artist and the study of contemporary criticism to arrive at aesthetic principles. We might, for our purposes, even define aesthetics as the relationship between criticism and art objects, for the relationship between artist and the objects is the problem of "creativity." (Obviously, some and perhaps the most telling art critics are artists themselves. For analytical purposes, however, we can divide these functions.)

The question is, then, are we interested in comparative creativity? If, as Westerners, we probably are, we must go to the creators of art for our information. But where do we get our information on comparative aesthetics: Aesthetics means the study of the relationships between art and all that bundle of attitudes and activities which we in the modern world call criticism. Comparative aesthetics would surely establish means of classification of such relationships and, on a practical level, means by which one set of relationship ideas can be made to supplement and differentiate any of the others. (85-86)

Further on, in describing what he considered an unsuccessful field inquiry into the art of the Tiv people of central Nigeria—"I kept chasing artists," he said (87)—Bohannon concluded: "However, I did learn this: I was wrong in my field work because, Western fashion, I paid too much attention to artists, and when the artists disappointed me I came away with nothing. When I return, I shall search out the critics" (94). Although he was speaking about the plastic arts, it seems reasonable to assume that his approach could be applied equally profitably to modern African literature and the criticism of it. This, then, is the purpose of my study: "to search out the critics." But how does one do this? Even this question has caused some confusion.

Joseph Okpaku was one of the first critics to consider, if not the identification of the critical standards by which Africans judged African literature, at least the methods by which one could go about it. He asked:

What then are these African critical standards? The logical place to go in search of them is the African aesthetic. In particular, we should examine our traditional artistic forms as well as genuine (not "studied") contemporary African tastes and attitudes towards the various art forms. . . . The next place to search for these standards would be an examination of those common aspects of life most frequently dramatized in the arts. This would include love, life, hate, honor, duty, death,

destruction, pride, prejudice, friendship, fear, violence, birth and reality amongst others. Different cultures not only have different conceptions of these but have different attitudes to them. Not only that,
they give them different emphases. All these different conceptions, attitudes, emphases, tastes and preferences constitute the basis on which
to build criticism. This is where the search for African critical standards
must begin. ("Culture," 4)

I am not certain I understand what Okpaku meant by "aesthetic," but I am
quite certain I disagree that it is "the logical place to go" in search of critical standards. It seems more feasible to try to induce an African aesthetic
from the eventual isolating and identifying of critical standards rather than
to deduce the standards from the aesthetic. And although critical standards
may well derive from aesthetics, I do not think that fact must determine the
methodology of the search for them.

I agree with Okpaku that a study of traditional art forms will be useful in
determining their impact upon more modern forms. I am more interested
here, however, in discovering the attitude African critics had toward these
forms and what, in their opinions, was the role these forms *should* play in
modern African literature. I hope this will be made clear in Chapter 4.

But I completely disagree with Okpaku that critical standards will be found
through an examination of those "common aspects of life" such as "love,
life, hate, honor, duty" etc. ("Culture," 4). It is clear that African love dif-
fers in its manifestation from Western love, as indeed Okpaku explained
("Culture," 4-5). The African critic has a duty to complain loudly if he or
she thinks, for example, that African honor is being misrepresented. However, I do not see the evaluation of the literary rendering of African love,
African honor, African duty, or what I shall call African "reality" as constituting a long list of separate critical standards (held by many African critics,
incidentally, as will be seen in Chapter 5), but rather the composite of a single standard—namely, that the African writer must not falsify this reality.

The importance of this critical concept in African thinking means that
African writers, and African and non-African critics alike, must be to some
extent anthropologists. That is, they must have some familiarity with the
culture out of which the literature grows. That this observation is true for
any critic, and especially the critic concerned with a literature other than his
or her own, seems obvious. What was not so obvious, perhaps, was the historical context in which the African critic worked in the two decades following World War II and how this context affected his or her criticism. This
will be made clear in the section on "The African Presence" in Chapter 3
dealing with the need of Africans to project this African presence into the
world. This has meant that, to an extent perhaps greater than in the Western
tradition, anthropological considerations have played a significant role in

African criticism—and that Okpaku was well within a developing African literary tradition in placing great importance on the accuracy of the rendering of this African reality. That it was not the only critical standard used by Africans in evaluating their literature will be made clear in the course of this study.

How can one determine whether in fact this was a critical standard, and how can one determine if other standards existed and, if they did, what they were? The other half of Okpaku's suggestion seems the only logical place to look for African critical standards: the "contemporary African tastes and attitudes towards the various art forms" ("Culture," 4), though Okpaku made the unfortunate statement that these must be "genuine," not "studied," which was perhaps a fair enough request on his part except that it was not clear what he meant. His terms *studied* and *genuine* give the impression that African critical standards exist inherently in the African critic and that they remain only to be discovered or that they are easily identifiable and recognizable by all "genuine" African critics. And he seemed to suggest that the "genuineness" of any given critic, or the lack thereof, was readily apparent.

I proceed, rather, from a belief that critical standards may best be inferred from the explicit critical statements made by the critics themselves—that is, that the Africanness or Negritude of a critic is existential rather than essential, that it creates the African critical tradition at least as fast as it can be discovered. As Jean-Paul Sartre has said of Negritude, "It makes you and you make it" (*Black Orpheus*, 59). Further, I assume that an examination of African taste—as opposed to the things tasted, such as love, hate, honor, duty—will reveal critical standards. The elements of African life will reveal much about African culture, but the attitudes toward how these elements are handled literarily will tell us much more, in my opinion, about the standards of African literary criticism. It is this latter examination, the examination of African critical taste, that I attempt here.

In the two decades following World War II, it was tacitly assumed by Africans and non-Africans alike that African critical standards for modern African literature did not exist, or, if they did exist, that they were unknown. Yet Africans have been writing literary criticism of modern African literature in increasing volume since the inception of the journal *Présence africaine* late in 1947. It seemed, therefore, that an analysis of this body of criticism would very likely suggest African critical standards that have actually been in existence, and in use, for some time, and, as Paul Bohannon pointed out, might provide a new dimension to the Western understanding of the African literary aesthetic. This aesthetic should not (or could not, for that matter) be adopted wholesale by Western critics, of course, but a clearer knowledge of it will allow Western critics a better—because it is more complete—frame of reference for the evaluation of an African text, as well as a better understanding of the culture in which the African writer has written. Critics and their criticism, after all, are as much a part of the cultural context as are artists and their art.

My procedure, then, has been, first, to identify, locate, and read as many critical statements as possible made by African critics about modern African literature in the two decades after World War II. This was not as easy a task as I somewhat naively presumed in the beginning. First, the number of critics and works cited will suggest that there was much more of this critical literature than one might have expected. Second, access to many African and French journals was difficult. African periodicals even as recent as the mid-1950s are all too scarce in American libraries. Some of the important but generally ephemeral student literary magazines have been researched, such as *Nexus* (Nairobi), but many more have not been found. I researched newspapers practically not at all, for reasons of time and because I believed that the fruits of my research into the literary journals had yielded enough criticism by Africans upon which some conclusions might be drawn regarding their literary tastes.

More basic, perhaps, was the question of what and who was an African critic. Aside from the difficulty of defining the term *African*, there is the question of the term *critic*. For my purposes, any discussion of African literature has been treated as literary criticism, with equal, if not special, emphasis given to applied criticism.

Beyond defining *African* in theory, there has been the practical difficulty of identification. Some of the major journals concerned with African literature provide biographical notes on their contributors, but this practice has not been uniform, nor has the information provided always been reliable. Furthermore, it is often ambiguous as to a critic's nationality—which has been one of my overriding criteria in the identification of African critics. The unwary reader might, for example, assume that Sangadore Akanji is an African critic. His book reviews in the early issues of *Black Orpheus* were very insightful, and his observations and critical standards were not unlike those of many other critics cited in this study. However, consider the biographical note on him in *Black Orpheus*, no. 4 (October 1958), which says that Akanji

> describes himself as a "detribalized Yoruba". Born abroad, i.e., outside Nigeria he lived most of his life in Europe and the Near East. He has recently returned to Nigeria in order to "rediscover his lost Yoruba self". He teaches literature. His most absorbing interests at the moment he describes as Beethoven's music and the worship of Sango. (63)

To prove the African or non-African nationality of this critic would require means and information not generally available, though the critic's African background is certainly suspect.

Other critics have been equally difficult to identify. A Valerie D'Cruz, for instance, reviewed several books for *Nexus*, the literary journal of University College, Nairobi. But one cannot rely on the treacherous science of names. Several of the prominent families of Togo and Benin today—d'Almeida, de Medeiros, Olympio, Santos—still bear linguistic evidence of the Portuguese presence in West Africa several centuries ago. Short of some sophisticated intercontinental detective work, it was difficult to decide whether to include this criticism. There may be other credentials open to question. However, I believe that a very large percentage of the critics cited in the course of this study are African by birth or experience and that any and all of the major critical standards arrived at would not be seriously invalidated even if a few non-African interlopers might be unmasked.

The second procedure was, upon reading this body of criticism, to note carefully those statements that seemed to suggest a literary value judgment by the critic, especially those statements that seemed to suggest that a literary work was "good" or "bad" or that a particular work was "better" or "worse" than another, and where these were made fairly clear, the reasons why; to note these evaluative statements. The third procedure was to attempt to classify them into the broad categories, which form the chapters of this study. This was perhaps the most crucial step in the study, since it was at this point that my own literary prejudices could conceivably creep into the work. All I can do, perhaps, is to plead innocent and hope that the reader's own experience and investigation will bear out my results. The critical tendencies of African critics are surely just that—tendencies. No attempt is made to suggest that they are rigid, with respect to either the present or past, and certainly not with respect to the future. As Justine M. Cordwell has said in a study on the aesthetics of the Yoruba and Benin cultures,

> Aesthetic judgments, for the most part, do not arise from a rational, conscious level, but rather from a subliminal level formed by cultural learning and idiosyncratic experience which shapes taste. Thus, while people are conscious of many of the criteria they use in aesthetic judgments, for the most part these are shaped by early training, individual experience, and idiosyncratic preferences based on the personality of the individual. (244)

She added a further point that should also be kept in mind in reading this study: "The fact that aesthetic standards may be interpreted in the light of ethical, religious, economic and even political standards as well is as true in West African cultures as in Euroamerican ones" (246).

And finally, this study, though it deals with a large number of statements made by African critics and suggests some of the trends that seemed to emerge from these statements, does not intend to suggest that there is a single, clearly unified body of African criticism any more than there is a clear African aesthetic or any more, for that matter, than there is a single, unified Western criticism or aesthetic. In fact, this study will conclude much as Cordwell did when she said, "The facts which emerged then were not definite criteria recognized and agreed upon as such by all members of Yoruba and Benin societies, but a consensus of opinion and behavior which indicated the range and type of standards in the selection of forms of graphic and plastic arts" (247). And it will be noted that within several of the following chapters there exists a more or less clear splitting into two or more distinct—in the case of Negritude, diametrically opposed—positions. Indeed, the occurrence of such divisions of opinion has been taken as especially strong evidence for the validity of the underlying element, the cause of the disagreement.

No attempt has been made to evaluate the substance of any of the statements made by the critics except to decide whether they were evaluative. Hence, there is no attempt to prejudge any critic or, as Okpaku wanted it, to rule on a critic's "genuineness" or "studiedness." All critics were weighted equally in the sense that no critic or statement has been dismissed out of hand or raised above the others. Thus a statement, for example, by 1986 Nobel Prize laureate Wole Soyinka carries on its surface no more weight for the purposes of this study than, say, that of an undergraduate student reviewing a novel in a student literary magazine. Indeed, the fact that both tend to use similar critical standards lends validity to the critical standards identified in the course of this study. The critical standards themselves, and not the critics as personalities, are of primary interest here.

The statements by the critics are not considered on the basis of any kind of preconceived validity, since validity is what I am trying to discover. That is, what were those elements that suggested aesthetic, literary validity to the African critics? Although I do not try in each case to define hard and fast critical standards, I did attempt to pay close attention to statements that suggest the existence of such standards. Thus I attempt a careful scrutiny not only of the more theoretical statements made by Africans but also of the criticism applied to specific works of African literature. Tied as it is to concrete examples available to all, applied criticism is what finally provides the common touchstones through which the critic can best communicate the rudiments of his or her aesthetic to another. It is hoped that by attempting to identify some of the touchstones chosen from African literature by African critics, and the reasons for them, the Western critic—and perhaps even the African—will have a clearer understanding of the cultural context of African literature. After reading this study, the Westerner will not come to see African literature through African eyes, certainly, but he or she will no longer be able to judge African literature as though no standards other than his or her own exist. The Westerner must, at the very least, give a condescending nod to the existence of other standards, much in the same way that, say, an

American teaching French literature might speak of the "French genius" of Racine while preferring Shakespeare. The least he or she has to do in this case, it would seem, is to explain that the French prefer Racine and why. This has not been easy to do for African works because the criticism has not yet been surveyed. Hence this study.

Some of the critical standards that emerged from the criticism seem to resemble certain standards of the Western literary tradition. For example, Chapter 5 will suggest the French concept of *vraisemblance* and the whole mimetic tradition in Western literature. I do not think this means that Africans have adopted a Western critical standard. Joseph Okpaku said, "An African critic trying to relate African literature or any other literature to Africans must do so against the background of African culture. He must draw upon the patterns of the African aesthetic. In other words, he must use African critical standards" ("Culture," 3). The difficulty comes when it is seen that the African critic's background is clearly different from that of Westerners, yet the standard used is the same. The communication breaks down when the Western critic then says, "You see? You're using a *Western* standard," to which the African critic, quite understandably, says he or she is doing no such thing. The quarrel could end amicably if the African were to realize that a critical standard used by a non-African is not, by definition, *un-African*; whereas the Westerner would do well to realize that there is nothing inherently Western in any of the critical standards he or she happens to use. It is Western because he or she uses it, not vice-versa.

It is equally clear that a critical standard need not necessarily be, in order to qualify as continental or national or cultural, unique and immediately recognizable as such, in the same way, say, that black skin is recognizable from white. At least three African critics stated as much, and it might be well to quote them here. In *The Mind of Africa* (1962), W. E. Abraham spoke of African philosophy in a way that would seem to hold as well for African literature:

> The question of the existence of an African philosophy is not a "uniqueness" question. There is no reason why, in order that there should be an African philosophy, it has to be different from every other philosophy. It is sufficient that philosophy should occur in Africa such that it is not derived from outside Africa. (104)

A. Bodunrin, while reviewing Abraham's book in 1966, said,

> When one speaks of the unity of African cultures one does not thereby imply uniqueness, one does not necessarily wish to say that there is a minimal complex of significant elements which are common to African cultures and which are such that they have never been seen elsewhere

before in the history of mankind. Such a claim would clearly be pre-
posterous. (Review, 46)

Gaetan Sebudani said the same year that while African works showed a
"world vision reflective of the African soul" (80), it was also apparent that
"the criteria which make up the originality of Negro culture end up simultaneously revealing its connection to the stream of a universal civilization"
(80-81*).

A particular critical standard, then, regardless of its resemblance, imag-
ined or real, to any standard chosen by any other critical tradition, becomes
African by definition, by virtue of its having been used by Africans.

PARAMETERS

I surveyed criticism written by Africans, in English and French, for the
most part between 1947 and 1966. My guess is that I found 80 to 90 percent
of the body of criticism written during this period. I am not aware of a more
extensive bibliography of this criticism than the one I compiled in 1973,
upon which this study is based. Because of my linguistic limitations, I did
not survey criticism written in Portuguese or African languages. I suspect
that a survey of this criticism would corroborate many, if not all, of the conclusions I eventually reached.

I chose to begin with the year 1947-1948 because two literary events occurred then that may be said to have been the beginning of modern African
literature. The first of these occurred in the fall of 1947. After several years
of planning among African and European intellectuals, the initial issue of
the journal *Présence africaine* appeared in Paris and Dakar. Alioune Diop,
its editor, said its purpose was to "define the African's creativity and to
hasten his integration in the modern world" ("Niam n'goura," 185) and
that it had been conceived during World War II by "a certain number of
overseas students, witnessing a stricken Europe questioning herself as to the
efficacy and genuineness of her values, [who] gathered themselves together
to study that same situation and to weigh the distinctive qualities of their
own being" (186). At the First International Congress of Africanists, held
in Accra in 1962, Diop explained the inspiration behind the journal's name:
"In France, the expression 'Présence Française' is a well-known euphe-
mism, denoting as it does . . . 'the authority of the French in the colonies' "
("The Spirit," 46), and added:

> The ordinary pre-war French bourgeois could conceive of the term
> "Présence Française" as meaning simply the presence in the colonies
> of French communities living in peace and harmony with the native
> community, their sole purpose being to bring the disinherited peoples
> medicine, education, technical and financial assistance. We know, in

actual fact, that things were far from being quite as simple and straight-forward. The plain truth is that European civilisation and culture are to be met with throughout the world. We use the languages of Europe at our conferences. We employ the techniques of Europe to give our lives a modern touch. The economic laws of Europe dominate our lives. The price of ground nuts or coffee is determined in the Western capitals, whose currency we use. . . . If we are to live in the modern world, we need to assert our presence in it, and that is the meaning of 'Présence Africaine'. ("The Spirit," 46-47)

Davidson Nicol of Sierra Leone said of it in 1964 that it

has played an important part in the literary renaissance of West Africa. It provided an opportunity for the world to see the work of young African writers and poets, some of whom have now gone on to become famous. It was an active mid-wife of Negritude. . . . In its complete-ness—sponsorship, editorship, publication, library and bookshop— Présence Africaine shows the essential apparatus required to bring the African mind directly to the notice of the public without foreign intervention at any point. (*Africa*, 68)

On the occasion of the First World Festival of Negro Arts, Alioune Sène, a Senegalese diplomat and critic looking back over the years, rendered the jour-nal "sublime hommage" as an "eminent ambassador of African Culture in the world" (14*). So in some sense, it may be said that *Présence Africaine* was a major event in the development of African post-World War II thought. If it produced little actual literary criticism until the mid-1950s, it did pro-vide a prime encouragement for African intellectuals.

The second important literary event of the year 1947-1948 was the publi-cation of Leopold Senghor's *Anthologie de la nouvelle poésie nègre et malgache de langue française*. Outside of his own *Chants d'ombre* (1945) and Leon Damas's anthology, *Poètes d'expression française (Afrique Noire, Madagascar, Reunion, Guadeloupe, Martinique, Indochine, Guyane), 1900-1945* (1947), Senghor's was the first major anthology to indicate that serious poetry was being written by enough Africans and poets of African descent to make continued ignorance or denial of it increasingly difficult. Indeed, like much of the poetry itself, the introductory essay, "Orphée noir," by one of Europe's ranking intellectuals, Jean-Paul Sartre, was no doubt equally influential—in its impact upon African writers, at least the French-speaking poets, as well as in bringing their work to the attention of the non-African world.

Paulin Joachim, a critic from Benin, suggested in part what Senghor's anthology meant to Africans: "Everyone knows the important role played by this book in the affirmation of African values. It came in the nick of time to fill a void that had been felt for a long time" ("Anthologie," 61*). Taken together, then, Senghor's anthology, Sartre's essay, and Alioune Diop's journal mark the beginning of a new era for African literature.

The year 1966 provided another African milestone, also of Senghor's design: the First World Festival of Negro Arts, hosted by the Republic of Senegal and held in Dakar, April 1-24. There was no shortage of Africans who commented on the significance of the festival. Father Englebert Mveng of Cameroun said it "will not be, as one assumed, a simple folkloric rendezvous. It is, on the contrary, one of the high points of the history of Africa in this century" (7*). Looking ahead, A Bodunrin of Nigeria said, "The end of the Festival should serve as the beginning of a re-thinking on African arts, culture and civilization" ("The First Festival," 29). Other events, too, such as the Nigerian Civil War, seem to have contributed to the ending of a significant period of African literature in or around 1966.

DEFINING AFRICAN LITERATURE

It is tempting to begin by assuming that everyone knew and everyone agreed on what was meant by *African literature*. As it turned out, things were not that simple.

One of the first African critics to offer a definition of African literature was the Nigerian writer Cyprian Ekwensi. In 1956 he wrote, "What then is African writing? To my own mind African writing is that piece of self-expression in which the psychology behind African thought is manifest; in which the philosophy and the pattern of culture from which it springs can be discerned" ("The Dilemma," 703). However, it was not until 1962, when Christopher Okigbo put the question before the Conference of African Writers of English Expression, held that year June 8-18 at Makerere University, that the matter was taken up in earnest.

There was no attempt to keep or publish an exact transcript of what was to become a seminal conference for African literature, but there exist at least three attempts to summarize the conference's attempt to come to terms with the question of defining African literature. Bloke Modisane of South Africa reported that

> Christopher Okigbo, the eccentric Nigerian poet ("I don't read my poetry to non-poets"), provoked discussion by posing three points. Is African literature that body of literature produced in Africa by African and non-African Writers? Is it the literature produced by Africans of African descent? Or is it the literature produced by writers from all over the world writing on and about Africa? This stormy session struggled with definitions which threw up more questions and more definitions. Arthur Maimane, South African short-story writer, submitted

that it was literature recording the experience as seen through the eyes of an African. Questions shifted to the qualification of African literature. What were the essential elements of the literature? Opinion emphasized "that feeling of being black" and this divided the conference on the concept of "Negritude"—which was defended passionately by the observers from French-speaking territories. Ronald Segal, a white South African, challenged the validity of "that feeling", submitting that feelings were universal, and that there was nothing like an exclusive African feeling. Subsequent discussion was inconclusive, but with the compromise acceptance of the unstated principle that the essential elements of African literature were the African viewpoint, a little of "that feeling", the moral values, the philosophy, and the customs of African society. (716)

Bernard Fonlon of Cameroun reported more precisely that Christopher Okigbo had said that to be African,

> a work must have its roots deep in African soil, must take its birth from African experience, must pulsate with African feeling; in brief, what made a work African was Negritude as first felt and expressed by Senghor and Césaire. It was not race, neither was it theme that made a work African: a foreigner could treat African material and an African writer could be devoid of authentic African feeling. ("African Writers," 42)

Okigbo himself was asked at the conclusion of the conference, "Are you convinced after the deliberation and doubts of the Conference that there is such a thing that might be termed African Literature?" He replied, "If and when the literature emerges, it will have to divine its own laws for its unity; its own form. Until this happens it appears rather premature to talk of African Literature in terms other than geographical" ("Transition Conference Questionnaire," 12). Fonlon then offered his own thoughts:

> The experiences and emotions of the African are essentially universal: colonial humiliation, frustration, sorrow, bitterness, hate, revolt, revenge, exaltation, joy, love—these are human experiences. To my mind what conferred upon these an African character was their expression, their manner. ("African Writers," 42)

What is significant here is Fonlon's emphasis on expression as the defining element.

Another leading African critic, Ezekiel Mphahlele, addressed himself to one of the more ticklish aspects of the question: whether white African writers, such as Nadine Gordimer and Alan Paton, came within the definition of African literature. He drew two interesting distinctions based on an author's identification with characters:

> There is a degree of identification in which a white writer in Africa like Mr. Paton or Miss Gordimer stands in relation to the characters and setting of his or her stories which indicates whether either of them is African. In both cases, one can distinctly tell they are on the white side of the colour line. For their identification is stronger with the white characters than with the black. This identification is a much closer and intimate relationship than the mere espousal of a cause which one's characters uphold in the context of a story; in other words, it is not just sympathy. It is a matter of belongingness in relation to the group represented by one section of characters one is portraying and the habitat of that group. What holds good for the white writer is true in the case of the Black one in his segregated world.
>
> This is the distinction between a non-African white writer and a white African writer on the one hand, and between a white and a black African writer on the other. ("African Literature," 220-21)

Mphahlele then cleared the air further, not by reporting on the Makerere attempts at definition but by speculating on the basic assumptions of the organizers of the conference:

> When we talk of African English writing then, I suggest, we cannot help but discuss literature coming from both black and white in the continent. And by "black" I am including African Arabs. But if I insist on the *cultural* context in which we use the phrase, I should then take in writing by black Africans south of the Sahara, leaving out both whites and Arabs. It is in this context that Mbari summoned the writers at Makerere. ("African Literature," 221)

Perhaps Mphahlele had advance information from Mbari as to its rationale for inviting some writers and not others—implying, in fact, a definition. It is ironic, then, that the conference went to such lengths in trying to define African literature and that, as Chinua Achebe said, it failed ("English," 27). Richard Rive, a South African writer, suggested this was so because "the answer was never defined because the answer *can* never be defined" ("No Common Factor," 55). He added that "it is easy to build up a mystique and speak authoritatively of the African personality, whatever that means. But what is the common factor uniting me with Ebrahim Salahi in Sudan, John [*sic*] Ngugi in Kenya and Camara Laye in Guinea" (55) and that "even our alleged common opposition to colonialism or neo-colonialism is different in texture and degree, and in some cases non-existent" (55). He concluded that "in fact the exciting thing about Africa is its richness in diversity, its difference, its lack of a common factor" (55).

Less than a year after the Makerere conference, two others were held successively, in March and April 1963, at the Faculté des lettres of the University of Dakar and at Fourah Bay College in Freetown, Sierra Leone. The theme of these conferences was "African Literature and the University Curriculum" and it led, quite naturally, perhaps out of the Makerere failure, to another attempt to define African literature.

It was a Canadian critic, T. R. M. Creighton, who proposed what eventually became the definition accepted by the Freetown conference: that African literature is composed of "any work in which an African setting is authentically handled, or to which experiences which originate in Africa are integral" (84). This definition has the merit, argued Creighton, of including Conrad's *Heart of Darkness* and Wole Soyinka's "Telephone Conversation," set in London, while excluding Graham Greene's novel *The Heart of the Matter* because it "might as well have taken place in Singapore or in Tooting as in Freetown" (84).

Responding immediately to this definition, Donatus Nwoga, a Nigerian critic, stated he would prefer to exclude *Heart of Darkness* while accepting "Telephone Conversation" as African literature because

> there are two elements pointed out which should, if they are present, give us the confidence to speak of African literature, elements of, let us call it, nationality and experience. If an African writes about an African situation, that is clearly African literature. If he goes to France for five years, and writes of his experience in France, then he is still writing African literature. And on the other hand, I would want to leave out Joyce Cary's novels, which are very good in their setting of Africa, but I would still prefer to call it English literature in an African setting, just as Wole Soyinka's poems based on his experience in London are African literature in an English setting. (Creighton, 85)

A not unconnected question—is this literature African, or is it an addendum to European literatures?—was raised by Ezekiel Mphahlele in a discussion paper at the conference:

> When someone talks to me about African writers, I react emotionally, and so think of the epithet "African" as referring only to black people in Africa. The epithet makes me impulsively think in general cultural terms, and so exclude Arabs and whites. If I said white Africans should be included in a conference specifically labelled "African writers," I should be reacting intellectually. But when we speak of African *writing* or literature, then I suggest that we need not be bullied by terminology of our own making. For what we call African writing, outside the unequivocally African literature that takes in all indigenous languages capable of being written, is really *primarily* English or French or Portuguese or Italian or Spanish literature, and only secondarily African.

The element of Africa in the concept is both geographical and cultural. ("The Language of African Literature," discussion paper 1)

This position was also challenged by Nwoga, who took the opposite view: "I would prefer to consider that what we call African literature is *primarily African* and *secondarily English* or *French* etc." (Creighton, 84).

The Creighton definition was eventually adopted by the Freetown conference. It had also been accepted earlier by the First International Congress of Africanists, held in Accra in 1962 (Creighton, 84). And it seems to have been accepted in very large part by the Ghanaian poet George Awoonor-Williams (more recently known as Kofi Awoonor), who wrote that "agreement is now being generally reached that African literature is that body of literature in which African experiences are integrally treated, imbuing the total creation with some large measure of authenticity" (5).

But the Creighton definition did not go unchallenged. It prompted this response from Cyprian Ekwensi in 1964:

> I do not agree with the stress which has been laid on experiences confined to the African continent, especially in these modern times when the most travelled man in the world is the educated African. My own definition of African Literature is literature based on African character and psychology. This means that the main theme may be anthropological, traditional or modern, but the traits, temperaments and reactions of the characters will be peculiarly African due to influences of tribe, culture and history. Thus the presence in the United Nations does not make literature based on him non-African because it is set on foreign soil. ("African Literature," 294-95)

To give full justice to Ekwensi's definition, however, it is necessary to quote from an earlier essay (1963) in conjunction with the one above:

> In my many years of writing I found that the phrase "African Writing" as used by critics does not necessarily mean writing by Africans. There still lingers in certain minds the idea that unless the subject matter be ritual murder, circumcision or the racial situation, the novel is not "African." . . . My own definition of African writing is writing which reveals the psychology of the African. I use the term psychology very broadly to embrace reactions to situations and to the social order, religious beliefs, interpretations of moral codes, inter-relationships within the family. These factors inter-acting create the African character which gives its stamp to African writing. The subject matter is incidental. ("Problems," 218)

On the matter of Graham Greene, Joseph Conrad, and Joyce Cary, Ekwensi went on to say that "African writing is unique. It can be written by no one else but the African" ("Problems," 218).

Agreeing at least in part with Ekwensi's reaction to the Creighton definition was Chinua Achebe, who wrote:

> I could not help being amused by the curious circumstances in which Conrad, a Pole, writing in English produced African literature! On the other hand if Peter Abrahams were to write a good novel based on his experiences in the West Indies it would not be accepted as African literature.
>
> What all this suggests to me is that you cannot cram African literature into a small, neat definition. I do not see African literature as one unit but as a group of associated units—in fact the sum total of all the *national* and *ethnic* literatures of Africa.
>
> A national literature is one that takes the whole nation for its province, and has a realised or potential audience throughout its territory. In other words a literature that is written in a *national* language. An ethnic literature is one which is available only to one ethnic group within the nation. ("English," 27)

In tying African literatures to national and ethnic concepts, and thus closely to language, Achebe raised another question that will be dealt with in another chapter: which languages—European or African—ought to be used as the vehicles of African literature.

In 1966 Mphahlele offered an addendum to his earlier definition, and accepted "black" or "Negro" as a defining element in much the same way Ekwensi seemed to: "A study of African literature (having made the point that it is still rightly *African* because it is written out of an *African experience*) is not complete if it does not include writing by whites who are native to Africa and write out of a situation of involvement in the life of the continent" ("African Literature for Beginners," 25). But he added that "we have to begin somewhere; again, the mood, idiom and imagery of negro African writing is not shared by the literature that comes from any of these whites" (25).

Definitions by French-speaking Africans were fewer. It seems likely that francophone Africans were less interested than their English-speaking counterparts in defining African literature because of their greater preoccupation with the term *Negritude*. It is very likely that they considered Negritude to be the definition of African literature. It is interesting to speculate as to how Negritude might differ, as a defining agent, from Mphahlele's "cultural context" and "mood, idiom and imagery," or from Fonlon's "expression" or "manner," or from Ekwensi's "psychology." Indeed, the definition offered by the Negritude poet David Diop sounded very much like Ekwensi's. Diop was here engaged in a debate in the pages of *Présence africaine* concerning a "national poetry":

> We do not believe that one form more than another can give a "national character" to poetry, and that it can enclose its inspiration in a form called "traditional" in order to baptize it "popular."

"National" in this domain is defined not by exterior marks but by psychological particularities, by habits of thought born of given living conditions which, through the personal genius of the author, reveal a common culture of men living in the same nation. ("Contribution," 113*)

It is also interesting to realize that the efforts of the English-speaking Africans led them at least in the direction of the concept of Negritude. It is perhaps superfluous to point out that any definition of African literature must first come to an understanding, however vague, of the term *African*.

Still another possible defining factor was suggested by German historian and bibliographer Janheinz Jahn:

Distinguishing characteristics of neo-African literature are due to Western influences. In contrast to Western literature, however, Neo-African literature has certain stylistic elements which stem from Negro-African oral tradition. It is this style which characterizes Neo-African literature and not the author's language (for the most part European), birthplace or color of skin. . . . Works written by Africans which lack these specific stylistic elements do not belong to neo-African, but to Western literature. ("Introduction," vii)

Jahn did not, however, elaborate on the distinguishing characteristics of this style. Nevertheless, at least one African critic, Romanus Nnagbo Egudu, agreed with him: "These stylistic behaviors which Jahn recommends as the distinguishing marks of African literature, are again pointed at by Achebe in his own views, and there is no doubt that these more than language are a more plausible means of characterising African literature ("The Matter and Manner," 75).

In contradistinction to whatever *African* means, the terms *Western* and *European* are often used in this study interchangeably. *European* is used more often, perhaps, in referring to languages and to the colonial powers in Africa; *Western* is used to denote a broader frame of reference to include, specifically, the term *American*. If the two terms are not used consistently, it may help to think of their more significant connotation as being *non-African*.

The adjectives *black* and *Sub-Saharan* have been accepted as working limits for this study—not necessarily because I think they are completely defensible but because they have helped to bring shape to what became a body of material much more ample than I had originally anticipated. A case can be made—though not an airtight one, perhaps—for the cultural entity of black, Sub-Saharan Africa. Indeed, Cheikh Anta Diop's *The Cultural Unity of Negro-Africa* (1955) attempted to do just that. Whether Diop succeeded is a matter of opinion. But there would seem to be enough evidence for such a unity—along with the implied acceptance of these terms by several black,

Sub-Saharan critics—to warrant a literary study based on these predefining terms. They have the further merit, along with nationality, of being identifiable and, further still, of not requiring a prejudgment, which would be necessary with such concepts as Ekwensi's *psychology*, for example. Such elements may be important, finally, in the definition arrived at for *African literature*, but they can hardly be used as working terms here, as the judgment by Africans is what is here attempted. If the critical standards suggested in the following chapters are valid for black, Sub-Saharan literature, and not for whatever shall be eventually defined as the term *African literature*, then this study will at least have had the merit of isolating the critical standards of a large subgroup within that term, during a particular period of time, against which the findings of parallel studies (North African, Muslim, white South African, and others) could be checked and collated.

2 The Languages of African Literature

LANGUAGE AND LITERATURE

An important argument relating to the definition of African literature has been the controversy surrounding the languages in which it is, and ought to be, written. What is the relationship between a literature and its language? In pursuing this question, African critics began to establish a critical standard.

Not many Africans approached the question as directly as did Nigerian critic Obiajunwa Wali. His 1963 article, "The Dead End of African Literature?" set off a lively debate. Wali's basic premise was that

> the whole uncritical acceptance of English and French as the inevitable medium for educated African writing, is misdirected, and has no chance of advancing African literature and culture. In other words, until these [African] writers and their western midwives accept the fact that any true African literature must be written in African languages, they would be merely pursuing a dead end, which can only lead to sterility, uncreativity, and frustration. (14)

One of the bases for Wali's position was that literatures are defined by language and, therefore, "African literature as now understood and practised, is merely a minor appendage in the main stream of European literature" (13). He explained further,

> The basic distinction between French and German literature for instance, is that one is written in French, and the other in German. All the other distinctions, whatever they be, are based on this fundamental fact. What therefore is now described as African literature in English and French, is a clear contradiction, and a false proposition, just as "Italian literature in Hausa" would be. (14)

Fifteen years earlier Cheikh Anta Diop had expressed the same idea:

Without underestimating at all the value of these Africans writing in foreign languages, does one have the right to consider their writings as the base of an African culture? Upon examination—even a superficial one—we must respond in the negative. In effect, we believe that all literary work belongs necessarily to the language in which it is written: the works thus written by Africans arise, above all, from these foreign literatures, and one would not know how to consider them as monuments of an African literature. ("Quand," 58*)

Another Nigerian, Ben Obumselu, had a similar thought in 1966: "An African literary work translated into the language of European literature almost immediately ceases to be African" ("Background," 50).

Two other critics supported the use of African languages for political reasons. A Zimbabwean critic, Patrick F. Chakaipa, listed some characteristics of the Shona language and observed that "it would appear that such a concrete language is especially fit for the writing of fiction." He cited the political value of writing in African languages: "It is almost impossible to build a great nation without vernacular literature" (52). Ngugi wa Thiong'o, known then as James Ngugi, expressed the feeling that because of his interest in nation building, "I have reached a point of crisis. I don't know whether it is worth any longer writing in English" ("James Ngugi Interviewed," v).

Wali's argument by no means went unchallenged. Ezekiel Mphahlele, the South African critic, countered immediately by saying, in reply,

If Wali is so particular about the use of names or categories, what would he call literature produced by eastern Russians—European or Asian? What would he call literature produced in Hawaii—American? South Americans write in Spanish and Portuguese because these are the languages spoken in that part of the world. Would Wali quarrel if we called the literature from there South American writing in Spanish and Portuguese? These were not the original languages of the indigenous people of South America. (Letter, 8)

Mphahlele went further in his reply, stating that the colonial languages were a unifying force within African nations:

English and French have become the common language with which to present a national front against white oppressors. Where the white man has already retreated, as in the independent states, these two languages are still a unifying force. By stages, each of the various states will need to find an African official language for itself. (8)

He then asked, "In the meantime are we going to fold our arms and wait for that kingdom to come? The creative instinct always runs ahead of social, political, and economic developments; and the creative impulse cannot wait for such developments before it expresses itself'' (8).

Leopold Senghor had had a similar thought, which he expressed in his opening speech at the Colloque sur la littérature africaine d'expression française in Dakar in March 1963. Defending the African writers' choice of French, he said, ''It is our *colonized situation* that imposed the colonizer's language on us, more precisely the policy of *assimilation*'' (''Négritude et civilisation,'' 9*). He then quoted Sartre in the same vein: ''As Jean-Paul Sartre says, we have chosen to turn the colonizer's weapons against him. The 'miraculous arms,' as Aimé Césaire puts it'' (9*). He concluded, ''This is why, if we had been given the choice, we would have chosen French!'' (9*).

Chinua Achebe put it even more explicitly. He argued that national languages, and not languages per se, define literatures, and that for better or worse the national language of Nigeria in 1965 was English:

> I have indicated somewhat off-handedly that the national literature of Nigeria and of many other countries of Africa is, or will be, written in English. This may sound like a controversial statement, but it isn't. All I have done has been to look at the reality of present-day Africa. This ''reality'' may change as a result of deliberate, e.g. political, action. If it does an entirely new situation will arise, and there will be plenty of time to examine it. At present it may be more profitable to look at the scene as it is. (''English,'' 28)

He added that part of this reality was that

> there are not many countries in Africa today where you could abolish the languages of the erstwhile colonial powers and still retain the facility for mutual communication. Therefore those African writers who have chosen to write in English or French are not unpatriotic smart alecs with an eye on the main chance—outside their own countries. They are by-products of the same processes that made the new nation states of Africa. (28)

Wali's other main argument for African languages was that the African writing in a European language would produce only a pale version of what he or she would be capable of creating in an African language. He said:

> An African writer who thinks and feels in his own language *must* write in that language. The question of transliteration, whatever that means, is unwise as it is unacceptable, for the ''original'' which is spoken of here, is the real stuff of literature and the imagination, and must not be discarded in favor of a *copy*. (14)

Here Wali touched on an argument that received much greater support among his fellow critics. In fact, the argument goes back to 1948, when O. K. Poku felt that the technical difficulties of writing in a second language were nearly insurmountable. He said,

> Africans can do little to furnish the palace of English literature. For the African's knowledge of English can never equal the knowledge that the Englishman has of his own language. Africans can never be Englishmen; can never speak English perfectly and can never fully understand its idioms. Better to start developing the African tongue to become masters of a true literature and the best interpreters of the African nature. (900)

In 1949, K. A. B. Jones-Quartey said, in the same vein,

> The majority of Africans can never employ the English language as the majority of Englishmen and Americans employ it; they can or should never build a national literature upon it, because the original language of a people carries with it that people's peculiar genius. And the African genius dwells as much in African languages as the Anglo-Saxon and Hindu spirits dwell in English and Hindustani. ("Our Language," 24)

The Reverend John S. Mbiti took a similar view when he spoke of attempts to preserve oral African literature in these terms: "By the time it is passed for publication, it has been polished and double polished by them [committees] to the extent that it is almost like a translation of a book written by an English or Italian author" (246).

Achebe challenged the argument that the African could not write effectively in a second language. Examining Christopher Okigbo's "Limits" and J. P. Clark's "Night Rain," he said:

> I do not see any signs of sterility anywhere here. What I do see is a new voice coming out of Africa, speaking of African experience in a world-wide language. So my answer to the question, Can an African ever learn English well enough to be able to use it effectively in creative writing? is certainly yes. ("English," 29)

Psychology

More cogent, perhaps, was the argument put forth by some critics to the effect that the African writer's choice of a second, non-African language as a literary vehicle raised questions of a psychological rather than a technical nature. Perhaps the first attempt to deal with this aspect of the question came in 1960, in this statement by Ghanaian poet Michael Dei-Anang: "In the long run . . . Africans, whether they be French or Portuguese or English by historical or political affiliation, can best express their innermost feeling in their mother tongue with the complex and expanding matrix of traditional life as a fitting background" ("Introduction," xi). Dei-Anang then pointed out the interesting situation in which Chaucer and Langland produced masterpieces in a very much out-of-favor language during the Norman occupation of England (xii).

Eldred Jones of Sierra Leone, while favoring the use of English, suggested that there might be psychological ramifications not always apparent in one's choice of language:

> Full-blooded Africans in French West Africa for several decades of French rule recited passages to the effect that their ancestors were tall, fair-haired Gauls. It would not take too much reflection to reject that particular idea, but there may be others more insidious. ("Nationalism," 153)

Practicalities

In spite of the psychological hazards attendant on choosing to write in European languages, several Africans pointed out the practicalities involved in such a choice. Chinua Achebe said, "There are scores of languages I would want to learn if it were possible. Where am I to find the time to learn the half-a-dozen or so Nigerian languages each of which can sustain a literature?" ("English," 28). It was Mphahlele who argued that national choices of languages were not really the writers' to make:

> It is not the writer alone who will redeem the situation. Wali should address himself to the education departments and universities of Africa. It is as much a pedagogical problem as a literary one. We have to wait a generation or two before more Africans outside South and East Africa can produce an adult literature in their own languages. But we as writers cannot be asked to leave off writing and engage in linguistics which are the basic concern of education authorities. (Letter, 8)

Cheik Hamidou Kane expressed similar feelings based on practicalities at the Freetown conference in 1963:

> Our languages need modernising and we need to learn to write them, we need to teach them and use them. But meanwhile, until this has all been done, are we to do nothing else? Are we not to live or express ourselves? Are we to call a halt to all evolution? My own answer would be no; nor do I think there is anyone whose answer would be yes. (Ousmane et al., 61)

There was also the practicality of using a world language, with its wider audience, that appealed to several Africans. Recalling a visit to Brazil, Achebe mentioned the impression made on him by Jorge Amado's novel *Gabriela, Clove and Cinnamon* and his surprise at the number of Brazilians writing in

Portuguese: "At their national writer's festival there were literally hundreds of them. But the work of the vast majority will be closed to the rest of the world forever, including no doubt the work of some excellent writers. There is certainly a great advantage in writing in a world language" ("English," 28). Achebe was following, though perhaps not consciously, a lead taken by Leopold Senghor, who as early as 1956 began to defend the choice of French as a literary language for Africans on the ground of its worldwide usage. He said, "We express ourselves in French because French is a language of universal usage, because our message is addressed *also* to the French in France and to other peoples, because French is a language of 'gentility and honesty' " ("Comme les lamantins," 120*). J. P. Clark felt similarly when he said he wrote in English—"a language that no longer is the copyright of any one people or nation, and which to my mind is a positive step back from Babel's house of many tongues" ("A Personal Note," viii).

Aesthetics

The underlying, unstated assumption implied by these critics was that, given a different set of more practical circumstances, they would gladly have chosen to write in their own African languages. Rare was the African who said he or she would use a European language because of its intrinsic superiority over African languages. Thus, Davidson Nicol's remark in 1958 was unique. He questioned the technical ability of the African languages to express the current situations with which the African writer might want to be concerned. He was asked in an interview, "Several black African poets say they write in French or English because their languages are no longer adapted to their inspiration; what do you think of this?" His reply was that "the old languages suited the old guard, but they sometimes lacked words to express reality. More, the black poets are sometimes more used to European languages and rhythms, especially when they are city folks" ("Le Progrès," 38*).

Senghor was likely the only other African to defend openly, for aesthetic reasons, the literary use of European over African languages, and no other African has done so as often or as eloquently. In his opening speech at the Colloque sur la litterature africaine d'expression française, held in Dakar in 1963, he said, "I say it [the French language] is, par excellence, a language of *communication*, 'a language of gentility and honesty,' a language of beauty, clarity, and rigor" ("Négritude et civilisation," 9*). Senghor elaborated more fully on the intrinsic values of the language in his essay "Le Français, langue de culture," in which he listed five reasons why Africans should use French: (1) the fact that some of them know French better than their maternal languages; (2) its rich vocabulary; (3) the conciseness of its syntax; (4) the French style, which is "a symbiosis of Greek subtlety and Latin rigor, a symbiosis enlivened by Celtic passion"; and (5) its humanism (840*). On the other hand, in a 1954 essay he had compared French and Wolof versions of *The Imitation of Jesus Christ* and found the Wolof version superior ("Langage," 160*).

Senghor was not widely challenged by his francophone colleagues, perhaps because of his stature as a connaisseur of the French language, although one critic, G. Towo Atangana, attacked him for his preference and said that for the African writing in French it "could only be a palliative, a temporary tool" (20*). Like Achebe and most other critics, then, Atangana made a distinction (though not the same one Achebe did) between the ideal situation and the present reality. They both seemed to agree that, ideally, African literatures in African languages were to be preferred.

EUROPEAN LANGUAGES, AFRICAN STYLE

Very likely as a result of the language question raised by Wali and taken up by others, an interesting and related line of thought began to develop. If the African writer, for whatever reasons, chose to write in a European language, could that language somehow be made "African"? Could French and English be "Africanized"? For many critics, the answer was yes.

Davidson Nicol of Sierra Leone was perhaps the first African critic to take this position. In 1956 he asked:

Is it possible for a West African to write poetry in English? Or in French for that matter? I think it is. It may not be acceptable always to some Europeans who may feel that it is unlikely an African or Asian can handle these languages sufficiently well for this purpose. However, other Africans when they read poetry in English or French by an African can understand and feel the poetic impulse and anguish coming through. ("The Soft Pink Palms," 116)

In the same year Cyprian Ekwensi mentioned two extremes available to the African writer while at the same time advocating an intermediate solution:

In Africa, communication on a mass scale must still be in the English language, and that leaves the African two and only two choices; depending on the character from whose lips the words are proceeding. The first medium, as I have said, is Queen's English—as it would be used in conversation by a normal Englishman. The second medium is pidgin English. But the injection of African idioms into spoken English so as to identify the dialogue as African, can still be achieved without recourse to dropped h's and g's or inclusions of "ain'ts" and "reckons." ("The Dilemma," 704)

Ghanaian philosopher W. E. Abraham expressed a similar opinion in *The Mind of Africa*: "It is proper for our new African novelists to do for Africa

what Hardy and Lawrence did for Britain. They can do this by putting their
vernacular behind their English and their French, by writing of the mass of
traditional Africa as though they were translating into English or French''
(99). Ezekiel Mphahlele, again responding to Wali, asked of the African
writer: "Why can he not be authentic simply because he is using a foreign
medium? He is bringing to the particular European language an African experience which in turn affects his style'' (Letter, 8). In another place Mphahlele
said about writing for an African rather than a European audience, "This
will have an effect on our style, we shant always be writing Oxford English.
We should be able to change . . . to experiment with style . . . give English
a new and fresh ring'' (National Educational Television, "Modern African
Writers,'' 61).

The use of standard forms of European languages was also discussed at
the Dakar conference of March 1963. Gilbert Ilboudo said that

> the writers attending the symposium all felt this need to grasp African
> reality when they spoke of "doing violence" to the French language.
> French, they say, cannot express all the shades of our feelings. Even at
> the risk of adulterating the language, it should be made to accord more
> closely to our way of feeling. However the direction in which this trans-
> mutation is to occur was not made clear. (31)

Two years later another francophone critic, Gaetan Sebudani, spoke not in
prescriptive terms but of an apparent fact: "Negro-African literature has
given French a new dimension'' (79*). He added that "the French language,
accustomed to translating rational thought, finds itself suddenly the vehicle
for emotional expression. And this convergence of currents betrays neither
the internal structure of French, nor the rhythm that marks the abundant
richness of the African soul'' (80*). Mphahlele and Ellis Ayitey Komey, in
introducing their collection, *Modern African Stories*, use language similar
to that reported by Ilboudo: "Although we cannot seriously claim that we
have evolved new styles as African writers, still less *un style negro-africain—*
whatever its promoters may mean by it—we are doing violence to standard
English'' (Komey, 12). In another place, Mphahlele offered this advice to
the aspiring African writer: "*A writer should listen closely to his people's
speech.* Then he should put it across in English, *without necessarily sound-
ing very English in idiom*'' (*A Guide*, 30), to which he added,

> In reporting dialogue in particular a writer should not strain at writing
> strictly grammatical and idiomatic English. What he should strive to
> do is *capture the mood, atmosphere and word pictures* or images of
> what a character is saying *or doing in his* (*the character's*) *own lan-
> guage*. Otherwise African characters will be heard to talk like English-
> speaking ones, which is false. (30-31)

Achebe spoke similarly of the African writer's position, describing the dilemma of trying to express African thoughts and feelings in a language that cannot seem to do so:

> Caught in that situation he can do one of two things. He can try and contain what he wants to say within the limits of conventional English or he can try to push back those limits to accommodate his idea. The first method produces competent, uninspired and rather flat work. The second method can produce something new and valuable to the English language as well as to the material he is trying to put over. *But* it can also get out of hand. It can lead to simply *bad* English being accepted and defended as African or Nigerian. ("The Role," 160)

Another Nigerian, Edward Okwu, used similar terms:

> There are then those swift and subtle turns of the mind, and those little catch-phrases that are peculiarly African, or Nigerian as the case may be, which, attributed to the wrong circumstances, at best look grotesque and misapplied. Our writers should then make the English language serve them the purpose of squeezing out of it the colour of African thought. (313)

These quotations have shown the various sides of the debate concerning the use of European languages for African literature. Obiajunwa Wali thought that languages ought to define literatures; Mphahlele raised several instances to challenge this view. Others felt African languages were important in nation building, although Mphahlele pointed out that this was not true in South Africa; Achebe argued that English *is* the national language of Nigeria. There was the feeling among some Africans that their literature must reflect Africa and that this can be done best—some would argue, *only*—in African languages. To this argument there was little rebuttal. Rather, the impracticalities of using African languages were pointed out, particularly the small economic market for a literature in any one African language, as well as the advantages of using a world language: not only an international audience but, more important, a means for intra-African communication.

There was the further argument that Africans could not produce a superior literature in languages they commanded only secondarily. The difficulties of learning a second language were played down by Chinua Achebe; by implication, the works of several authors were said to provide additional proof that second languages were not an insurmountable literary problem.

It was argued that, even granting a technical command of a second language, there were psychological hazards that might occur in using the language of the colonizer. To this argument there was little direct rebuttal; however, a strong rebuttal by implication lay in the thinking of many that the African writer, in using the colonizer's language, used it in such a way as to bring out the Africanness of the context in which it was used, thus gaining the advantages of a world language and audience, something important to many, without endangering the integrity of the African experience.

LANGUAGE AS A CRITICAL STANDARD

Aside from these theoretical statements, what is more interesting to note is that the African writer's use of European languages led to the creation of a critical standard by many African critics, who applied it to particular works of African literature. It is interesting to note some of the various ways this was done. But first a word of caution and explanation is necessary. The quotations in this section are direct statements and judgments made by African critics. They are offered to indicate one thing only: that a significantly large number of critics felt the choice and use of language to be significant and used it as a critical standard. I offer no comment as to how the critics used this standard or whether I agree or disagree with either the use of the standard in general or the application of it in any given instance. That would be the object of a much more subjective work. No judgment of the critics is intended, therefore, since my goal is to arrive at a better understanding of what tools the critics were using rather than the skill with which they used them. It seems fair to assume that there are good and bad critics the world over—in all countries, in all languages, and of all races. While determining which standards were being used by the good and bad critics from Africa, it will remain for the reader to decide which were used poorly and which were used well.

Tutuola

The most obvious instance of the application of language as a critical standard were the early works of Amos Tutuola, mostly because of the reception of his first "novel," *The Palm-Wine Drinkard and His Dead Palm-Wine Tapster in the Dead's Town* (1952).

Despite the furor raised in African circles by the European reception of *The Palm-Wine Drinkard*, Cyprian Ekwensi's early review of it, apparently the first by an African, suggested much of the later, more sober Tutuola criticism that seemed to prevail. Among other things, Ekwensi applied the standard of language, saying, "The language is simple and if it sometimes lapses into the ungrammatical ('I lied down awoke'), it is graphic in places ('. . . his body was almost covered with long hair like a horse's tail') and musical in many" ("A Yoruba Fantasy," 713). This seems to have been the only review by an African before the appearance the same month of Dylan Thomas's famous review. Thomas found it a "tall, devilish story" written in "young English" (7).

Two years later a British critic, Eric Robinson, reviewed Tutuola's second book, *My Life in the Bush of Ghosts* (1954), which precipitated a lively debate in the pages of *West Africa*. Babasola Johnson said that the *"Palm Wine Drinkard* should not have been published at all. The language in which it is written is foreign to West Africans and English people, or anybody for that matter. It is bad enough to attempt an African narrative in 'good English', it is worse to attempt it in Mr. Tutuola's strange lingo" (322).

Another critic, I. Adeagbo Akinjogbin, though he claimed not to have read Tutuola's first two books, was equally dubious of Tutuola's language: "I would suggest that undue prominence is being given to these two books which, as far as I can gather, are of no literary value in spite of the 'author's written style' being unique among present-day writers' " (513).

Later detractors included Mphahlele, who remarked in a 1962 interview, "I think that *Tutuola* is not a great writer. You begin, as he does, by telling a story that has been told a thousand times, and then you simply change the sequence of events and write them in bad English . . . and you have Tutuola" ("Entretien avec Ezekiel Mphahlele," 57). Another detractor, Mbella Sonne Dipoko, said, "The English language is mutilated and grammar writhes in pain on the gallows of this Nigerian's pen" (Review of *Seven African Writers*, 31). Mark N. Eze was another, who said of a Tutuola short story, *"Don't Pay Bad for Bad* is a pretty folk tale with a pretty moral told in a pretty manner. [But] the story lacks the movement which comes from the correct use of language" (14). And, finally, Taban Lo Liyong told the colorful story of some proud Nigerian students lording it over some other African students one day at Howard University, "talking about their Achebes, Ekwensis, Njokwus, Clarks, Soyinkas, Okaras, and would have bored us stiff with the catalogue if somebody had not interrupted. . . . He reminded the Nigerians that they have an Amos Tutuola, too. That shut their mouths" ("Can We Correct," 5).

Tutuola also had his supporters. Alongside Akinjogbin's letter was a more favorable one. Ade Sodipo wrote, "To me, the language employed in the two books does not (without being influenced by fondness of palm wine) read strangely" (513), and added that "Mr. Tutuola writes on folk tales; to write these successfully demands real ability on the writer's part so that he can carry his readers with him. To do this his style must attune to the subject matter. Mr. Tutuola has, in my opinion, achieved this; the style is romantic" (513).

Four years after his original review, Ekwensi reiterated his appreciation of Tutuola's language, saying, "He writes in the direct manner of African expression, sharp and stripped of all trimmings, yet not devoid of feelings and beauty" ("The Dilemma," 702). Davidson Nicol also commented on the language of *The Palm-Wine Drinkard*: "It has been translated into French,

German, Italian and Yugoslav, though one wonders how much of the un-
usual flavour of the book can be carried over; since its semi-distortion of
English words is one of the chief factors lending power to it" ("The Soft
Pink Palms," 112).

Achebe was another enthusiastic critic. He said, "Those who can do the
work of extending the frontiers of English so as to accommodate African
thought-patterns must do it through their mastery of English and not out of
innocence. Of course, there is the obvious exception of Amos Tutuola"
("The Role," 160). George Awoonor-Williams said that Tutuola "writes a
language that has freshness and charm because it lacks the conventionalism
of English as we know it" (9). And J. O. Ekpenyong said Tutuola and Etok
Akpan belonged to the "folklore category" of African literature and that
"though they may ignore grammar and idiom they often succeed in making
quite a gripping impact upon the reader with their boldness in coining words
and introducing new usages for familiar English words" (147). Eldred Jones
used English style as a standard when he wrote, of the African reading
Tutuola, "The language is likely to be as puzzling to him as to a European,
for Tutuola's merit is *not* essentially linguistic, though few can fail to thrill
at some of Tutuola's more fortunate coinages—'drinkard' and 'gravitiness'
being two of my favourites" ("Turning Back," 30).

Certainly Tutuola presented a special case in the use of European languages by African writers and drew a mixed response. Whether or not one
agrees with British critic Gerald Moore that "Tutuola's books are far more
like a fascinating cul-de-sac than the beginning of anything directly useful
to other writers" (*Seven African Writers*, 57), it is a fact that long after the
publication of *The Palm-Wine Drinkard*, few African writers have emulated
him.

Pidgin and Krio

Inadvertently, Tutuola was responsible for the raising of another interesting aspect of the language question: the literary possibilities of Pidgin English, as spoken in Nigeria, Cameroun, and Ghana; and Krio, spoken in
Sierra Leone. Eldred Jones seems to have been the first, if not the only,
African critic to have considered this question seriously. In 1957 he wrote,
concerning the large number of Krio speakers, "Thousands of people in this
country are completely cut off from at least one source of aesthetic experience, because they are not sufficiently in command of the language which
they are compelled by circumstances to speak" ("The Potentialities," 40),
and added, "I think that there is a place and a need for vernacular literature
in Krio now" (40). Five years later Bernard Fonlon reported that the matter
was discussed at the Makerere conference in 1962. Of Pidgin English, he
said that "some strongly disapproved of it as found in the works of Cyprian

Ekwensi; they said it was not pidgin English at all for his version of it was spoken nowhere" ("Challenge," 48). Fonlon then reported that Langston Hughes, also at the conference, said he had learned from his writing of American black English that "if dialect was written exactly as it was spoken it would be very difficult to read; to reduce it to writing it had to be modified by being brought a bit nearer to English especially in spelling" (49). Fonlon's Cameroun journal, *Abbia*, carried a debate on the adoption of Pidgin English as the national language for Cameroun (see J. A. Kisob), but the matter was soon dropped. (However, see Abioseh Michael Porter's bibliography of the literature in Cameroun.)

Somewhat later, Mphahlele also had doubts about the efficacy of Pidgin, while suggesting more potential for Krio. In 1964 he said,

> I do not think pidgin has a chance of developing beyond this talkative, if expressive level. It has no fixed grammar, like for instance, Kriol [sic] as spoken in Sierra Leone. Pidgin is not spoken in West African homes, as Kriol is. ("The Language of African Literature," *Language and Learning*, 267)

Interestingly, however, Mphahlele commented favorably on Frank Aig-Imoukhuede's poem "One Wife for One Man" because he said the author "uses pidgin in a very expressive manner" ("The Language of African Literature," discussion paper 4).

Dapo Adelugba commented on the use of Pidgin in Wole Soyinka's play, *The Trials of Brother Jero*, saying, "In the creation of Chume and Amope, Wole Soyinka has shown that potentialities of comic dialogue lie inherent in 'pidgin' English" (74). And J. P. Clark said, "The character using pidgin must be in a position to do so in actual life, and there must be a special purpose served. That is, there must be propriety" ("Aspects," 125). He also commented on Soyinka's *Jero*:

> In Mr. Wole Soyinka's *Brother Jero*, however, the disciple Chume oscillates between "pidgin" and the so-called standard or Queen's English. The excuse might be that at one time the situation demands that he speaks straight in English that is Pidgin English as befits an office messenger, while at another it requires him to speak in his original Nigerian tongue here translated into appropriate standard English as we have said. ("Aspects," 125-26)

On the other hand, Joseph Okpaku said of the Pidgin used in Achebe's *A Man of the People*, "Achebe's pidgin English is good low Pidgin though by no means anything like the High Pidgin English of the Nigerian Midwestern provinces. It is adequate and only fails once or twice" ("A Novel," 78-79). And finally, in a review of Ferdinand Oyono's *Houseboy*, Mofolo Bulane seemed surprised that Pidgin was not used. He said, "One should have expected the author to use pidgin in portraying his minor characters. He has effectively done so by other techniques" ("Cameroon! Cameroon!" 216).

From these critics' remarks, we may conclude that there has not been any systematic tendency to use Pidgin English in African literature. Tutuola does not seem to write anything approximating a standard form of Pidgin, and other authors have used it mainly for its comic effect. Nor has any African critic dealt with the question at length. However, the critics' comments suggest the beginning of a critical standard.

Transliteration: Gabriel Okara

Another intriguing aspect of the language question taken up by the critics was the linguistic relationship of the African languages to the expression of African literature in European langauges. How can African content be expressed in a European form without losing some of its Africanness? This problem led to one other case in African literature that may also, along with Tutuola, be described as special. This concerns the discussion surrounding the process of transliteration that was raised upon the publication of an experimental novel, *The Voice* (1964), by Nigerian writer Gabriel Okara. Okara described his method of composition in his novel thus:

> As a writer who believes in the utilisation of African ideas, African philosophy and African folk-lore and imagery to the fullest extent possible, I am of the opinion the only way to use them effectively is to translate them almost literally from the African language native to the writer into whatever European language he is using as his medium of expression. (15)

Further on he said:

> In order to capture the vivid images of African speech, I had to eschew the habit of expressing my thoughts first in English. It was difficult at first, but I had to learn. I had to study each Ijaw expression I used and to discover the probable situation in which it was used in order to bring out the nearest meaning in English. (15)

Three African critics reacted to Okara's linguistic experiment. Mphahlele said, "Okara's experiment is too strenuous and is still not available to the person who is outside his language group: English becomes the slave of the African language" ("The Language of African Literature," *Language and Learning,* 273). Emmanuel Obiechina was more favorable:

> His experiment with language is even more interesting for whereas Achebe and other West African novelists are content to translate oral

tradition into English by keeping as close as possible to the original meaning, Okara is the only writer who actually goes so far as to transliterate, even to the extent of reproducing syntactical form. This gives the action of his story a peculiarly heavy-footed and tortuous movement which again seems to fit the serious moral tone and pessimistic mood of the story. (62)

And yet in the same review Obiechina said of Nkem Nwankwo's novel, *Danda* (1964), that the author "contents himself with using his natural style to reproduce traditional speech in English. He makes much less tedious reading than Okara" (63), and concluded that "when Mr. Okara has pondered his 'folksy' style a little longer, he may have to decide whether it will not be better for him to write simply as Gabriel Okara and reserve transliteration to only the actual dialogues" (63).

Ben Obumselu, like Mphahlele, had reservations. Speaking of the Wali-Achebe debate, Obumselu said they

> both conclude that African writing in English or French should attempt to secure closer verisimilitude by rendering African speech literally into the metropolitan language. If this recommendation is implemented with Mr. Achebe's self-effacing skill, the result should be both agreeable and imaginative. But that the principle itself is mistaken is evident from its impoverishing influence on Gabriel Okara's *The Voice*. ("The Background," 51)

More specifically, Obumselu pointed out that "when Gabriel Okara makes an Ijaw man say: 'Thou keepest quiet? Answer me. I know nothing thou sayeth'; the English reader is not, and cannot be, introduced by this into the peculiarities of the Ijaw mind or the Ijaw syntax. The syntax is that of Biblical English" ("The Background," 52). He added that "there is no escape from contexts and associations of one language into those of another" (52).

Donatus Nwoga indicated some works that he believed were successes and failures of the transliteration process. He said of Okara's *The Voice* and Nwankwo's *Danda* that "these attempts are not fully successful because the reader is often being called upon to make unjustifiably drastic readjustments to language elements during the process of reading" but went on to say, "There is no doubt however that the attempt to bring English deep into its African environment is justified. Christina Aidoo's story 'Cut Me a Drink' and P. I. Buahin's 'This Is Experience Speaking', in their various ways, show how exciting and convincing can be the result of the experimentation and adaptation" ("West Africa," 15). What is especially interesting here was the critic's application of the same standard to arrive at both positive and negative conclusions.

The process of transliteration would seem to differ from writer to writer, depending in part upon his relative fluency in the two languages in question. And whereas Okara had to "eschew the habit of expressing [his] thoughts first in English," the Ghanaian poet George Awoonor-Williams claimed that "we all think in our own vernaculars. And even for someone who thinks in an adopted language, when his basic emotions are called upon, he will express them in his native tongue" (9). He added, "It may be a good experiment, no doubt limited in some respects, to express our thoughts in a transliterated English, keeping as close as possible to the vernacular expression. For there are a number of things in our languages which defy translation into a conventionally idiomatic English" (9).

A Nigerian writer, John Munonye, described the process he went through when he had difficulty expressing himself:

> One thing I do in such circumstances (apart from walking out of the house) is to resort to the vernacular, in my mind, and then translate into English on paper. I must say that I have found this very rewarding. It leads to some personal style.
>
> This is particularly so in the dialogues. In a story where the characters are Nigerian the dialogues should, I think, be as close as possible to the emotions, style and idiosyncrasies of the people. (78)

Upon asking himself whether African writers write directly in European languages or translate from African ones, Davidson Nicol decided that "they probably do both as the situation warrants" (*Africa*, 69), and asked, "Is this process of translation an obstacle? It may be a hindrance to expression; on the other hand it may lead to more care in the use of words, and, with the highly literate African, a more finished and polished piece of prose" (69).

Lewis Nkosi described what he considered a successful linguistic experiment by Mphahlele that exploited the willingness of African languages to borrow and adapt from other languages:

> I am thinking of words like "situation" which is a term of abuse for members of the African middle-class trying to "situate" themselves above the masses. And so is *"sitshuzimi"* which is an adaptation of the phrase "Excuse me," also used in a satirical vein to refer to pretentious half-baked Africans trying to ape the ways of white folk by a repetitive use of similar phrases.
>
> So far as I have been able to gather from such evidence as I possess, what Ezekiel Mphahlele has been trying to do is reclaim some of these words from the African languages back into the English where they have their origin anyway; and simultaneously he exploits the new connotative element they have since acquired by their association with the

African languages: in doing so he manages to give them a slightly ambivalent satirical content which they would not otherwise possess. Or
he merely makes African idioms and speech rhythms stand behind his
English, something which Nigerians do all the time. ("Fiction," 50)

One African critic, however, objected to this kind of experimentation. In
the newsletter of the American Society for African Culture, Samuel K. Opoku
was reported to have objected to

the use of English in an elaborate, periphrastic form by one writer, A.
A. Opoku, in order to imitate Akan speech. "That is not the sort of
style that we teach our students at school and I, myself, don't think it
is the sort of style that is going to make any contribution to world literature." ("The African Literary Scene," 3)

But this reaction got little or no support from other critics.

Achebe

Tutuola and Okara represented two unique cases of language use; certainly
no others have generated as much discussion. Chinua Achebe, however,
seemed to find the happy middle ground that critics wanted, somewhere between the Victorian English of the British colonial forms and the "young
English" of Tutuola. In fact, Achebe's use of English became widely accepted as a standard, with only an occasional demurral, as a look at the critics'
comments will indicate.

In reviewing *Things Fall Apart* in 1959, Ben Obumselu said the African
writer "is not merely to use but to expand the resources of English" and that

the verbal peculiarities of *Things Fall Apart* suggest that Chinua Achebe
has reflected much on this problem. His solution is to attempt literal
fidelity, to translate wherever possible the actual words which might
have been used in his own language and thereby preserve the native
flavour of his situations. Such an experiment requires both imagination and originality. And though Mr. Achebe does not carry it off
with distinction, he does so with credit. His experiment is a very positive contribution to the writing of West African English literature, and
I believe it will make the work of subsequent authors easier. (Review,
38)

A Ghanaian critic, G. Adali Mortty, also reviewed the novel in 1959 and
said of Achebe, "He knows and uses English with consummate skill" (49),
and "His language has the ring and rhythm of poetry. At the background of
the words can be heard the thrumming syncopation of the sound of Africa—
the gongs, the drums, the castanets and the horns" (49). Eldred Jones said,

"One of the significant successes of the book is the author's sensitive use of English so that it reflects the African environment. This he achieves by drawing his images out of his surroundings and from traditional African sources instead of plucking them ready-made from British literary English" ("Language," 39).

George Awoonor-Williams was equally enthusiastic about Achebe's English. He asked, "In writing, instead of 'good night' why shouldn't the Akan writer using English say 'May it dawn on us'?" (9). His answer was:

> I think it more beautiful and expressive. It also gives English a new dimension, a certain freshness. I think Achebe's *Things Fall Apart* achieves this overall effect of freshness by the translating of Igbo thoughts and words into English, giving his story a remarkable authenticity. Proverbs are woven into speech and dialogue. Far from being a desecration of the English language, which seems to have come to stay, this transliteration of thoughts, concepts and images gives the language a freshness and a new scope for which I am sure the native speakers of English will thank us. (9)

J. P. Clark also used Achebe as a standard, saying that if "there is a faithful reproduction of the speech habits of one people into another language as Mr. Chinua Achebe does significantly in English with the Ibo dialogue proceeding by technique of the proverb, then I think the artist has achieved a reasonable measure of success" ("Aspects," 125).

Others

Achebe was no doubt the writer whose language was most often used positively as a standard. Other writers were also cited, however, although not always positively. For example, A. Bodurin saw a dissociation in Wole Soyinka's English: "This dissociation of content from expression is partly responsible for the difficulty in appreciating Wole Soyinka's plays. I am strongly convinced that if 'A dance of the forests,' the most intriguing of his plays, were written in Yoruba, much of the obscurity would disappear" (42). And Ben Obumselu said of Soyinka's play *The Strong Breed*, "The reader could wish that the experiences of the play were more fully realized in language. Except in the retrospective passages (which are perhaps too misty), Wole Soyinka attempts to make do with inexpressive realistic dialogue in a play that calls for lucid poetic statement" ("The Background," 56-57).

Still other writers drew similar comments, favorable and unfavorable, from the critics. Writing in 1959, Nontando Jabavu said of a passage in *One Man—One Wife*, a novel by T. M. Aluko, that

> such a passage was sheer delight to me, for that's how you would interrupt and speak if an old woman at home; . . . And whatever the literal

rendering may be in the Nigerian language concerned, the English rendering: "I bore her," exactly fits in my language. Yet in English for native English people, it would sound odd to express yourself like that. (421)

The early date of this critique is of some interest. Of more interest, perhaps, was the phenomenon of a West African writer's succeeding for a South African critic where "African English" was concerned. Though from obviously disparate linguistic backgrounds, Aluko's English sounded "African" to Jabavu.

Similar observations occurred in francophone Africa. Jacques Rabemananjara, writing of the poetry of a fellow Malagasay writer, said, "Rabearivelo has assimilated French so well that, instead of being its servant, it serves him" ("Préface," 21*).

And Gilbert Ilboudo, reporting on the conference proceedings at Dakar in 1963, singled out a particular work for its Africanized French. Speaking of the desire to transform standard French into a vehicle for African literature, he said,

However the direction in which this transmutation is to occur was not made clear, although there is a work which could have served as an exemplar for serious discussion on this point: Nazi Boni's novel *Crépuscule des temps anciens*. . . . I think this is an interesting example of the manner in which the French language might be moulded to conform more closely to our thoughts. (31)

CONCLUSIONS

Although many African writers agreed with Wali that it would be ideal if African literature were written in African languages, there were many overriding practical considerations that suggested the continued use of European languages for some time to come. It was also very clear that the use to which the African writer puts a European language must capture the rhythms, idioms, and feeling of an African language. And in doing this, it was understood that the resultant form of the European language would deviate from the standard form of the language as spoken by Europeans.

The language question surrounding African literature made it apparent that a standard form of African English was evolving. The case for African French was less clear. Although the French-speaking African critics were occasionally interested in linguistic questions, they did not seem to have pursued the matter with quite the vigor of their English-speaking counterparts. One possible explanation might be the different attitudes toward language among the British and the French and how these attitudes became part of the education policies in their respective colonies.

3 African Literature for Whom? The Question of Audience

Much has been written on the African writer's problem of audience. What has not been noted, insofar as I am aware, is the effect this question had on African literary criticism in its early years. The fact that African critics took up the question, however consciously or unconsciously, means that the eventual impact on the literature itself will be even more profound than one might otherwise have expected, for criticism has the double function of expressing the past—in this case, a concern with cultural identity—and of affecting—and effecting—the future directions in which African literature is likely to move in response to it. The restlessness with which African critics have dealt with the problem of audience indicates the pervasiveness of the question of cultural identity and autonomy in contemporary thinking. Even more significant is the fact that the critics' discussion of this problem has not remained academic and theoretical; it has been put into practice. The question of audience was in fact applied by African critics as a critical standard by which specific works of African literature were judged in the two decades following World War II.

African literary criticism, like everything else, did not develop in a vacuum. In fact, the world milieu in which it did develop was so politically and emotionally charged—not to say economically and culturally controlled by the West—that African critics encountered difficult problems in establishing the standards by which they evaluated African literature. In some cases, these standards seemed to be, if not contradictory, at least superficially difficult to reconcile with one another. The question of African literature for whom? has been one such area of confusion. Should this new, emerging literature be directed toward the West? Should it be directed inwardly, toward Africa itself? Or, what is a more confusing but tempting possibility, should it be aimed in both directions at once? A survey of the criticism suggests that

African critics, caught between these necessities, have vacillated between the two while attempting to recognize the validity of each.

Modern African literary criticism as a conscious movement toward the articulation of critical standards applying to African literature probably began in the 1930s with Aimé Césaire, Léon Damas, Léopold Sédar Senghor, and others formulating, somewhere on the Left Bank, the theoretical basis of Negritude. The criticism takes on more concrete form with the founding of the journal and publishing house, Présence africaine, in 1947, and in the publication the following year of Senghor's *Anthologie de la nouvelle poésie nègre et malgache de langue française*, with its introduction, "Orphée noir," by Jean-Paul Sartre. We are clearly concerned, then, with a beginning. What I will demonstrate are the two distinct directions in which this beginning moved: outward, toward the West in particular, and inward toward Africa.

No critic would be likely to say that writers should aim their efforts expressly away from the culture and people with whom they identify as human beings. And, in fact, many African critics have insisted on just the opposite. Yet there may be good reason for writers to want to reach an audience well beyond their own culture and people. Certainly many African critics have agreed on this necessity as well. What must be kept in mind is the extent and depth of the complex position in which African critics found themselves, particularly in the years just prior to and after independence. Confronted with a burgeoning literature and with a desire to foster an accurate image of Africa abroad while encouraging a concern for Africa's immediate internal problems, Africans have produced a body of criticism that reflects precisely this complex and fluid situation.

THE AFRICAN PRESENCE IN THE WORLD

The premiere issue of *Présence africaine* appeared at the close of 1947. Its Senegalese editor, Alioune Diop, said the journal would consist of "authoritative studies of the culture and civilization of Africa by well-known scholars" and that "there will also be searching examinations of the methods of integrating the black man in western civilization" ("Niam n'goura," 185). Diop was no doubt unaware at that time that he was inaugurating a standard by which African critics would later come to judge African literature, but this is in fact what occurred. Two factors explain why.

First, independence for the British and French colonies had not been seriously considered and was in most instances thirteen years in the future; second, the prestige surrounding the creation of *Présence africaine*, with the assistance and cooperation of such Western intellectuals as Jean-Paul Sartre, André Gide, Albert Camus, and Richard Wright, was enormous. The journal was, of course, a reflection of a powerful creative drive in those Africans who had come into contact with Western civilization, found it both seductive and lacking, and felt the double urge to rediscover Africa's values and then to present them to the rest of the world, to correct what Leopold Senghor would later call the theory of *tabula rasa* (Makward, "Negritude," 41): the belief that Africa had no culture or history and was, rather, a "blank page" on which Europe would create its own version of Africa. *Présence africaine* would no doubt combat the *tabula rasa* myth, and Diop set forth one of the ramifications of the "African presence" when he spoke of "the obligation to create in communion with others a universal order with universal values" ("Niam n'goura," 189). This universalizing, through the introduction of the African presence into a world that had not only lacked it but denied its existence, led easily to Leopold Senghor's concept of a "civilization of the universal." Between them, Diop and Senghor went on to develop a cohesive politicocultural position. In fact, in the year after the founding of the journal, Senghor took up the concept when, in his introduction, he reminded readers that his *Anthologie* was published as part of a series of works celebrating the centenary of the Revolution of 1848. Senghor further reminded his readers that included in this revolution was the decree of April 27, 1848, abolishing slavery and said of the Negro peoples that "thus they have been able, despite the regression of the Second Empire and the Third Republic, to make their contribution to the French humanism of today, which is truly universal because it has been nourished by the milk of all the races of the earth" ("Introduction," *Anthologie*, 1*).

Perhaps Senghor's most succinct statement of his position (he has reiterated it on countless occasions) was the following, made in 1961:

> If European civilization were to be imposed, unmodified, on all peoples and continents, if could only be by force. That is its first disadvantage. A more serious one is that it would not be *humanistic*, for it would cut itself off from the contemporary values of the greater part of humanity . . . it would be a universal civilization; it would not be the Civilization of the Universal. ("What Is Negritude?" 1211)

A few years later, Senghor took note of the African presence in Europe as fact rather than a theory of wished-for necessity. Speaking at the opening of the First World Festival of Negro Arts in 1966, he made the following observation on the impact of Africa on the twentieth century:

> Being unable . . . to deny Negro art, one wished to minimize its originality under the pretext that it had a monopoly neither on emotion nor on the analogical image, nor even on rhythm. And it is true that every true artist takes advantage of his talents, his race, his nation, whatever they may be. And yet, it was necessary that Rimbaud make use of Negritude, that Picasso was staggered by a Baoule mask, that Apollinaire

extolled wood fetishes before the art of Western Europe consented, after two thousand years, to abandon the *physeos mimesis*, the imitation of nature. ("Discour," 20*)

Diop and Senghor undoubtedly did much together to create the African presence as a critical value. However, many other critics, both anglophone and francophone, expressed a similar value, though perhaps not at such length or as systematically as these two.

It might be assumed that because of the widespread influence of Senghor and the influence of *Présence africaine* on French-speaking Africa, especially in its early days, the need for an African presence was not shared by English-speaking Africans. However, the split among Africans over the issue of an African presence—or, for that matter, of Negritude—has never been as clear-cut along linguistic lines as some would have us believe. One finds this value being promoted, in fact, by a number of anglophone Africans.

As early as 1950, for example, the Nigerian writer Cyprian Ekwensi called for an African presence when he identified the "first task for the West African writer: development of the ability to write *of* his people *for* the world" ("Outlook," 21). The Reverend John S. Mbiti, speaking at the Second Congress of Negro Writers and Artists (Rome, 1959), told of his collecting of the verbal literature of the Akamba people and favored an African presence when he pointed out that "there is a desperate need to save this verbal literature, and to make known to the world, the powers of creative thinking of the African mind" (260).

Ezekiel Mphahlele, with Senghor one of the most prolific and cogent of critics, sponsored the value of an African presence when, speaking of the advantages of using colonial languages, he said, "We can . . . make African symbols and images available to the rest of the world, and thus the fusion of cultures takes a more natural course" ("Out of Africa," 62).

Several other critics made similar statements of theory that reflected their desire to foster an African presence. To quote them all would make tedious reading, but what is particularly interesting is whether African critics willingly and consciously applied this standard to particular works of African literature; whether they in fact applied the theory, thereby making it a concrete critical standard. Clearly Africans indeed applied such a standard on many occasions.

The African Presence as a Critical Standard

Francophone Critics. Alexandre Biyidi (better known as Mongo Beti, the Camerounian novelist and critic) was one of the first to apply the African presence as a critical standard to a particular literary work. He disliked Camara Laye's first novel, *L'Enfant noir*, because, among other things, it would mislead the non-African. Writing in an early issue of *Présence africaine*, he put it this way: "The *Black Child* is not at all a testimony—my God! When I think of the conclusions that will be drawn by the kind of person one knows" ("L'Enfant noir," 420*).

A Zairian critic, Paul Mushiete, in referring to the authors he had selected for his anthology, *La Littérature française africaine* (1957), said, "The greatest preoccupation of these authors has been to remind the world of the reality of a world that has been set aside from the history of nations. The poet stands proudly erect and revalues the ignored Africa and communicates to us his faith in a powerful Africa" ("Introduction," 4*).

Paulin Joachim applied the standard on several occasions. Referring to *Un Piège sans fin*, a novel by Olympe Bhely-Quenum, as well as to his own future work, he said that "the writer tells us that the whole of his literary work will have Dahomey as its subject and will draw from it all its substance, because he wants fervently for this part of Africa to be well-known and regarded as one of the peaks of the African *spirit*" ("Un Piège," 41*). Of Cheikh Hamidou Kane and his novel, *L'Aventure ambiguë*, Joachim said, "These are the men, this is the kind of demonstration and work that free Africa must show to the world that expects so much from her, that waits now to know the resources of the Negro African genius which the colonial regime has so long smothered" ("L'Aventure ambiguë," 21*). To still another work, he applied the same standard: "In his finely-textured *Contes d'Amadou Koumba*, Birago Diop exhumes the cultural values of the black race that have so long been stifled by colonialist oppression, and imparts to them a pearly luster for all mankind to see" ("Contemporary," 298).

Another critic, Octave Ugirashebuja, praised Leopold Senghor for his contribution to an African presence: "He knew how to sing the genius of a people in the tongue of another people. And he contributed thereby, in an extraordinary efficacious way, to realize his program: to make known to the world the riches of the African soul" (333*).

Bakary Traoré, in a preface to a play by Cheik A. Ndao, said the play fulfilled the requirements of Negro-African theater, one of which was "to make African civilizations recognized, through a consciousness of the uniqueness of our problems" as well as its being "a raising of the consciousness of the world" ("Preface," 10*).

Anglophone Critics. Anglophone critics were equally ready to apply the African presence as a standard to specific literary works. The first to do so may have been I. Adeagbo Akinjogbin, who reacted negatively to Amos Tutuola's first two novels and the translation of one of them into French, because

> most Englishmen, and perhaps Frenchmen, are pleased to believe all sorts of fantastic tales about Africa, a continent of which they are profoundly ignorant. The "extraordinary books" of Mr. Tutuola (which

must undoubtedly contain some of the unbelievable things in our folk-tales) will just suit the temper of his European readers as they seem to confirm their concepts of Africa. (513)

Davidson Nicol of Sierra Leone, on the other hand, took a more positive view of Tutuola while applying the same standard. He said, "He has certainly put West Africa on the map of the literary world, and for that he is to be congratulated" ("The Soft Pink Palms," 113). But Ben Obumselu, a Nigerian critic, sided with Akinjogbin rather than Nicol, saying, "It is not easy to escape the suspicion that European admiration of Amos Tutuola's novels comes out of a supposition, conscious or unconscious, that the Freudian nightmare into which Mr. Tutuola takes his readers is a true picture of the jungle which is the African mind" (Review, 37). Still applying the same standard, Obumselu arrived at a positive judgment of Chinua Achebe's *Things Fall Apart*, in part because "it is assured a world market" (Review, 38).

Another critic, Adisa Williams, liked Achebe's third novel, *Arrow of God*, because of its portrayal of African rural life and because "in this way he has not only widened the horizon of fellow Nigerians but he has also, culturally speaking, taken the rest of the world into our confidence" (43). And, finally, J. P. Clark expressed the standard when he spoke disparagingly of "the Italian film producer who wants to shoot Ekwensi's *Jagua Nana* because the old tart and her cut-throat politician lovers are symbols of the new Africa!" to which he added, "A pity I have lost my cannibal ways for how I tremble to wring the man's neck for vomiting such mess" ("Our Literary Critics," 81).

Anti-African Presence as a Critical Standard

There were, on the other hand, some Africans who were uneasy with the desire to project an African presence at all. Indeed, Achebe, in his essay "The Black Writer's Burden," tried to discourage any cultural effort intended as a self-justification, arguing that no group of human beings should have to justify their existence to anyone. Wole Soyinka was also concerned about African self-consciousness throughout his essay "And After the Narcissist?" in which he said:

> In any culture, the cycle of rediscovery—*negritude* or Renaissance enlightenment or pre-Raphaelite—must, before the wonder palls, breed its own body of the literature of self-worship. African writing has suffered from an additional infliction; apart from his own rediscovery, the African writer has experienced discovery by the external eye. It is doubtful if the effect of this has any parallel in European literature. (56)

Where Achebe and Soyinka saw self-justification and self-consciousness in the desire for an African presence, Eldred Jones of Sierra Leone saw a detrimental nationalism. He noted that adverse criticism of a novel like *Jagua Nana* in Africa is sometimes based not on any artistic failure in the novel, but on the supposition that it shows Nigeria to the outside world in a bad light. . . . It is to be hoped that writers in Africa will be undeterred by such narrow nationalistic theories of literature as the best writers elsewhere have been; otherwise our writers will produce not literature but propaganda. ("Nationalism," 155)

A. Bodurin was equally explicit in denouncing literature intended as propaganda:

> I know it can be argued that the African author writing in a European language reaches a bigger and more international public which is an advantage for African culture. This argument implies that literature is propaganda not culture. The logic of the situation is ineluctable. If African literature is destined for a European-speaking African elite or if it is produced for European anthropologists then this literature has inflicted a double defeat on itself by contributing nothing to either African or European culture. (42)

Bodurin's solution was the adoption of African languages as literary vehicles.

Mohamadou Kane gave a historical perspective to the need for an African presence while declaring that in 1966 the need no longer existed: "In the past there was the need to have talks with the colonizers and to show Negroes in a light that he felt to be an honest one. Today, with utterly different conditions of political and cultural promotion, it is amazing to see that our writers are prepared to stay in the old rut" (19).

And finally, in the same year, one critic seemed actually to have applied an "anti-African presence" as a critical standard. In reviewing Achebe's fourth novel, *A Man of the People*, Joseph Okpaku said that, after the opening pages, "We no longer see the diligent yet irrelevant attempt to demonstrate a thorough mastery of the Queen's English—nor the commitment to explain the complex culture of 'our Country' to the people outside, though once or twice this threatens to rear up its head" ("A Novel," 77).

Thus it is clear that by 1966, Diop's and Senghor's clarion call two decades earlier for an African presence was being resisted in some quarters. And paralleling the outward-looking standard of the African presence was an inward-looking standard—that of the African audience.

THE AFRICAN AUDIENCE

The critical value which balances that of the African presence in the world is the widely accepted dictum that the African writer must write first and foremost for Africans: African literature for the Africans. This is not a surprising or revolutionary concept; it is very likely an unspoken criterion of the literary criticism of any literature.

The hard fact for the African writer and critic was that almost all the publishing machinery in the 1950s and 1960s was located in the West and was controlled by Westerners whose decisions were based on a knowledge of, and dependence upon, Western customers. The fact that Présence africaine was not only a journal but a publishing house as well, with editorial decisions made primarily by Africans, is a fact that should not be underestimated. But Présence africaine-the-publisher was the exception, not the rule, in the first two decades of African literature.

The East Africa Publishing House began publishing creative work in the middle 1960s, and André Deutsch, Longmans, and Oxford set up operations in Africa with varying success. But it is clear that the control of the publication of African literature, certainly before 1960, was almost entirely in non-African hands. Even Présence africaine seems to have published only six or eight volumes before that date, beginning with Bernard Dadié's *Le Pagne noir* and Antoine-Roger Bolamba's *Esanzo; chants pour mon pays* (both 1955). It remains true that non-Africans have continued to control much of the publication of African literature from 1960 to the present, though less exclusively.

Non-African control might not have been significant if it had not been for the fact that the book market in Africa in the period under discussion was limited. A Western publisher who took on an African manuscript had to keep in mind that almost all its prospective buyers would be Western, not African. And this, of course, was the very market the publisher knew best. Hence the scene was set that would encourage a particular form of African literature.

The African writer and critic had yet another difficulty. There was a great desire to project into the non-African world an accurate image of Africa. Africans then had to reach the very people for whom the Western publisher was prepared to tailor an African literature that would reinforce, rather than combat, their stereotypes. African writers wanted to reach a Western audience but on their own terms; yet they were not in a position to dictate those terms. They had to write for a Western publisher; they wanted to write for a Western audience; but they had also to write for an African critic who told them they should write for an African audience.

Cheikh Anta Diop was perhaps the first African to address this predicament. In 1948, speaking of African writers, he said that "we are obliged to recognize that it is essentially a European public to which they address themselves, that their goal is to shine in the eyes of the Europeans, all the while defending incidentally an African cause" ("Quand," 58*). A year later, T. M. Aluko put forth a call to the writers, saying that "we shall want stories and novels written by African writers with an essentially African background and atmosphere, and for an essentially African reading public" (1239).

Several other critics made similar pronouncements, and various groups and gatherings of writers lent added weight to this criterion. One such example was the resolution arrived at in Rome in 1959 at the Second Congress of Negro Writers and Artists. The Congress said that "this writer meets with serious publishing difficulties in the modern and Western conditions in which he finds himself; his audience is therefore most often limited" ("Résolution," 388*).

To cite all the critics who theorized about this predicament would be tedious. As in the case of the African presence, it is the application of the matter of audience that is more interesting, and more pertinent, to the study of African literary criticism. The fact that African critics chose to evaluate literary works on this basis concerns us more directly, and the critics have produced many such examples.

Audience as a Critical Standard

Peter Abrahams, a South African writer, was perhaps the first to apply the African audience as a standard when, reviewing Cyprian Ekwensi's *People of the City*, he made it obvious that he preferred it to Amos Tutuola's *Palm-Wine Drinkard* because the Drinkard's world was "likely to appeal more to non-Africans than to Africans. For the literate African today lives, and is more interested in, the real world of Mr. Ekwensi's Sango" ("A Literary Pioneer," 975). Abrahams in turn had the French translation of his *A Wreath for Udomo* reviewed favorably by Hadj El Mukrane, who chose to use the same standard, after lamenting the African writer's dilemma of having to write exotically and falsely to satisfy a European audience (238). South African critic Nontando Jabavu implied the same standard when she said of T. M. Aluko's *One Man, One Wife*, "How like my own home background! I already felt identified as an African reader with the story this writer promised to unfold; I therefore settled in the receptive aura born of this identification" (427).

On the other hand, Phebean Ogundipe reacted in part negatively to an Ibadan University performance of two Wole Soyinka plays because, she said,

> Just as I had suspected that the dance-drama at the beginning of *The Lion and the Jewel* had been devised only to impress a London audience, so I found in *The Swamp Dwellers* some things which appeared to me a glamourized portrayal of African life which can be expected to appeal to European rather than African audiences. (29)

But the critic qualified her use of the standard, distinguishing between two different Nigerian audiences in this way:

The question here is, what type of Nigerian audience was it meant for? Professor Mahood suggests that the audience reaction at the February performance shows a failure in communication, "as if Mr. Soyinka had forgotten what does and does not move Nigerian playgoers". But I think he did not mean it for the new Nigerian audience—the audience composed of educated Nigerians who know and appreciate good European literature, and can understand the language as well as the artistry of a play like this. The instances of wrong reaction which struck Professor Mahood probably belong to some of the standards of the old Nigerian audience, who expect quite different things of their plays . . . but as the writer cannot have been writing for this type of audience (the type who would very likely prefer Ogunde or Ogunmola) we cannot blame him for such reactions. (30)

In 1961, J. Chunwike Ene reviewed Achebe's *No Longer at Ease* and said of the "discerning African" that "he feels strangely disappointed when an African novelist tends to direct his story specifically at the European audience, as Achebe does sometimes" (43). The same year, Paulin Joachim said of Camara Laye's *Le Regard du roi*, "The world awaits Africa's distinct contribution to a common heritage. And it is not at this time that an African creator will choose to be a Kafka or a Picasso. Let us do as President Senghor and write for our people and not for the approval of a foreign public" ("L'Ecueil," 7*).

Ezekiel Mphahlele applied audience as a critical standard in 1962 when he said of the African writer: "He slips into prosy explanations of his setting and gets bogged down in anthropological information. Examples of this kind of literature are William Conton's *The African* and Onuora Nzekwu's *Wand of Noble Wood*" ("The Makerere Writers' Conference," 7). The next year, Mphahlele said more specifically that Conton "seems to be addressing himself to the outside world and advertising the African way of life" ("African Culture Trends," 134).

In 1964 George Awoonor-Williams singled out some of the same writers Mphahlele had criticized for writing for the wrong audience:

It seems to me that a few of the novelists are writing mainly for an external audience in the mistaken conviction that they have a duty to tell Europe and America how we Africans live. Ekwensi, Nzekwu and Conton are, to some extent the worst offenders in this respect. Of course the conditioning factor of a Europe suddenly interested in an awakened Africa has led many publishers to make unreasonable demands on African writers. This can only be changed when African writers know that they are writing first and foremost for their own people, and only secondarily for the outside world. This knowledge can come when African countries have their own publishing houses which ensure a good and useful distribution of African writing. (8)

Lewis Nkosi criticized Bloke Modisane's autobiographical novel, *Blame Me on History*, for similar reasons. He said, "Bloke Modisane is very dear to me; so when I came to those passages of the book which were contrived, false and melodramatic, which seemed to have been written entirely for foreign consumption, for those, so to speak, who did not know the truth, I was truly revolted" ("The Sting," 54). Also in 1964, G. Kahari applied the same standard to a novel written in Shona, a Zimbabwean language. He said of *Feso*, by Solomon Mutswairo, "On several occasions, I have found it extremely difficult to know whether Feso is meant to be read by people whose mother tongue is Shona or for Europeans. His constant use of such phrases as *chinonzi . . . zvinonzi . . . yainzi*, meaning 'what is called', has left me in no doubt that the book is not only written for the Mashona people" (102).

In 1965, Alfred Hutchinson, a South African critic, reviewed T. M. Aluko's *One Man, One Matchet* favorably because he didn't "explain his characters to potential foreign readers: there is no need because his characters are universal" (114). Paulin Joachim spoke favorably of the Senegalese writer Sembene Ousmane and, with a barb directed at certain others, said,

> It is precisely because he knows the length and breadth of his African world and its modest intellectual resources that the Senegalese writer strives continually, as he says, to "render more primary his literary creation", because he estimates that 80% of all Africans are incapable of following literature as it is conceived and created by the black writers of the white West. ("Les Lettres africaines," 47*)

And finally, Olympe Bhely-Quenum was critical of Camera Laye's third novel, *Dramouss*, and said of its second chapter, "White Night,"

> The chapter in question corresponds too exactly to the questions several French publishers ask their African authors living in France: "Tell us of your impressions of your first time in France, of Paris, of the French people, the snow, the cold. How did you picture the French before your arrival in France, the difference between those in France and those of the colonies, etc. And of course, the sympathetic M. Laye answered all these questions, while giving very flattering answers that will fill the hearts of the French people with joy. ("*Dramouss*," 50*).

Anti-Audience as a Critical Standard

A handful of critics questioned audience as a viable critical standard. Chinua Achebe, who at times favored the projection of an African presence and at others the primacy of an African audience, at least on one occasion seemed to reject audience as a standard altogether. Asked in 1964 by Lewis Nkosi whether he was beginning to be able to write more consciously for an African audience, Achebe said, "Yes, I think you're right. Although I must say that I don't think I was consciously working with an audience in mind in my first book" (Nkosi, "Some Conversations," 21), and added, "But now I feel I don't have to worry over-much about who understands what I'm saying or who doesn't. I feel that there will always be enough people interested in a good story" (21). John Nagenda was another rare instance of the African critic questioning the value of audience as a critical standard. Reviewing James Ngugi's novel, *Weep Not, Child*, he wondered

> whether a novel written for an East African market needs to be as well-finished, as sophisticated, as if it had been written by another author for another, more sophisticated audience. I think that in this present case the answer is that Mr. Ngugi did not have, should not have had, an exclusively East African audience in mind (why should he?)—and in any case no serious *creative* writer is going to set himself these geographical limits—even when he has a local situation in mind, his intention will be to reach this, but to acquire a universal sense, and stage, in doing so. (69)

But these remarks constitute a small minority when considered in relation to the criticism as a whole.

CONCLUSION

A clear duality manifested itself early in modern African literary criticism. African critics took pains to look outward toward the rest of the world and considered—and often prescribed—the impact that literature had and should have on the world. But the critics (often the same critics) looked inward as well, saying that African literature must be written primarily for Africans. The task of the critics (let alone the writers) was not easy, particularly in the years just preceding and following 1960. This is not to suggest this criticism needs an apology; my purpose has been to describe only one aspect of the growth of this criticism and to suggest that the "mental tightwire" (to use Mohamadou Kane's phrase) of the audience question lent a unique urgency to this criticism. The question of whose African literature forced Africans to approach their literature in a manner that has long been taken for granted by other critics writing of other literatures.

4 The Making of a Literary Tradition

AFRICAN LITERATURE, WESTERN CRITICS

When modern African literature began blossoming in the late 1940s and early 1950s, it was primarily for European consumption. An essay by a leading European intellectual ("Orphée noir" by Jean-Paul Sartre) and the establishing of an African-run journal and publishing house, Présence africaine, in Paris and Dakar, under the patronage of a group of Western intellectuals whose names read like a *Who's Who* of the period, were two early developments that helped bring about this peculiar writer-audience relationship. Certainly the paucity of a literate and literature-reading audience and a lack of publishers in Africa also contributed to this state of affairs. Thus it was inevitable, perhaps, if not desirable, that Westerners became involved very early on in the criticism of this new body of literature.

The Western critic was also filling a vacuum of sorts, a cultural lag growing in the wake of the literature due to the lack of a written critical tradition. Oral criticism is no doubt as old as oral literature, though we know little about it and await eagerly a definitive study of it. But it seems clear that the carry-over from oral to written criticism is more complex and less obvious than the carry-over from oral to written literature. And the bulk of written literature to this time would hardly have warranted a critical tradition. A chronological analysis of Jahn and Dressler's *Bibliography of Creative African Writing* (1971) reveals that the number of items published for the years 1965-1966 equaled the entire publication record prior to 1950. Thus B. W. Vilakazi could say in 1942 that Zulu literature had "no governing body which could decide on any classic in our Bantu languages in South Africa today. We have no critical opinions of men of taste and knowledge, whose qualifications today enable them to judge a work by certain positive standards" (274).

Vilakazi's comment is interesting from another standpoint as well. He lamented a lack of critics rather than "certain positive standards," but his standards were very likely those of white South Africa, if not of the entire Western literary tradition. The problematical nature of the relationship of African literature to this tradition was to be raised later and is treated at some length below. The relationship became problematical because of the nature of this early Western criticism, which must be understood if one is to appreciate the importance of the reaction to it in establishing an African literary criticism.

The most unfortunate aspect of this early Western criticism was that very few of the Westerners knew much about Africa (the state of affairs that had led to the choosing of "Présence africaine" as a title). Sartre's own essay indicated little specific knowledge of African culture; it was, rather, a brilliant psychological study of the colonizer and the colonized, even if stated in Marxist terms that today seem a little stilted. One could make much, perhaps, of the fact that Sartre chose *not* to become a major Western critic of African literature.

Undaunted, less timid minds forged ahead into the field, until it became apparent to increasing numbers of Africans that something was drastically wrong: the criticism of the literature was being based on the assumption that, because it employed European languages, African literature in French and English were therefore, respectively, branches of French and English literature, and that one need only apply the underlying principles of Western literary criticism in assessing the new literature. Thus Chinua Achebe found himself the grand-nephew of Joseph Conrad, and the mark of T. S. Eliot and Gerard Manley Hopkins was ferreted out in many African poets. Judgments by comparison to Western writers and values became common practice, which allowed Westerners to "locate" African writers in terms they understood—in terms, that is, of the Western literary tradition. But the practice was predicated on the false premise—an old Western failing where Africa was concerned—that, beyond the mastering of a few anthropological details, there was little about the literature or the culture it sprang from that demanded serious study. And so, as in so many other areas of twentieth-century life, Africa's literary situation—or rather the understanding of it by non-Africans—came to be compared to a seemingly similar institution in the West. More often than not, Africa's institutions, because they did not correspond exactly to their Western counterparts, were thought to be "underdeveloped," if not inferior or nonexistent. Thus the oral tradition was seen merely as a precursor to writing, as it was in medieval Europe—the implication being that since written literature was relatively new to Africa, it had a lot to learn before one could speak of an African literary tradition and, worse, that the African tradition, when it did develop, would perforce develop along the lines of the Western tradition since it was clearly "behind" in its "evolution."

Faced with this cultural hegemony, African critics began to question the inevitabilities voiced by Westerners and soon experienced a *prise de conscience* that led to a reexamination of the relationship of Africa's newly written literature to the traditions of the West. It is this reexamination that I here wish to explore, as well as to show that, not only was the relationship reexamined, but became itself a standard by which critics judged individual works of the literature.

The criticism indicates three major stances by Africans vis-à-vis the Western literary tradition: reliance upon it, avoidance of it, and a synthesis of Western and African elements. That there was not total agreement on the question need not surprise us any more than the variances on other questions have not. It was, rather, an indication of the complexity and importance of the issue in the critics' minds.

Although African literature increased dramatically in volume, particularly after the publication of Senghor's *Chants d'ombre* in 1945 and the advent of *Présence africaine* in 1947, it was inevitable that Western critics, armed with their ready-made literary tradition, had a head start in the criticism of the new literature. Neither should their political (colonial) advantage be underestimated. Senghor wrote in 1950,

> Europe has developed the critical spirit in us, which is more method than invention. Levy-Bruhl considers "invention" an essential virtue of the "primitive." Thus the critical spirit is, above all, perception, objective comprehension of all aspects of a problem. But for the European there is more, there is this glow, this warmth, that underlies the method and brings about a solution. ("L'Afrique s'interroge," 438*)

Yet a few years later, Senghor himself opened the attack on Western criticism of African literature. Writing in 1956 of a Westerner's critique of the poetry of Aimé Césaire, he said, "To criticize Césaire and others for their rhythm, their 'monotony,' in a word their style, is to criticize them for being born 'Negroes,' West Indians or Africans and not 'French' or Christian; it is to criticize them for having remained themselves, totally sincere" ("Comme les lamantins," 118*).

The attack was taken up in earnest a few years later by two Nigerian writers, J. P. Clark and Chinua Achebe, in *Nigeria Magazine.* And the attack became general in tone. Writing in 1962, Clark delineated three types of "non-link" Western critics. The first were those who "go for what to them is exotic and unspoilt," such as the critic who doted on Tutuola,

> lisping and lapping the poor fellow out of breath until he got out of step with the flow of *The Palm Wine Drinkard* that had brought them

upon him. "Oh, the man has begun taking lecture notes from Wolsey Hall," they complained and swept aside *The Brave African Huntress* and all the old master's later efforts. ("Our Literary Critics," 79-80)

The second was the type who "goes for anthropology," who sees no difference in quality in the works of Cyprian Ekwensi, Chinua Achebe, or Onuora Nzekwu, and who "has conveniently tacked all three together as explorers of the theme of cultural conflict" (80). The third type was those who went "the Paul Gauguin way" (80), and who, "because they need a guide, . . . would swallow everything a so-called expert tells them" (81).

Three months later Achebe took up the question and, speaking for his fellow Africans, said, "We are not opposed to criticism but we are getting a little weary of all the special types of criticism which have been designed for us by people whose knowledge of us is very limited" ("Where Angels," 61). Achebe also arranged the Westerners into three categories, though somewhat different from those of Clark: "the peevishly hostile, what-do-they-think-they-are Honor Tracy breed. These are angry with the new-fangled idea of colonial freedom and its gross ingratitude for colonial benefits" (61); those who "are amazed that we should be able to write at all" (61); and a group "which is fully conscious of the folly of the other two and is bent on restoring a sense of balance to the argument," of whom Achebe said, "This is the group with which we could hold a dialogue, with frankness on either side," but he added also that "this group annoys us by their increasing dogmatism" (61).

About this same time, several Africans (Achebe and Clark among them) were gathered at a Conference of English-Speaking African Writers at Makerere University in Kampala, where an attitude toward Western critics seems to have crystallized. Reporting on the conference, Bernard Fonlon said that "strong disapproval was expressed from the very start, at the attitude of some Europeans who, considering themselves as experts in Negro literature, lay down canons on what this literature should be, and dismiss as not African any work by an African that does not conform to their dogma" ("African Writers," 42). And while attending the conference African Literature and the Universities in Freetown a few months later, John Akar, a Sierra Leone critic, gave a particularly vexing example of this dogmatism. He told of a friend's sending a novel to several publishing houses and that "one in particular wrote and said 'Very interesting novel, but it did not sound African enough'. . . . Now who is to say that it does not sound African enough— the publishing house? An African is writing about his own personal experience" ("General Discussion," 130).

Some years later Joseph Okpaku, in the initial editorial in his *Journal of the New African Literature and the Arts*, made a similar comment:

Much of African literature has been severely restricted to what the Western world would like to classify as purely African or authentically African. The result of this limitation which essentially has been an imposition on the African writer by those who prefer to preserve what they claim is the characteristic eroticism and exoticism of African culture, is that African literature has been frozen in this anachronistic mode and thereby deprived of the opportunity to grow and develop along with the growth and development of the African society. ("The Philosophy," 1-2)

In more concrete terms, Robert Serumaga summarized the responses of the British critics to a London production of Wole Soyinka's *The Road* and was critical of a remark by Gerard Fay in *The Guardian*, which was that "when [Soyinka] knows, or perhaps more accurately when he can make us others know what he is trying to say, he will be going places" (ii). Serumaga replied, "But it may at least equally forcibly be argued that the shoe is on the other foot. When Mr. Fay can understand at once what a play set in a different culture is all about, he will be going places. On the evidence of the review he may not even be trying" (ii). Serumaga preferred the *Daily Mail* critic, who, he said, "struck a note that augers well for a continued dialogue between cultures: 'I do not myself pretend to have understood half of Soyinka's play. I am sure for one thing that I have got the plot all wrong. But throughout the evening I was thrilled enough to want to understand' " (i).

Lewis Nkosi, as well as others, described a different danger in Western criticism: while it may be accurate, it may also be patronizing. He said, "What is threatening to ruin most of us [African writers], including some writers of genuine promise, is over-exposure and over-praise. The reputations of some writers have simply been 'manufactured' by busy-body students of African affairs determined to find something exciting and new to study and write home about" ("Where Does," 8). George Otieno echoed this sentiment upon reviewing some of J. P. Clark's poems: "Most foreign critics and publishers are still reluctant to judge our writers purely on merits; they must judge them as African writers, and this tendency sometimes leads to an unhealthy patronisation which can only kill the creative impulse" (43).

Mohamadou Kane summed up the position perhaps as well as anyone else. He spoke of the "misunderstanding" caused by European criticism, which had been able to hold sway because

between the African public and itself there is no established African opinion to intervene with the same persuasion. Its sympathy towards Africa in general and towards our literature in particular is undeniable. Its good intentions are those which pave the way to the worst hells for, finally, such criticism leads to imposing its views or to the total falsification of the meaning of a work. ("African Writer," 20)

Kane's positive suggestion was that

the only attitude this [Western] criticism could take which would help in promoting our writing would be in maintaining a stronger conviction that the future of our writing will become concrete in the continent itself. African literature, expressed in any form whatever, cannot, for innumerable reasons, be considered as the common property of Europe and Africa but must be appreciated for itself as an element of cultural solidarity. (23)

AFRICAN LITERATURE AND THE WESTERN LITERARY TRADITION: A CRITICAL STANDARD

The comments by Africans on Western criticism are legion. Of more interest is the discussion, not of the Westerners themselves, but of the tradition that lay behind them. What was the relationship between African literature and the Western literary tradition? What should it be? These questions provoked serious discussion among Africans and became, finally, a criterion used in the evaluation of individual works of African literature. Let us consider first the critics who recognized the influence of the Western literary tradition on African literature and who considered such influence as good, in and of itself.

Pro-Western Critics

The earliest of these comments came from a South African, D. D. T. Jabavu, who wrote a small book on the subject, *The Influence of English on Bantu Literature* (1948), based on a speech made in 1943. In it, he said of B. W. Vilakazi's poetry, *Inkondlo kaZulu* (1935), that it was

the one great book of poetry in Zulu that attains to the rank of a classic. It is English influence *in excelsis*, by reason of its outright imitation of English modes (metres long, short and common; all varieties of stanzas, elegaics, sonnets, rhymes, and even the heroic couplet, reminiscent of Pope and Dryden) all punctiliously observed. Even the titles remind one of Keats in disguising their subject, ensuring that *ars artem celare est*. (11)

Jabavu concluded his study saying, of A. C. Jordan's novel, *IngQumbo yemiNyanya* (1940), "If the influence of English on Bantu literature will inspire further classics of this calibre, then its continuation is worthwhile" (26).

Another large problem was recognized at the First International Congress of Black Writers and Artists, held in Paris in 1956. Senghor had spoken of African rhythm, which prompted the following statement from N. Damz:

> I would like to ask Mr. Senghor one thing: if we listened—for example—to the African griots, who compose this music, which delights us, and which is the basic element of the art they compose, I think we would perceive that their aesthetic nuances are governed by European aesthetic nuances. . . . I mean that, in general, all the problems we face here are affected by our European education, that is, by the stamp of our European education upon us. ("Débats," 83*)

The impact of European education on African thinking and aesthetic feeling is much too complex a question to be dealt with here. It is clear, however, that the problem Damz posed was discussed at this important conference.

Less problematic—but perhaps more dogmatic—was the comment some years later by Paulin Joachim, who favored the Western tradition by implication when he criticized Charles Nokan's *Le Soleil noir point* (1962) for not conforming to any "traditional" (read Western) literary genre. He said, "This is neither a novel nor a tale nor a short story, but a little of each, a formless, incoherent mixture. But why this penchant for innovation and for looking for ways to express oneself in forms so far removed from the traditional ones? Is this the only way to express one's originality?" ("Le Soleil noir point," 58-59*).

Pro-Synthesis Critics

More reasoned, perhaps, were the comments by critics who argued for a syncretic relationship with the West. One of the earliest expressions of this view seems to have been made in 1956 by Antoine-Roger Bolamba, a Zairian critic, who said of the Malgache poet that "the great achievement of Flavien Ranaivo is that he remains true to the genius of his race while respecting French thought and technique" ("Flavien Ranaivo," 119*). Joseph Miezan Bognini of the Ivory Coast was another critic who accepted a syncretic relationship with the Western tradition. Reviewing Bernard Dadié's novel, *Un Nègre à Paris* (1959), he said,

> I do not think this book seeks to transplant Western development—a part of whose culture we have acquired—into Africa. The issue is one involving her individual evolution confronted with Western culture, because it must be said that she can only evolve in terms of what she has received. This does not mean a mere copying but a synthesizing of her own in order to acquire her own individuality. (156*)

Joachim, modifying somewhat his earlier position on Nokan's work, applied a similar standard when he quoted comments on a Senegalese writer: "[Abdoulaye] Sadji was the extreme, the product of the shock of the two civilizations. The Senegalese found him too Europeanized and the French a little too casual about the requirements of assimilated life. But Sadji was a cultured man. He had roots in the soil, his head and heart open to the winds of Europe" ("Trois livres," 39*).

Bernard Fonlon noted in 1966 two trends of African literature, one largely a protest literature influenced by European education, which "arouses little or no interest among the African literate public and remains largely unread" ("A Word," 10), and the other that "looks for approval not from foreign critics who judge according to the canons established by the European literary tradition, but from the African readers who are better qualified to pronounce on its authenticity" (11). He went on to say that a more powerful African literature will come about when these two trends merge, and he then applied the idea as a critical standard when he said, "Already the merger of these two tendencies is being effected by some writers. The novel of the Western Nigerian writer, T. M. Aluko, *One Man, One Matchet*, is a skillful blend of both" (12).

In his Ph.D. dissertation, Romanus Egudu sanctioned the mixing of Western and African elements when he concluded of the poetry of Christopher Okigbo, J. P. Clark, George Awoonor-Williams, and Lenrie Peters that "these poets seem to believe (and this author agrees) that while making use of their indigenous poetry (vernacular and colonial) and experiences for creating works of art, they can still tap foreign sources of experiences, which are made accessible to them by their acquisition of a second language" (269).

Anti-Western Critics

Such statements, however, were clearly outnumbered by those directed against the Western literary tradition, by those who saw it as a danger and threat to the ultimate integrity of African literature. Perhaps the first of such comments was by Ben Obumselu, a Nigerian critic, who, upon reviewing Achebe's *Things Fall Apart* in 1959, was at least mildly reproachful because he said Achebe had overlooked "implications in our music, sculpture and folklore which the West African novelist cannot neglect if he wishes to do more than merely imitate a European fashion" (Review, 38).

Another critic, using the same standard, implied a different evaluation of Achebe. Christina Aidoo commented on Gerald Moore's early critical work, *Seven African Writers* (1962), asking rhetorically, "How far should one go with Moore in viewing the work of Chinua Achebe as an African development of the English literary tradition that includes Conrad?" (46).

And once again, the Benin critic, Paulin Joachim, could be found using this standard, albeit in some contrast to those instances already cited. He compared the first two novels of Guinean writer Camara Laye and thought that *L'Enfant noir* was superior to *Le Regard du roi* because the latter "is less interesting, principally because its form is no longer original or African and it approaches too closely current European writing" ("Contemporary," 298). He concluded his review by saying, "The African novel will begin an authoritative existence the day its writers abandon a sterile imitation of Western forms of expression and return to their native land to search for originality and a specifically African style" (300).

The novel was not the only genre to draw out the critics in this regard. The drama also led Africans to warn against the encroachment of Western tradition. Viewing two Soyinka plays in 1959 in Ibadan, Phebean Ogundipe had the following misgivings: "I was afraid that they might be just another of those pseudo-original pieces of literature where the English framework on which they are built is only too painfully obvious, and that they might turn out to be a re-hash of Shakespeare or Rattigan, thinly clothed with Nigerian names and settings" (29). A. Bodurin criticized Soyinka for writing drama too closely allied to Western literary techniques. After saying, somewhat contradictorily, that "Soyinka is our best playwright," he then compared him unfavorably with another Nigerian:

> When we compare the qualified successes he [Soyinka] received in London for his latest play *The Road* with the overwhelming reception accorded to Duro Ladipo's *Oba Koso* we have to conclude that something is lacking in him. This something is dramatic skill. He tries to put the cinema on the stage failing to appreciate the spatial and temporal limitations of the latter. His use of uneasy verse adorned with highly esoteric symbolism further reduces the dramatic impact. (40)

Bodurin gave slightly better marks to J. P. Clark when he said, "To a lesser degree the same criticism can be validly applied to J. P. Clark's theatre although Clark suffers in addition from over-reliance on classical Greek tragedy" (40). Lewis Nkosi echoed this judgment in saying that

> with our playwrights and poets trained in a totally Western tradition we are in great danger of being offered an Oedipus of the tropics whom we would be encouraged to adopt as our own archetypal figure. What this means is that there are enormous dangers likely to attend the modern syncretist movement in Africa. (*Home and Exile*, 50)

Poetry also elicited the same critical standard. In very Senghorian terms, Octave Ugirashebuja complimented Senghor's poetry while denigrating European techniques: "Some forms of Western poems seemed to him purely mechanical, child's play. How can one, without treachery, compress a true inspiration into fourteen verses, the grouping and rhymes of which are already fixed? The triumph of mathematics!'' (338*).

Another critic applied the same standard but reached an entirely different conclusion of the same poet. W. E. Abraham said, ''Senghor does not, in my opinion, write as an African poet. What he does is to write French poetry which is interlarded with odd African illusions. Any Frenchman can do that'' (Nkosi, ''Some Conversations,'' 17).

Some early Ghanaian poetry elicited the wrath of Lewis Nkosi, who said:

> Most Ghanaian poetry is not only appallingly romantic; it utilizes some archaic forms of expression, and borrows heavily from the lush imagery of eighteenth and nineteenth-century English poetry. Sometimes a Keats or Wordsworth seems to have been removed from the English soil lock, stock and barrel. (''Contemporary,'' 293)

Awoonor-Williams saw a more recent threat from Europe, saying of an unnamed poet,

> This sounds like T. S. Eliot. But it is from the pen of a Nigerian poet. One asks, has there never been in this poet's making the native sensibility, the ethos from which he has emerged and which is perhaps the permanence in him as an African with traditions and customs behind him? The superficial nature is clear. He must imitate, and show that he has absorbed, and has become a member of the elite whose heritage stretches from Euripides to Ezra Pound. (10)

Commenting on the poetry of Christopher Okigbo, Ezekiel Mphahlele raised the same standard and was bothered by the same influences, asking, ''Should African writers not be a little more choosy about the models they adopt in English writing? For instance, one of the first and most obvious things that strikes me in Okigbo's poetry is how close he is to Pound'' (''Postscript,'' 83).

It is impossible to arrive at any final certainty regarding the African view of the Western literary tradition. Literary criticism—like literature itself—is in a constant state of flux. One can speak of tendencies during limited periods of time, by smaller or larger groups of critics—being aware that, even then, one is dealing subjectively with a very complex phenomenon. That need not detain us, however, nor cause those of us in the humanities to apologize (as we are prone to do). It is surely of importance, to both Africans and non-Africans, to understand that during the 1950s and 1960s, African critics were extremely aware of Western criticism and the Western literary tradition as they bore on African literature. The richness of the dialogue they engaged in ensures that, whatever position is eventually taken, it will have been arrived at with care. From the earliest discussions, however, one can conclude that African critics were aware of the problematic nature of the relationship of their literature to the West and that it often became a standard of their criticism.

Awoonor spoke of the African "with traditions and customs behind him." It remains now to understand how African critics affirmed these traditions and customs in establishing an African literary tradition.

THE AFRICAN TRADITION

African critics seemed to agree that African writers should pursue the African tradition and avoid the European tradition as much as possible. However, this proved more difficult than it seemed. What was, after all, the African tradition? Did it exist? Thomas Melone, a critic and scholar from Cameroun, suggested that it did not exist:

> The writer's craft assumes a long literary tradition, a heritage of formulae, thoughts and sensibility, of types and views of the world accumulated by the ancients and which, for the present generation, constitute an essential source. Neither Senghor, nor Césaire, nor Birago Diop, nor Elolongue Epanya have a Cervantes in front of them, as Corneille had, nor a Hugo. ("The Theme," 167)

However, Melone's was a lonely voice among a chorus that proclaimed the existence of a healthy and vigorous African tradition. Senghor was probably the first to make such a claim, however tentatively, in 1947: "Although our research in Senegalese poetry is not yet finished, we believe we can now affirm the existence in Senegal of a rich oral poetry, possessing its own techniques, however subtle" ("L'Afrique noire," 219*).

The next year Cheikh Anta Diop wrote of Africa's tradition of written as well as oral literature. He said, "There exist written—not only oral—African literatures that follow a well defined poetic art: the epic Wolof literature concedes nothing to European epic literature, it even has a certain superiority of form" ("Quand," 61*). In 1949 J. H. Nketia translated some Akan poetry and offered this advice to future African writers: "It's important that our traditional poems, reflecting our life, and embodying our ideas and sentiments, are collected before they are forgotten" (Osadebay et al., 158), and added that "for those who are aspiring to write literature, they should provide the structure on which to base their literary activity" (158).

In the early 1950s Samba Birame defended the oral tradition in the pages of *Présence africaine*: "We know that the music, the songs and dances, the poems, the stage sets of this older theatre were not written. But this in no way diminishes their original value" (305). A student at the time, Birame said further that African students needed "to absorb without hesitation the essential virtues that the African traditions teach" (305).

In 1957 Joseph Ki-Zerbo noted with concern the dangers attending African culture in the face of an aggressive West bringing its technology into the continent. He asked, "Should we therefore expect a phenomenon of pure and simple cultural destruction?" and then assured the reader that "to forecast the extinction of these cultures would also be to underestimate the conscience of an ever-increasing number of young Africans who deeply feel an historical mission to liberate their country by preserving its traditional culture" (13). In the same year Amadou Moustapha Wade saw a different danger—that of not knowing well enough what the African tradition was. He asked, "Who among us has sufficiently penetrated our poetic universe, our languages, to be able to choose which elements to marry to another prosody" (84)?

The Second Congress of Negro Writers and Artists (Rome, 1959) agreed on "the necessity to defend these oral literatures that constitute the real base of Negro-African cultures" ("Résolution," 387*). Also in 1959, Michael Dei-Anang echoed the sentiments of fellow Ghanaian J. H. Nketia in reiterating the value of an African tradition for the writer. He said, "These Africans who want to write Romantic, imaginative stories could not have a richer treasure than the *Ananse* stories. . . . As for music and poetry, the true and sincere cadence of powerful words and melody, we have a reserve that is probably richer than any other in the whole world" ("La Culture," 6*).

In a comment now heavy with irony, Camara Laye saluted then-President Sekou Touré of Guinea (because of whom he went into exile) and made clear the role of African tradition in 1963:

> Under the guidance of our President, His Excellency Sekou Touré, the first thing we did, after independence, was to take hold of ourselves again. Very quickly, we picked up again our own music, our own literature, our own sculpture; all, that is to say, that was most deeply implanted in us and that had been slumbering during the sixty years of our colonisation. That is our new soul. ("The Soul," 73)

In 1964 David Rubadiri spoke of his feeling for an African tradition: "Now when I sit down to write, I don't consciously make an effort to try to adapt some so-called African forms. The echoes of the African tradition come to me subconsciously. I hear them, and perhaps this is the only African influence that I can confess to" (Nkosi, "Some Conversations," 15).

On the other hand, Abiola Irele, while reviewing the first four volumes of the Oxford Library of African literature, called for a more deliberate effort:

> It is impossible for the modern African writer to take his "Africanness" for granted; on the contrary, it is imperative for him to rethink

and refashion his art with reference to his own heritage and in conformity with a native cultural authority. The present volumes indicate that such a tradition exists, affording a solid frame of reference to the modern individual artist in search of a new, living idiom. I must therefore recommend them as indispensable reading not only for students and scholars, but indeed primarily for African writers themselves. (Review of *A Selection*, 468)

By 1965 Donatus Nwoga could say that "West African writers, particularly the poets, are more confidently allowing elements of traditional and folk imagination into their work" ("West Africa," 15). He concluded that "a proper appreciation and criticism of their poems depends more and more on an understanding of the folk poetry and the folk imagination behind the poets" (16).

On the other hand, Lewis Nkosi, while implying the value of the African tradition, was concerned because black South African writers did not avail themselves of it enough. He said, "Behind most of their writing there appears to be nothing in the way of background or tradition other than the monstrous workings of the apartheid system" ("Annals," 164). It is possible that this was a mental reaction in the black South African writer against what Ezekiel Mphahlele saw as the use of Bantu culture as a "means of oppression" by the South African government to further its policy of apartheid (*The African Image*, 193).

Mphahlele's thoughts on the African tradition were also developed in a booklet written expressly for the aspiring African writer, *A Guide to Creative Writing* (1966). In his introduction, he said of the new African short story that "it can no longer be the fable or legend that we have told among ourselves from generation to generation without changing the subject. . . . It can no longer be the story in which the music of the words plays an important part" (2). Nevertheless, Mphahlele by no means advocated abandoning the oral tradition. He saw its value for written literature clearly: "We should however record our fables, legends and myths and oral poetry before they are completely forgotten. Recording these stories in print and on tape will help us to know better where we came from. This in turn must show us which way we are going with the new forms" (2-3).

It could be argued that one of the objects of the whole Negritude movement was to encourage the expression of the African tradition in the arts—that, in fact, Negritude *was* the African tradition. However, this notion was largely rejected by English-speaking Africans. Ben Obumselu stated this position perhaps more succinctly than anyone else:

If we wish to insist that the literary works which our contemporaries are now writing should be described as "African" with the object of characterizing some quality in the literary works themselves and not merely the racial origin of the authors, we ought, I think, to imply among other things that these works appeal to an imagination created in a large measure by the tradition of African literature. ("The Background," 47)

Further on he reiterated more pointedly that "if there is continuity of African literary imagination, it will be found that this continuity is maintained by learning and not by the activity of some occult racial principle" (55). In its place, he offered some suggestions as to what might and might not be used. Negatively, and opposed to Rubadiri, Irele, and others, he said, "I do not believe that modern African literature can learn very much from folklore. Its imaginative range—I distinguish folktales from legends and myths—is too narrow" (55). More positively, he said he believed "that myths and legends are more promising" (58) and added, "But apart from a few Nigerian experiments, the possibilities of mythical material have not so far been exploited—perhaps they have not been discovered—by our writers" (58-59).

   J. P. Clark suggested a corresponding source for Nigerian drama:

As the roots of European drama go back to the Egyptian Osiris and the Greek Dionysius so are the origins of Nigerian drama likely to be found in the early religious and magical ceremonies and festivals of this country. The *egungun* and *oro* of the Yoruba, the *egwugwu* and *mmo* masques of the Ibo, and the *owu* and *oru* water masquerades of the Ijaw are dramas typical of the national repertory still generally unacknowledged today. ("Aspects," 118)

M. J. C. Echeruo pointed to what he saw as a significant gap between the African tradition and modern Nigerian poetry. Echeruo chided the African poets for their neglect of their tradition: "Our poets, we should say, have so far refused to commit themselves to any kind of form that would answer to the tradition of the popular epic in traditional literature" ("Traditional," 150).

   Mohamadou Kane saw the use of the African tradition as essential while attributing the lack of its influence to a gap between the African writer and an African audience. The African writer went astray, he said, in writing for a European audience; "The solution offered, if not original, is one calling for common sense and a strengthening of relations between traditional African writing and the new. In other words, for the new trends to be thoroughly embedded in a cultural reality which is African culture" ("The African Writer," 13). But he warned that this process could not be superficial:

He [the African writer] sings of the wealth and soul of our culture and praises the hundred qualities in it but is careful not to delve into tradition and illustrate such treasures. He leaves us with the disagreeable impression of being a preacher unconvinced himself, a skilful handler of myths. Experience shows us, however, that those writers known to Africans and esteemed by them are the ones who realize their work will be worth something only if it is rooted in a traditional literature in which the writer, even though he may know it perfectly well, at times feels ill at ease. (28)

Kane also saw the problem of invoking the African tradition prematurely:

The trouble is that we have been summoned to a meeting with the universal too early and it is characteristic of our times to be impatient and to insist that every man must be ready to cope with this meeting. We must of course see in this invitation the implicit recognition of the value of our cultures but must not lose sight of the need at this first stage not only to consolidate the authenticity of our culture and literature, but to act in such a way that our spokesmen absorb this fully from the outset. (31)

To undertake a description of the African tradition—primarily oral—is well beyond the scope of this study. The astute scholarship that has gone into the several volumes of the Oxford Library of African Literature will alone attest to this fact. Other studies by African critics are numerous and equally detailed. Many have been cited above and will be below. What was pertinent to the developing canons of African literary criticism was the critics' awareness of the African tradition, not only of its existence but of its aesthetic detail. More to the point was their willingness to apply their knowledge of this tradition to their evaluations of modern African literature.

THE AFRICAN TRADITION AS A CRITICAL STANDARD

Birago Diop

If modern African literature may be said to have begun with Senghor's *Anthologie* (1948), then modern African literary criticism began with it as well. Senghor used the African tradition as a standard for evaluation in his introductory note, "Birago Diop," when he said, "He does what all our good storytellers do: on an old theme, he composes a new poem" (135*). Diop drew comments from other critics as well for his use of the African tradition. Senghor said of Diop in 1958, "He has lived, as only the Negro African listener knows how, the stories of the Griot; he has rethought and written them as an artist both Negro and French, remembering that 'traduttore traditore' ("Préface" to Birago Diop, 7*). But, using the same standard, Senghor criticized Diop at another point in the same essay for altering the tradition, saying, "Birago Diop suppresses the opening and closing formulas because they are contrary, no doubt, to French taste, and this is unfortunate" (10*).

Paulin Joachim was equally enthusiastic although less explicit than Senghor in his praise of Diop. In reviewing Diop's *Contes et lavanes* (1963), Joachim said, "Birago Diop's credit is to have had the idea of fixing in writing this ancestral tradition that is being lost in the sand, this simple and direct manner, both didactic and entertaining in educating a young being, in preparing him for life and to fertilize his life with poetry" ("Contes," 51*).

Mohamadou Kane also saw merit in Diop, along with Achebe and Ivory Coast writer Bernard Dadié, because of their common respect for African tradition. He said, "We can only attribute the success of Diop, a Dadié or the Nigerian Achebe to the desire to delve deep down into tradition and there is nothing surprising in the parallels to be found in their writings" ("The African Writer," 30).

Senghor

Senghor's poetry also elicited a substantial amount of critical comment for its use of African tradition. In 1953 A. R. Bolamba saw in Senghor's poetry two aspects of the African tradition: its oral quality and its intended accompaniment by African instruments ("Poésie négro-africaine," 10*). In 1964 Davidson Nicol showed a preference for the French-speaking poets, and especially Senghor, to the English-speaking Africans because, he said, "The French-speaking poets are more closely tied to their local African traditions than those who speak English. In reading French African poetry, we are struck by the use made of symbolic factors in the poets' tribal background, like blood, the natural elements and their spirit ancestors" (*Africa*, 73). Ben Obumselu said, "The best example of the modern praise song is, of course, to be found in Senghor's poetry" ("The Background," 49).

Tutuola

There were anglophone writers as well who led the critics to solidify the African tradition as a critical standard over a period of years. When Amos Tutuola's *The Palm-Wine Drinkard* appeared in 1952, Cyprian Ekwensi applied the standard when he said Tutuola's novel was valuable "as representing the transition-point between folk-lore and the novel as a literary form" ("A Yoruba Fantasy," 713). Another Tutuola admirer was Mabel Jolaoso, who applied the same standard in her review of *My Life in the Bush of Ghosts* in 1955, saying, "This book is pure fantasy, but fantasy built on the age-long beliefs of the African" (42).

Lewis Nkosi also saw the African tradition as one of Tutuola's assets, noting that "his fantasies are in the best tradition of the African oral idiom" ("Some Conversations," 11). Ben Obumselu was another critic who recognized Tutuola's (and D. O. Fagunwa's) debt to African tradition, which, he said, should be pointed out to correct the erroneous tendencies of Tutuola criticism:

> Tutuola's *The Palm-Wine Drinkard* was written under the influence of Fagunwa; and like Fagunwa, Tutuola stands within the Yoruba tradition. Not only do they both make extensive use of the material of folklore, but the formal organization of that material is modelled on the folktale about the hunter who ventures into the bad bush or the wrestler who takes his mortal challenge to the denizens of the spirit world. It is important to emphasize the traditional sources of Tutuola's art as a corrective to those readers who approach *The Palm Wine Drinkard* as if it were medieval or Jungian allegory. ("The Background," 57)

However, Obumselu gave considerably more thought as to how Tutuola used African tradition, and he concluded that, to a significant degree, Tutuola misused it. For example, Obumselu saw a corrupting effect in the "modern" elements Tutuola brought into his narrative alongside those more traditional: "How lapsed from its folk purity Tutuola's sensibility has become may be judged by comparing these metaphorical allusions with the opposite manifestation: with those of Shinega in Sahle Sellassie's *Shinega's Village* who meeting a clothed friend finds him 'wrapped up like an ear of corn' " ("The Background," 58).

Achebe

Another writer who caused considerable comment among critics for his use of African tradition was Chinua Achebe. It is interesting, and no doubt significant, that these remarks were more or less equally divided between the influence of African tradition on Achebe's form and content.

G. Adali Mortty was perhaps the earliest to comment on the African tradition in Achebe's work. In his 1959 review of *Things Fall Apart*, he said, "Proverbs, which according to the Ibos, 'are the palm-oil with which words are eaten', stand out as gems on a string of beads in Achebe's prose" (49). K. E. Senanu expressed a similar evaluation two years later. After quoting an early section of *Things Fall Apart*, in which Okonkwo's wrestling prowess is established, Senanu said, "The similes in which the contestants are compared to the cat and the fish, we may notice in passing, are almost literal translations of vernacular proverbs; but the important thing is that they are expressive and strictly functional in the context" ("The Literature," 179-80).

J. P. Clark, in a 1962 critique of the Western criticism of African literature, chided those critics who saw Ekwensi, Achebe, and Onuora Nzekwu in the same class. And although Clark did not say specifically who he thought was the best of the three, it is clear that the African tradition was the standard he was applying: "Which of them uses the proverb, that Nigerian contribution to the art of dialogue, to convey the entire grammar of his people's philoso-phy and poetry or of the very ultimate in their system of values which some have called ancestral worship" ("Our Literary Critics," 80). Mphahlele made a similar observation: "Chinua Achebe . . . uses plenty of African proverbs in his writing. But he does it cleverly, so that a proverb is not sim-ply dragged into the story" (*A Guide*, 28).

In 1966, Clark took favorable note of a different aspect of tradition in Achebe. After pointing out the traditional debt of Nigerian drama to var-ious rituals and festivals, he said:

> In each case given above, the story derives directly from an ancestor or founder myth well-known to the audience, and the development is not so much by logic and discussion as by a poetic evocation of some re-ligious experience shared alike by performer and spectators.
>
> A similar drama is described with tremendous power by Mr. Chinua Achebe in *The Arrow of God*. This is *The First Coming of Ullu*, as celebrated in the market-place of "the six villages of Umuaro" to the clamorous beat of the *ikolo* and *ogene*. ("Aspects," 119)

Others

In addition to Senghor, Diop, Tutuola, and Achebe, the critics singled out other writers and works for their use of African tradition. A few exam-ples will illustrate the range of the critics' concerns.

In an essay on the Malagasay poet Jean-Joseph Rabearivelo, E. Ralaimi-hoatra commented favorably on the poet's evolution from French to Mala-gasay influences:

> *Traduit de la nuit* published in 1935 marked a capital turning in Rabe-arivelo's literary production. Before that, almost all his French works were written in classic verse and treated themes that inspired the poet from somewhere outside. *Traduit de la nuit*, written in free verse, like *hain-teny*, is a whole other genre and reveals another Rabearivelo who has moved from objective to subjective poetry. (526*)

Condotto Nenekhaly-Camara felt similarly about the work of Guinean poet and choreographer Keita Fodeba, saying, "He draws from songs, stories and traditional legends of the Mandingo country" (14*).

The collecting and publishing of Senghor's essays in 1964, as *Liberté I: Négritude et humanisme*, made it apparent, if it was not already, that the Senegalese poet-president had written a sizable body of literary criticism, both theoretical and applied. One of the standards informing this criticism was the reliance upon African tradition. In his 1955 preface to Antoine-Roger Bolamba's first poems, *Esanzo; chants pour mon pays*, Senghor said, "He has not read but rather listened during the nights to the tam-tams and *lokoles*"

("Préface," 9*). In a review appearing in *Diogène* the next year, Senghor saw in the work of the Congo (Brazzaville) poet, Gerald-Felix Tchicaya U Tam'si, a special aspect of the African tradition—its obscurity: "His poems often begin with a vision or a gnomic sentence" ("De la poésie," 9*). Another traditional quality was that "his poems just as often begin or continue a story, as in the old Black stories. In Africa, poets are tellers, reciters of 'hidden things' " (9*). And in his 1963 preface to the French translation of Peter Abrahams's novel, *A Wreath for Udomo*, Senghor noted that "if Peter Abrahams' reknown is such, if he is a great novelist, it is because he is, first, a *great writer. A classic* who borrows less from Europe than from Africa. . . . Abrahams has rediscovered the *style* of African stories" ("Peter Abrahams," 427-28*). These examples show that the African tradition was one of the most, if not the most, important critical standards for Senghor.

A Zairian critic, Paul Mushiete, compiled a smaller Senghor-like anthology in 1957 and in a biographical note said of Malagasay poet, Jacques Rabemananjara, "He began his literary activities in making the Romantic, Parnassian, Symbolist spirits his, but very quickly he returned to the source of popular Malagasay poetry" (*La Littérature française africaine*, 12*). In the same collection, Mushiete evaluated a long epic poem, *La Divine pastorale* (1952-1955), using much the same standard. He said, "The Abbey Alexis Kagame gives us more than a testimony. It is the richness of our world that he reveals to us. The ensemble of his works constitutes a challenge to the skeptics—black as well as white—who do not believe there could exist any values worthy of interest in the African tradition" (37-38*).

J. P. Clark applied the standard to Senghor's work, however reservedly, to which the "pamphleteering" poetry of Dennis Osadebay was compared unfavorably. After quoting from Osadebay's poem, "Young Africa's Plea," Clark said, "Of course, the chant, the monotone and the sonority as of incantation of words melting into melody and therefore requiring to be sung to the cora to 'pass into tradition,' as preached and persistently practised by Senghor, are all lacking in this type of poetry" ("Poetry in Africa," 21). Clark went on, however, to credit other English-speaking Africans for having taken up their African tradition. To make his case, Clark quoted from Gerald Moore and Ulli Beier's introduction to their anthology, *Modern Poetry from Africa* (1963):

> "It is interesting to see the use which has been made of vernacular poetry by two of these English-speaking poets, George Awoonor-Williams of Ghana and Mazisi Kunene of South Africa. Both have understood and assimilated the cryptic, rather oracular quality of much vernacular imagery. This has given both freshness and weight to their language." (25)

Clark was himself target as well as critic. George Otieno heralded what he saw as Clark's successful use of tradition, at least in his poetry. Otieno said,

"Throughout *A Reed in the Tide* there is a strong sense of natural spontaneous rhythm which J. P. Clark shares with his Agbor dancer, and with African traditional dancers all over the continent" (43).

Mofolo Bulane commented on a similar element in Mazisi Kunene's poetry in these terms: "He is not, like so many of us mentally castrated in the Western tradition, a caricature of European culture. This is clearly demonstrated by the idiom and cadence of his poems which are steeped in the traditional Zulu oral poetry" ("Raymond Mazisi Kunene," 111).

Wole Soyinka preferred Christopher Okigbo's poem "Distances" to the poetry of Senghor because it represented

> a deeper subsumption of the self into vision and experience. And although this applies to all poetry, we may insist that this is the true African sensibility, in which the animist *knowledge* of the objects of ritual is one with the ritualism, in which the physical has not been split from the psychic, nor can the concept exist of the separation of action from poetry. ("And After," 64)

Soyinka concluded by saying of Senghor's work, "Self-sacrificial in the process, Senghor's art has coursed a lifetime calling forth the essence of a new poetic heritage, but it is not itself the essence" (64).

Attention should also be drawn to what was the only statement found in the course of this study that suggested the African tradition ought *not* be used as a critical standard. This occurred in a review of J. W. Abruquah's novel *The Catechist* (1966), by Joe de Graft, who liked it because it was "not larded with folk wisdom congealed in proverbs" (63).

CONCLUSION

The cumulative effect of these examples indicates the importance an African tradition held for many African literary critics from the 1940s through the 1960s and their willingness to apply it as a literary standard in their criticism. What the African tradition was, and how it could best be incorporated into the body of modern African literature, was not always agreed upon. What is significant here is that certain elements elicited a positive response from the critic when they were recognized, while, conversely, the too-overt reliance on a non-African tradition drew a negative response. African critics may not have defined the African literary tradition, but they were able to identify some of the elements they would include in it and apply them as critical standards. Their invoking of a tradition, however vague at times, indicated their strong desire to create one.

5 Realisms, African Reality, and the African Past

In the two decades following World War II, many African writers and critics felt a compelling urge to further an African presence in the world as a way of refuting the European myth of a primitive, savage Africa. In addition, African critics have in large numbers followed the doctrine of *la littérature engagée*. In both instances, there is a similar concern with the nonliterary realities in which African literature found itself after World War II. In the former, the African reality was used to combat an erroneous and often arrogant view of the superiority of European culture; in the latter, to publicize and then attempt to solve the various social, economic, and political problems that Africa faced. At the outset of modern African literature these problems were readily laid at the feet of the colonial powers; later, *engagement* came to mean more the facing of the internal problems of independent African nations. In both cases, however, the realism required for the projection of an African presence into the world, both at home and abroad, may be seen as readily consonant with the term *littérature engagée*.

It is interesting to speculate as to whether this set of attitudes led to what might be called the Creighton definition of African literature, proposed by Professor T. R. M. Creighton and accepted at both the First International Congress of Africanists (Accra, December 1962) and the Freetown conference of 1963 or whether this definition influenced the direction of subsequent African criticism. Quite probably both situations are true, though in what proportion is difficult to say. In any case, a strong leaning toward realism can readily be seen in a statement that says African literature is "any work in which an African setting is authentically handled, or to which experiences which originate in Africa are integral" (Creighton, 84). And while the Creighton definition does not seem to have been widely accepted by African writers and critics, this chapter will suggest that it at least had the merit of reflecting one of the major concerns shared by many of those same writers and critics.

In 1955 A. A. Kwapong heralded the publication of Cyprian Ekwensi's novel, *People of the City* (1954), and noted a situation that could only be improved upon by upcoming African authors. He said:

> The post-war period of political and social ferment and change has seen an influx of foreign observers into the West African scene: by the very nature, however, of the length of time these visiting journalists and professional writers spend in West Africa, by their unfamiliarity with the languages and strange customs and ways of life here, most of their findings tend to be superficial or sensational or pander to pre-conceived notions. And now, at last it would seem, young African writers themselves are taking up the challenge of this literary invasion and are writing about themselves and their country. (24)

As some of the critics cited in this chapter say, literary realism is necessary in order to deal with the problems confronting Africa. Another group, smaller but nevertheless substantial, argue that realism is not the best mode for African literature to assume and that there are others equal if not superior to it—notably surrealism. Finally, the critical discussion of African reality concerns itself with the role of the African past in projecting the reality of the African present and the direction of the African future.

It will be noted that a distinction is made between realism and surrealism, two methods of literary presentation, and African Reality, the actuality and content upon which African literature is based (realistically or otherwise). Some critics insisted upon accuracy of detail without necessarily specifying realism as the literary method of the author, while others seemed to call for realism without dwelling on the accuracy of the facts and details presented.

REALISM

As we will see in the case of Negritude, two African critics, Ezekiel Mphahlele and Leopold Senghor, were ranged more or less against one another: Mphahlele the realist, Senghor the surrealist. Mphahlele was by no means the first to have proclaimed realism as the literary doctrine for African literature; however, he was the most persistent and most consistent critic to do so.

Mphahlele

In 1960 Mphahlele commented on William Plomer, a white South African writer, saying, "Plomer was the first writer to give South Africa a healthy realism that could inspire contemporary writing" ("Black and White," 342). Mphahlele often made the distinction between the situations of the South and West African writer, usually wishing that the South African situation led less naturally to realism, while feeling that West African writing would do well to move further in that direction and become "a realism which includes poverty, sickness, class-consciousness, the black man's inhumanity to those of his colour, etc." ("The Cult," 52). This can be seen as the beginning of Mphahlele's rejection of Negritude: it leads away from realism into romanticism. In another place he said, "Indeed, one finds a good deal of romanticism and rhetoric in French African poetry of the negritude school," and added, "And yet French African fiction, like the novels of Camara Laye, Mongo Beti and Ferdinand Oyono, has social realism, although it treats of a peculiarly African experience. These novelists write about the black-white encounter with a devastating irony that has no parallel in English African prose" ("Writers," 12).

In a joint introduction to their *Modern African Stories* (1964), Mphahlele and Ellis Ayitey Komey noted that their contributors were painfully aware of their Western backgrounds. This caused them to look back to their past, a factor about which Mphahlele usually felt negatively, but the two editors said in this case, "It is important to know that it is a sober retrospect which, although it may tend to idealize traditional beliefs, mores and rhythm of life, never romanticizes them" (Komey and Mphahlele, 10).

For some time a reporter for *Drum*, a Johannesburg magazine, Mphahlele more than once wrote of the effect of its racy style on his own prose, and on one occasion used it as a means to attack Negritude:

> It must be said that much of the *Drum* material written by Africans who came under its influence is escapist writing, and that when these same writers and the more serious and independent South African non-white writers are being resourceful, they infuse their writing with a freshness and robustness born out of the African experience, and without any pretensions to what some of the French-speaking African writers would like to call *un style negro-africain*, whatever that is. ("The Language of African Literature," *Language and Learning*, 271)

In another attack on Negritude as an anti-realism, made at the Dakar conference in 1963, Mphahlele said, after reiterating some less-than-savory aspects of African life,

> The image of Africa consists of all these and others. And *negritude* poetry pretends that they do not constitute the image and leaves them out. So we are told only half—often even a falsified half—of the story of Africa. Sheer romanticism that fails to see the large landscape of the personality of the African makes bad poetry. ("A Reply," 24)

Perhaps the crux of Mphahlele's realism came out in his small booklet, *A Guide to Creative Writing* (1966). In it, speaking to the would-be African writer, he attempted to discourage the use of folklore for material:

So let us put the folk tale where it belongs and turn our attention to the real world in which we live today. If a writer wants to use the subject of a folk tale or one out of the supernatural world, he has to relate it to our world of reality. He must do it because he wants to throw some light on a situation in real life. (6)

It is obvious, then, that, under Mphahlele's tutelage, African literature would take on a decidedly realistic tinge.

Others

Another writing manual of sorts, "Réflexions sur la technique de la nouvelle," by Jacques Nzouankeu, a Cameroun writer, discussed realism in more philosophical terms. Nzouankeu said,

The so-called realist story is nothing but an exact reproduction of things described. It is simply a reproduction that considers itself true to the objective truth, that tends to convince, thanks to the gamut of techniques the Realist and Naturalist writers have elaborated, such as exact descriptions of place and detail, the impersonal tone, the sober language, as well as elements whose purpose is to give the reader the *impression* that the story is based on the real. One has seen that the short story owes a great deal to this realistic art. (158*)

Quite aside from these how-to statements, however, a number of Africans declared specifically their preferences for a literature of realism on a philosophical plane, quite apart from the implications of such a position in the numerous critical commentaries on the need for an *African* reality. No doubt many of these critics who argued for a realism were equally committed to an African realism, but the critical argument was offered vigorously on both levels.

In 1955 Mongo Beti, signing himself "A. B." (Alexandre Biyidi), asked, "What will be the tone of the African novel, realist or non-realist?" He answered his question thus:

Given the modern conceptions of the beautiful in literature, given at the very least these essential conceptions, if a work is realistic it has many chances of being good; if not, supposing even that it has formal qualities, it risks lacking resonance, profundity, that of which all literature has the greatest need—the human; from which it follows that it has much less chance of being good—if only it had some—than a realistic work. (A. B., "Afrique noire," 135*)

The next year Bernard Dadié, taking part in a discussion on "conditions surrounding a black people's poetry" in the pages of *Présence africaine*, sounded a realist note when he said of the African writer, "The essential thing for him is that he be of his time, of his place" ("Le Fond," 117*).

Thomas Melone took a similarly pejorative view of romanticism when he said, "The World dichotomy, or Manichaeism, between the criminal-white colonialist and the innocent-Negro colonized no longer allows a certain literary romanticism to survive in Africa. The Negro is not, of course, that innocent and pure; he can colonize his own people, exploit them, and fail to lead them to noble objectives" ("New Voices," 65).

Cyprian Ekwensi was one writer who, in 1964, while indicating a critical preference for realism, also pointed out a political difficulty attending it:

> If there is one problem which the Nigerian writer must prepare to face it is the over-sensitiveness of his public to truth. The novelist must mirror society as it is if his work is to have any value. Unfortunately, this is an age of dreams and no mirror has yet been designed to reflect dreams. The result is that his work often represents a conflict between the image as visualized in the minds of the ardent nationalists and the true image reflected in the mirror. ("Literary Influences," 476)

AFRICAN REALITY

Far more numerous were those critics who sought, not realism in the abstract (if that is not a contradiction in terms), but a concrete reality reflecting specific elements of Africa. One of the first post-World War II critics to do so was O. K. Poku, who asked in 1948 that African writers "become masters of a true literature and the best interpreters of the African nature" (900). A year later T. M. Aluko said:

> We shall want stories and novels written by African writers with an essentially African background and atmosphere, and for an essentially African reading public; stories in which the characters will have familiar African names—Ajayi, Codjoe and Momo Kano; and in which the places are familiar West African towns and villages, with the names of well-known streets in say Ibadan or Kumasi coming in. (1239)

Peter Abrahams expressed a similar sentiment in 1952. He said of the African writer,

> First, he must know his land and its people so truly that when he writes of them they become real and living, even for those who do not know his land and people. He must have looked at them so closely that, almost, he can pick the unexpressed dreams and hopes from their hearts and put them down on paper. ("Challenge," 387)

In the same year Ekwensi said, in the same vein, "I would like to see the West African scene and way of life projected through the medium that is available to the creative writer: namely, poetry, and the novel" (Letter, 607).

The Reverend John S. Mbiti wrote of his reaction to a statement in an English children's book, which perhaps is still another explanation of the

African penchant for realism. Reverend Mbiti's childhood book said, " 'This book is specially written for English boys and girls. They will enjoy reading it more than any foreigner would; and will appreciate it more readily' " (244). This statement caused him to say, "I have always, since then, wanted to see books written by Africans, about our country and life, and with local colour" (244-45).

Paul Mushiete expressed his preference for an African reality: "The libraries are full of wise 'approaches' to the morals, the African ethnicity, and travel stories abound; but there exist few works describing in a realistic manner and sentiment the conditions of our daily life" ("La Littérature," 161*).

Chinua Achebe demonstrated a concern for African reality in a 1962 essay, "Where Angels Fear to Tread." He castigated a European critic for saying of Cyprian Ekwensi's novel *Burning Grass* (1962), "This is truly Nigeria and these are *real* Nigerian people" (62). Then, rather than questioning the limits of African reality, he went on to accept it implicitly by saying:

> She did not say what her test was for sorting out *real* Nigerians from unreal ones and what makes say, Jagua less real than Sunsaye. And as if that was not enough this critic went on to say that Ekwensi was much more at home in a rural setting than in big cities! (62)

Achebe did temper his acceptance of strict African reality a little further on in the essay, however, when he said:

> I would not dream of constructing theories to explain "the European mind" with the same "bold face" that some Europeans assume in explaining ours. But perhaps I am too diffident and out [ought?] to have a go at it. After all a novel is only a story and could be as tall as an iroko tree; in any case one couldn't do worse than the author of *Bride Scorners* [by Robert O. Halles] who invented an Ibo hero with a Yoruba name. (62)

In another place Achebe recalled a personal reaction that led him eventually to writing. Speaking of Joyce Cary, he said:

> If I may say so, perhaps he was—he helped to inspire me, but not in the usual way. I was very angry with his book *Mr. Johnson* which was set in Nigeria, you see. I happened to read this, I think, in my second year [at University College of Ibadan], and I said to myself, this is absurd. And if somebody without knowledge, without any inside knowledge of the people he's trying to describe can get away with it, perhaps I ought to try my hand at it. (National Educational Television, "The African Writer," 13)

In the initial issue of *Abbia*, Bernard Fonlon said of African writers that "if they really spring from African soil, if they are kneaded and leavened by

African experience, their manner, their expression, will bear an African imprint, whatever their theme may be" ("African Writers," 43). He was particularly excited by Nigerian literature because, he said, "one has only to read the works of Chinua Achebe or of J. P. Clark or of Gabriel Okara to see how rich this rising literature is with the substance of Nigerian soil" ("African Writers," 50). In another place Fonlon described what he considered to be an important connection between a realistic literature and *la littérature engagée*. He said:

> Once you have aroused in a people a thirst for reading by fashioning for them a literature like Eve was fashioned from Adam, a literature from their own flesh and blood, a literature from a substance that touches them most intimately, a literature in which they can see themselves as in a mirror, a literature which speaks a language they can understand—then, subsequently, the other literature which strives to rouse political consciousness, which seeks to be a weapon against injustice, an instrument for social change or moral reform, will meet minds already prepared, minds athirst for more and more literature. ("A Word," 11)

Writing on the situation of the theatre in Africa in 1964, Michael Dei-Anang said, "It is a most deplorable circumstance that no one ever endeavours to give African life and thought a fair trial in dramatization" (*Ghana Resurgent*, 184). Bob Leshoai had a similar thought the next year when he said, "I wish to stress that more African playwrights must come forward to interpret the way of life of the African both as it really is and as it should be" (45-46). Sonar Senghor was also concerned that African theatre be realistic. Speaking of the writers' workshops he began in Senegal, he said they "must permit us to create an African repertoire in French based on certain Senegalese themes—themes of the national *prise de conscience*, themes borrowed from our everyday problems" (57*).

J. P. Clark seemed to agree with Senghor when he chided Nigerian teachers for their impatience with modern poetry dealing with Nigeria. He said:

> The average teacher of poetry in Nigeria, trained only in the appreciation of traditional English poetry, exhibits very strongly built-in reactions against modern Nigerian poetry, indeed against all modern poetry, and therefore cannot easily accommodate novelty. Possessed of reflexes, conditioned as those of Pavlov's dog, he reacts readily to any item out of the double vistas of the Classics and the Bible that, according to [Sir Herbert] Grierson, inform English poetry. But the slightest reference to the religion, history and oral traditions of his own peoples leaves him sniffing at one for explanations. ("A Note," 64)

According to Paulin Joachim, Senegalese writer Sembène Ousmane felt he knew the African reality as well as any African writer, to which claim Joachim replied:

One needs only to read his collections of stories gleaned from the four corners of the continent to give him this credit. And it is precisely because he knows the length and breadth of his African world and its modest intellectual resources that the Senegalese writer strives continually, as he says, to "render more primary his literary creation." ("Les Lettres africaines," 47*)

The readiness and willingness of African critics to apply the precepts of realism to African literature is an interesting phenomenon that invites certain hypotheses about the literature and criticism. No other single factor seemed to have been applied as often or as consistently as a critical standard. One explanation might be that the literary critic, like the writer, like most people, prefers to operate from a position of strength, from a base of what is known; and, given the fact that modern African criticism was even younger than modern African literature, what more logical base to build from than the "African reality" with which one was already familiar? Add to this the tremendous desire of the West to discover the "realities" of Africa, and the African critic's and writer's equally strong desire to assure that these Western "realities" were not merely the reinforcements of a superiority complex that led first to colonialism and then to nazism—and the demand for realism in African literature may be seen as inexorable.

This is not to subscribe to some evolutionary theory of criticism by which we must pass from an African Aristotle, through an African Taine in order to arrive at an African Jacques Derrida; it is to suggest that criticism is as tied to reality as is literature—no more, no less. And if African literature and criticism were contemplating their respective navels, as Wole Soyinka suggested ("And After"), and if the French, British, and American "realities" no longer call for realism, this is just another reminder that we are not all born in the same place in the same time.

Even granting an evolutionary criticism, one must be allowed the privilege of "adolescence" or whatever stage one is at (to extend the metaphor) and not be chided for not being something else. Wherever they were in the 1950s and 1960s in relation to Western literature and criticism, the Africans felt a strong need to be true to themselves.

African Reality as a Critical Standard

Whether it is called Realism—with a capital R—or African Reality, African critics found themselves from the late 1940s into the 1960s in relative agreement on the need for the depiction of African life—and on the need for accuracy in that depiction. Perhaps the term *African Realism* reflects both needs as well as any. It is particularly interesting to note that these needs were not confined to theoretical statements; they were applied to a host of individual literary works, and they cut across all genres.

Novel. Not surprisingly, the novel provoked as much application of the standard of reality as any genre. One of the first to invoke the standard was the South African critic D.D.T. Jabavu, who in 1948 said of A. C. Jordan's work, *IngQumbo yemiNyana* (1940), that "the novel is likely to remain unchallenged for a long time in Xhosa literature, for it reflects actual life to a detail and in a wholesome fashion" (26).

A few years later, in 1954, came Alexandre Biyidi's (Mongo Beti's) review of Camara Laye's first novel, *L'Enfant noir*, possibly the most well-known review in all of African literary criticism. Biyidi's main thrust was for *engagement* and will be examined in the next chapter, but he very likely helped to set the tone for later criticism vis-à-vis African realism as well. He said of Laye's Africa,

> Despite the appearance, this is a stereotyped image—therefore false—of the Africans of Africa who he is so intent on showing: idyllic universe, childish optimism, stupid and interminable celebrations, carnival initiations, circumcisions, excisions, superstitions, uncle Mamadous whose unconsciousness is equalled only by their unreality. (A. B., "L'Enfant noir," 420*)

Biyidi continued his insistence on an African reality even more strongly in his review of *Le Regard du roi*, Laye's second novel, the next year. He said:

> "L'Enfant noir" would have us believe in an idyllic Africa, one which is unbelievable, because the white man plays no part in it. In "Le Regard du roi," the white man is there, he is called Clarence, but he is a caricature. He is naive, docile, patient, curious about others: you might as well say that never has one seen his likes on African soil. (A. B., "*Le Regard du roi*," 144*)

From 1955 on, other critics began applying the standard of reality in earnest. A. A. Kwapong reviewed Cyprian Ekwensi's *People of the City* that year and liked it in part because "Ekwensi has a feeling for the climate of the Lagos of the night-clubs, ambitious politicians, grasping traders and ordinary folk which I find promising" (24). Another review of Ekwensi's *People* followed in the next year. Davidson Nicol admired the novel partly because "it is set chiefly in Lagos and it gives a vivid description and atmosphere of the demi-mondaine of a modern African city" ("The Soft Pink Palms," 113).

The year 1958 saw the publication of Chinua Achebe's first novel, *Things Fall Apart*, and African fiction—at least in English—seemed to move into a new stage, and the criticism with it. Ben Obumselu was one of the first Africans to review the novel. He noted that "*Things Fall Apart* will be seen as a first novel, not simply in the personal sense, but in the more important sense that it is the first English novel in which the life and institutions of a West African people is presented from the inside" (Review, 37). Obumselu applied the same standard when he criticized Achebe for a lack of fidelity on another account: "The form of the novel ought to have shown some awareness of the art of this culture. We do not have the novel form, of course, but there are implications in our music, sculpture and folklore which the West African novelist cannot neglect if he wishes to do more than merely imitate a European fashion" (38). He added, "I am in particular disappointed that there is in *Things Fall Apart* so little of the lyricism which marks our village life" (38).

G. Adali Mortty reviewed the novel in *Black Orpheus* and, interestingly, found a universal quality in its particularity. He said, "The theme of the novel is the kind which, while having a clearly recognizable local setting, breaks loose from its place limits. It is West African; it is African; and yet it is even more universal than that. The Ibo village of the story might well be any village of rural Africa" (48).

The Nigerian novelist Onuora Nzekwu applied the standard when he reviewed *Things Fall Apart*, T. M. Aluko's *One Man, One Wife*, and Ezekiel Mphahlele's *Down Second Avenue* and said, "All three books have succeeded in one thing: they give an insight into the life and feelings of African peoples" (107).

Achebe's second novel, *No Longer at Ease*, was published in 1960 and elicited several reviews, including one by J. Chunwike Ene, who noted the authentic flavor Achebe achieved through his use of proverb and myth. Ene concluded his review by saying of the book: "It is another brilliant contribution to that rare class of literature; the African writing on Africa from the inside" (43). Kojo Senanu said of it, "It attains at times a brittle evocation of scenes in urban West Africa—the dirt amidst which food is sold along the streets in the slums of Lagos, the sweat and the chaos of the highlife dance-hall of Saturday nights, the colourful pageant of the mushroom religious sects" ("A Rebel," 153).

Ezekiel Mphahlele was another critic who applied African reality consistently as a critical standard. His realist bent began to show in 1957 when he discussed several white South African writers and found them lacking. He said, "The story of Africa has not been told yet," and went on to criticize the unrealistic qualities of several white South Africans:

> Olive Schreiner, in spite of her strong sense of justice, regarded the non-white as part of the setting, passive and waiting for some individual philanthropy. William Plomer was so cynical about white civilization that he romanticized and idealized African character from a superficial knowledge of it. Sarah Gertrude Millin (of *God's Stepchildren* fame) regarded her Hottentot and half-caste characters as grovelling helpless victims of a fate: accidental or self-imposed mixed marriages. Alan Paton sentimentalized his black characters in order to prove the effectiveness of a liberal theory that he posed. ("What the," 175)

In another essay he commented on the lack of realism in Thomas Mofolo's *Chaka* and Sol T. Plaatje's *Mhudi*, saying, "These two novels were characteristic of the writing of their time: a romantic backward glance in response to the breakdown of traditional moral standards as a result of urbanization, the use of migrant labor, and political and social repression" ("African Culture Trends," 127). He continued in a more optimistic vein: "The two decades beginning with the last war have seen an increase in antiblack legislation in South Africa. Romance has given place to realism in prose writing." He added, "Mr. [Peter] Abrahams stands as an antithesis of writers of the Rider Haggard tradition as well as of the African romantics reviewed above" (128). A page later, Mphahlele also commented on the literary stance of his former co-writer on *Drum* magazine: "Can Themba's writing penetrates excruciatingly to the bone when it is journalistic but it is theatrical and escapist when it is fiction" (129).

Paulin Joachim for many years contributed book reviews to the Dakar-based magazine *Bingo*. In these can be seen his consistent concern with African reality. The earliest to exhibit the use of this standard is his 1961 review of *Un Piège sans fin* by fellow countryman Olympe Bhely-Quenum. Joachim said, "*Un Piège sans fin* is a book of great interest. It is above all a book authentically African. The first to our knowledge. It renders for us all the sensibility, all the emotional power of the Negro-African people" ("*Un Piège*," 41*). Joachim was critical of Leonard Sainville's *Anthologie de la littérature négro-africaine: romanciers et conteurs* for not having given proper recognition to Paul Hazoumé's *Doguicimi* (1938), "instead of consecrating endless pages to young African writers raised in Europe and seriously cut off from African reality" ("Anthologie," 61*). In Bernard Dadié's *Patron de New York* (1964), Joachim apparently saw not a physical but a metaphysical reality to approve. In the book, said Joachim, "one makes discoveries that are almost crown jewels and illustrate brilliantly the unique way the African observes the world" ("Un Livre," 45*). In considering Camara Laye's first novel, he made an evaluation quite different from Biyidi's: "In it, he [Laye] recreates the image of traditional African with its magic spells, its legends, and its passionate poetry" ("Contemporary," 298).

Olympe Bhely-Quenum, Joachim's fellow countryman and fellow editor (*La Vie africaine* and *L'Afrique actuelle*), also on several occasions displayed a concern for African reality. In reviewing Sembène Ousmane's *L'Harmattan* (1964), Bhely Quenum noted that, even when its action slowed, Ousmane's talent saved the book "because it is here that Sembène Ousmane is truly admirable, reveals his talent as an African writer careful with all African realities" (" 'L'Harmattan,' " 40*).

Wole Soyinka made his critical debut in print, so far as I can determine, in 1962. In that year, his essay "From a Common Back Cloth" did much to further the standard of African reality, for in it Soyinka reviewed the work

of several African writers in terms of their ability to use the "back cloth" of
that reality. Of Mongo Beti's *Mission to Kala* (1958), Soyinka said

> Mongo Beti takes the back cloth as he finds it, asserting simply that
> tradition is upheld not by one-dimensional innocents, but by cunning
> old codgers on chieftancy stools, polygamous elders, watching hawk-
> like the approach of young blood around their harem, by the eternal
> troublemaking females who plunge innocents, unaware, into memor-
> able odysseys. Hospitality is not, as we are constantly romantically in-
> formed that it is, nearly so spontaneous. There is a mercenary edge,
> and this, alas, is not always traceable to that alien corrupt civilization.
> ("From a Common," 394-95)

Soyinka concluded his essay with a strong call for realism, saying, "Ideali-
zation is a travesty of literary truth; worse still, it betrays only immature
hankerings of the creative impulse" (396).

Achebe's third novel, *Arrow of God* (1964), was reviewed in 1964 by Adisa
Williams, whose favorable comments continued the use of African reality
as a standard. Williams said, "Achebe's great achievement in this book is
his success in presenting traditional rural African life from the inside" (43).
Eldred Jones of Sierra Leone saw in the book the same characteristic he had
seen in Achebe's first novel: "Like *Things Fall Apart*, this novel employs
the imagery laden style, full of metaphors, proverbs, and Igbo saws which
give it a particularly African flavour" ("Achebe's," 177). Abiola Irele also
reviewed *Arrow* along with James Ngugi's first novel, *Weep Not, Child*,
published the same year, and said, "Both these books . . . participate in a
concrete unity in so far as the authors offer us, from inside, the image of
African society during a period of convulsion" (Review of *Arrow*, 234).

Ngugi's novel was approved by other critics who also admired it for its
fidelity to African reality. Taban Lo Liyong said, "He [Ngugi] has admirable figures of speech such as calling a chief 'big' because he 'used to eat
with the Governor.' There are others inappropriately used, however, such
as use of the proverb 'a lamb takes after her mother' to describe tigerish
qualities. For comic relief, he gives us realistic classroom scenes" (Review,
43). Alex Chudi Okeke liked the novel in part because "though Ngugi has
not used local proverbs such as you find in Chinua Achebe's writings, he
has nevertheless used certain proper names of existing places like Mahua,
Kikuyu and Kipanga which indeed give an aura of reality to the fiction" (4).

Yet another novel published in 1964, Gabriel Okara's *The Voice*, gave
critics occasion again to apply the standard of reality. In this case, however,
the remarks were primarily negative. Lewis Nkosi said of it,

> *The Voice* repels me with its contrived air of prophecy and portentous-
> ness. Parables are a great favorite with critics searching for "signifi-
> cances" in the human condition, but there is always a strain between

the moral and realistic frames unless the parable grows naturally out of the realistic details of the novel and is not a layer artificially imposed from above. ("Where Does," 8)

Sunday O. Anozie applied the same standard, saying of Okolo, the novel's hero, "The hero appears modelled after an obscure existentialist vision. And this makes Okolo either a wild beast or a god in his traditional village, and the novel itself so destitute in the concrete African sense of life" ("Theme," 62).

Other novels also led critics to invoke the same standard. They are far too numerous to cite in their entirety; a few examples should illustrate that the standard was not reserved only for the better-known writers.

Erisa Kironde, though she had serious doubts about the merits of William Conton's novel *The African*, was so moved by the realism of it that she said, "But Mr. Conton is such an excellent writer and his sense of invoking Africa so good, 'her till of (Kamara's mother's shop) a cigarette tin', that overall faults must be forgiven" (67).

Lewis Nkosi liked Chukwuemeka Ike's novel *Toads for Supper* because "Mr. Ike not only has a fine comic touch, but a talent for invoking interesting detail and the right metaphor. Authentic African imagery and sayings add to the richness of his prose" ("Where Does," 11). Absalom Ndyanabo wrote favorably of Onuora Nzekwu's *Blade among the Boys* because of "the African background, the vivid pictures and the puzzles it presents to one's mind" (64).

Poetry. Perhaps as much as the novel, poetry also led critics to express their concern for fidelity to African reality. Leopold Senghor was the leader of a movement away from conventional realism in African literature, but his quarrel was more with method than content. His concern for realia (as opposed to Realism) was apparent in his statement, "It is not true that realism is the best means of expressing the real" ("Le Réalisme," 11). It is not surprising, then, to find Senghor, as early as 1954, evaluating a writer using as his measure the adherence to an African reality. In his essay, "Langage et poésie négro-africaine," Senghor said of one poem, "It is thus speckled with images like the skin of a panther. Simple images, whose force nevertheless is that they are borrowed from the soil: from the animals, plants, natural phenomena, in the life of our country people" (154*). Also in 1954, Antoine-Roger Bolamba, editor of *La Voix du Congolais*, seemed to have an African reality in mind when he said of the Malagasay poet Jean-Joseph Rabearivelo, "His inspiration was all Malgache and came from the spirit of his ancestors" ("Le Poète martyr," 689*).

In 1956 Davidson Nicol applied the standard to poems of three poets—Crispin George of Sierra Leone, Dr. R. G. Armattoe of Ghana, and Dennis Osadebay of Nigeria—and found that "Osadebay's poetry has the closest connection with modern Africa" ("The Soft Pink Palms," 117).

Rabearivelo, who committed suicide in 1937, enjoyed a brief revival in 1960. Two critics wrote articles on him in the *Bulletin de Madagascar*, and his poems were republished with a preface by another Malgache poet, Jacques Rabemananjara. All three critics applied the standard of reality in their praise of Rabearivelo. Rabemananjara said, "Like *Vielles Chansons, Presque-Songes* could only have been born in the Imerina country. When one knows the fierce and sensual attachment that Rabearivelo avows and professes to his native country, one can only know the nature and sense of his poetic effort better" ("Préface," 15*). E. Ralaimihoatra noted favorably that the poet drew from a "poetic Malgache foundation" and that "it is in *Imaint-soanala*. . . . It appears in the symbolic value attached to Malgache plants, such as the *aviavy*, which represents grandeur; the *zahana*, love; and the mango tree, the security of the village" (525*). Gabriel Razafintsambaina referred to Rabearivelo as "Singer of the Malgache soul" and said, "He knew how to create a universe in which a people found its own echoes" (635*), adding, "In poetry he affirmed strongly that it was necessary to remain Malgache" (635*).

In 1963, at the Dakar conference, Ezekiel Mphahlele commented on Negritude and dwelt for a moment on the realism in Senghor's poetry:

Sheer romanticism that fails to see the large landscape of the personality of the African makes bad poetry. The omission of these elements of a continent in turmoil reflects a defective poetic vision. The greatest poetry of Leopold Sedar Senghor is that which portrays in himself the meeting point of Europe and Africa. This is the most realistic and honest and meaningful symbol of Africa, an ambivalent continent searching for equilibrium. ("A Reply," 24)

In 1964 Lewis Nkosi commented on another poet, saying, "In Gabriel Okara's poem 'One Night at Victoria Beach,' there is a passing reference to 'haggling sellers and buyers,' but for those who have ever been in West African cities or villages, an entire world is evoked" ("Contemporary," 288). In the same year Olympe Bhely-Quenum approved of Edouard Maunick's *Les Manèges de la mer* (1964) because, "Isn't it precisely this irrevocable attachment to his native land that gives a lot of truth and authenticity to Maunick's words?" ("Les Manèges," 51*).

A year later, in 1965, Theo Vincent felt similarly about Glory O. Nwanodi's *Icheke and Other Poems*, saying, "Mr. Nwanodi's poems are rooted and steeped in the culture, beliefs, traditions and rituals which he knows only too well" (58). The next year George Otieno had a similar observation to make on J. P. Clark's poem "Agbor Dancer": "Anyone who has ever seen African traditional dancers will admire the way in which J. P. Clark describes the excitement at that moment when music works magic in the dancer and they lose themselves in sheer rhythmic ecstasy" (43). Phillipa

Christie, a poet-critic writing before Zimbabwean independence, had the same standard in mind when she said of the poetry of Noeline Buttress, "She often ends with a couplet which contains the real meat of her poetry and has the very essence of Rhodesia in all her poems" (76).

Short Story. The use of the standard of reality was applied even to the short story, although this genre's neglect by African critics seems to have been as widespread as in other literatures.

Alioune Diop was perhaps the first to apply the standard to the short story when, in his preface to Bernard Dadié's *Légendes africaines* (1954), he spoke directly to Dadié, saying, "You not only have unquestionable talent, you are well rooted in the heart of your soil, sharing with your people their fight and their labors, their laughter and their innocence" ("Préface," 7*). M.J.C. Echeruo was concerned in 1962 with the direction being taken by Nigerian short fiction. He said,

> The short story in Nigeria has not realised itself for two reasons. Having been based on the wrong models, it did not, in the first place, realise, as Erskine Caldwell has pointed out, that it is "possible to find the materials of fiction in the everyday life around us,"—hence the search in several Nigerian short stories for the fantastic and the mysterious, as if the more magical the motivation, the more important the performance. There have, truly, been successful stories of this kind.
>
> J. P. Clark's *At the Waterfront*, Michael Chukwudalu's *A Tuesday Fifteen Years Ago*, and Miss Soba Ibiama's *The Mysterious Letter-writer* are examples. Altogether, however, the tendency has been either to despise "everyday life" or to think that the *commonplace* is the same as the *everyday*." ("Incidental," 11).

In 1963 the Cameroon journal *Abbia* published a short story by Jacques Muriel Nzouankeu, "Le Dame d'eau." In publishing it, however, the journal implied the standard of reality in this statement at the head of the story: "The somber pessimism of this work is contrary to the humanism and the optimism of the African vision of the world" (Abbia, "Note," 101*).

Drama. Perhaps drama received less criticism than any genre, but even here we find, for example, Peter Nazareth implying an African reality as a standard. Gerald Moore, the British critic of African literature, had suggested that James Ngugi's play *The Black Hermit* should not have been written in verse ("The Black Hermit," 34). Nazareth disagreed:

> The ritualistic quality of the verse makes the audience feel the ritualistic slow-moving quality of life in the village; it makes the audience feel that life in the village has roots. This is contrasted with the jazzy but "rootless" rhythms of life in the city. The contrast between the movement of the verse and the prose makes the audience feel that Jane,

for all her sincerity, could never comprehend life in the village and what it means to Kiarii. When the Elders come to the city to take Kiarii back to the village, the play shifts back to verse for a moment. The tautness of the verse makes the audience feel that the hold of the tribe over Kiarii is no intellectual abstraction—it is real. ("Verse," 5)

Oyin Ogunba applied the standard to James Ene Henshaw's plays, *This Is Our Chance* (1956), and claimed that "one can say that apart from the incidence of the story there is not much else that is West African about his plays" (81). A similar impatience led K.A.B. Jones-Quartey to say of R. S. Easmon's play *The New Patriots*,

> Even for an African girl brought up in England, and even in the rebellious mid-twentieth century, it is almost impossible to discover in Africa the likes of Mahmeh, a daughter who would talk to her father in the words, the tone of voice, the utterly out-of-context belligerence and contempt in which she is made to talk to Fred Byeloh, her stage-father. (" 'The New Patriots,' " 18)

The prominence of realism in African criticism and the insistence upon accuracy in the depiction of African reality were large, almost overriding factors in African literary criticism in the two decades after World War II. Only the concept of *engagement* might be said to challenge them for supremacy. Like most of the other issues prevalent in African criticism, however, realism and African reality were not absolutes. They were challenged, in one way or another, by several African critics. Realism was more often and more readily challenged than African reality. After all, no critic is likely to advocate a conscious falsification of a "reality" for its own sake—in any literature.

In several instances, I have pointed out that a critic noted a factual discrepancy between a literary text and the critic's own experience. No African critic, to my knowledge, has advocated a deliberate misrepresentation of fact or praised an African writer for committing one. Rather, the attack was made, if at all, on the literary technique. African reality, then, was unanimously or almost unanimously accepted in principle. The argument arose around the question of determining the best ways of translating the African reality into literature.

SURREALISM

Senghor

Leopold Senghor once said, "It is not true that realism is the best means of expressing the real" ("Le Réalisme," 11*). Not surprisingly, he has been the major opponent of realism in African literature, advocating the use of surrealism as the best literary technique for representing African reality. As early as 1939 he said, "What the Negro has is the ability to perceive the supernatural in the natural, the sense of the transcendent and the lively abandon that goes with it, the abandon of love" ("Ce que," 298-99*). In 1947 he elaborated, pointing out the difference between Western and African realism:

> What moves the Black is not the exterior aspect of the object, it is the *reality*, or better—since "realism" has become sensualism—its *surreality*. Water moves him, not because it cleanses, but because it purifies: fire, because of its destructive powers, not because of its warmth or color. The brush that burns and then grows again is life and death. Because here the surface, being understood in its singular particularities, is only the sign of the essence of the object. "The Creator says: Here is the sign." This means that the Negro is a mystic. ("L'Afrique noire," 166*)

In another essay Senghor distinguished between "European surrealism, which is uniquely empirical, and Negro-African surrealism, which is equally metaphysical, which is *supernatural*" ("Langage," 154*).

In his preface to Birago Diop's *Les Nouveaux contes d'Amadou-Koumba*, he said, "The real attains its density, becomes *true* only in breaking the rigid rules of logical reason, in freeing itself in the extensible dimensions of the surreal. We mock in passing the short-sighted logic of Bouki-the-hyena and his factual 'experience' " ("Préface to Birago Diop, 15*). In a 1952 essay, Senghor tied surrealism to Negritude, saying, "The Surrealist revolution . . . will alone have allowed our poets to express their Negritude in French" ("L'Apport," 142*). In 1955, while reviewing Camara Laye's *L'Enfant noir* and Lamine Diakhaté's *La Joie d'un continent*, Senghor again contrasted European and African forms:

> The merit of Romanticism, and especially *Surrealism*, is to have reversed engines, to have transcended the reason-imagination antimony, in restoring [imagination] to its primary place. It happens that Black Africa did not commit the error. It did not leave the Childhood Kingdom of art and poetry. From this comes the major contribution that it has brought to the revolution of the 20th century, to surrealism. ("Laye Camara et Lamine Diakhaté," 3*)

Others

Senghor had few African disciples in the matter of his surrealism, in relation to the number of avowed realists. Camara Laye was one of the few other Africans to advocate a surrealist technique. In a 1963 interview Laye admitted that he admired the work of Franz Kafka because "in his novels you can never distinguish between dream and reality. In Africa, it is exactly the same"

("Entretien avec Camara Laye," 56*). When asked, "And are you of the opinion that the surreal dimension is the fundamental trait of African art?" Laye responded, "Yes, but I will go further. I think that it is not possible to make only that of art without referring to the surreal side of things. Every work of art is finally surreal and this is true for European art as well as for African art" (57*). In another place Laye asked rhetorically, "Is the world only what we see when we look at it casually? Isn't the reality of the world precisely other than what our casual glance perceives?" and a page later, echoing Senghor's words, he gave this answer:

> The visible world shrinks suddenly before my eyes; I watch it dwindling
> into what it is, a dream and yet not quite a dream. But the sign, the sign
> of what exists beyond, of what is higher, infinitely higher, than the sign
> which itself is only appearance, is nothing, nothing that can satisfy. . . .
> I see the invisible rise up and confound our poor little reason which
> can only claim so tiny a place; I see the inexplicable elevated once more
> to its seat which is supreme above all. ("The Soul," 70)

For Laye as for Senghor, however, it was realism, and not African reality, that was opposed. At the Dakar conference of 1963, Laye said, "I am for a literature which conforms to Africa, and to the deepest aspirations of African people" ("The Black Lion," 129).

Another writer-critic, Tchicaya U Tam'si, indicated his preference for surrealism in this direct question: "Why is it necessary, each time one sings, to recite a grammar or logic lesson?" ("Tchicaya U Tam'si," 44*).

Anti-Surrealism

Even fewer critics attempted to attack surrealism directly, perhaps feeling that a strong realism was the better approach or that surrealism did not pose a serious threat to African reality and could therefore be ignored or tolerated. Condotto Nenekhaly-Camara, while not attacking it directly, saw far less importance in it than in the language issue. He said, "It is true that surrealism preached the dislocation of the traditional techniques of French poetry. But because the Negro-African uses the French linguistic instrument, he can only be a real poet if he respects the lasting genius of the French language. If not, there is a crime against Poetry" (15*). Mustapha Bal was even more direct. He saw surrealism as a means of escaping, rather than representing, the real. As he put it, "But if the real is too cruel? If there is no effective hope for liberation, the poet can take refuge in words, because there are words that liberate. Failing to change reality, we can change our vision of reality. Behind surrealism there is this tacit admission of impotence" (21*).

Surrealism as a Critical Standard

There were very few instances of African critics applying nonrealist criteria as literary standards. It might be interesting, nevertheless, to review the few examples that occurred.

Perhaps the first that might be remarked was not a literary judgment in the strictest sense of the word. Rather it involved an author's handling of African religion in an anthropological study. The critic was Leopold Senghor. Commenting on Maximilien Quenum's *Au Pays des Fons* (1938), he applied surrealism in this manner: "This is a work of incontestable literary qualities. Unfortunately, the rationalism that inspires it makes it particularly superficial in its treatment of religious facts, where we expected a 'profound vision' " ("L'Afrique noire," 234-35*). In his *Anthologie*, Senghor said of Birago Diop's literary method, "The story is poetry by way of its contempt for the real, or rather the everyday fact. It aspires neither toward the anecdote nor toward the 'slice-of-life'; its object, in giving us a vision of the surreal from beyond appearance, is to make us understand the profound sense of life in the world" ("Birago Diop," 135*). Reviewing Camara Laye's *L'Enfant noir*, Senghor called it a poem: "Laye Camara's greatest merit is to have made of his novel a long poem, as do the Negro-African storytellers. Poem it is by its symphonic rhythm and by its power of naming. It is enough for him to name beings and things that they burst into suggestive images and take part in surreal life, their true life" ("Laye Camara et Lamine Diakhaté," 157*).

Another francophone critic, Lamine Diakhaté, joined Senghor in applying the standard to one of Senghor's own poems. He said, "In Senghor's country, one dances for its own sake, one dances life. Dance of life and death, in surreal rhythm. Rooted in the surreal" ("Contribution," 60*).

THE AFRICAN PAST

In conjunction with and closely related to the debate on African reality was the discussion of the African past. In the throes of colonialism, Africans had been led to believe that they had no viable past, and thus the study of it was largely neglected during the first half of the twentieth century. With the coming of independence, however, came a renewed interest in the question of what, in fact, was the real Africa of 1960. This led quite naturally to a desire to rediscover what it had been.

The relationship of this past to modern African art was more complicated, since art is in a sense a conscious effort, whereas the making of history can be said to be controlled by conscious efforts totally outside itself—except, perhaps, for those recent American presidents who have developed the habit of guarding their documents for their historical value, to be housed in presidential libraries.

If the phrase "art for art's sake" is a comprehensible aesthetic stance (though largely rejected by African artists), history for history's sake would seem far less tenable. Hence the relationship of the past to the present is of particular interest in the realm of the arts. The African artist, faced with a blank canvas or piece of paper, or block of wood, was faced with the questions "Who am I?" and, more to the point, "How does whoever I am create?" Did Africa—the African artist—have to rediscover what pre-colonial Africa was in order to create an authentic Africa of the future? Or was that a romantic cul-de-sac that should be avoided, which had nothing to do with the more "real," more accessible colonial Africa, upon which a future Africa would best be based? Could a balance between these two approaches be achieved?

This discussion might have been included as part of Chapter 4, "The Making of a Literary Tradition." There, however, the scope was limited to more technical matters relating to the development of a literary tradition distinct from that of the West. This chapter will examine the past conceived of as content. It will not often address itself to the details of that content, but rather what the critics felt the past-as-content should mean to the African writer in the present.

African critics were sharply divided on this question. The majority seemed to favor the use of the past in modern African literature; there was, nevertheless, a vigorous and not-so-small minority that argued, essentially, that the past was dead and that African literature would best be served by "getting on with it." Let us examine the former argument first.

Use of the African Past

A South African critic, Woodroffe Mbete, was one of the first to call for a rejuvenation of the past when he quoted from P. S. Joshi's opening remarks at a non-European artists' conference held in Johannesburg in December 1945. Joshi said, "We must seek inspiration from the glorious past and create *authentic history*; we must sing the deeds of our great men and infuse eternal pride and manly respect among our people. We must *write* our folklore to *preserve our traditional and cultural heritage*" (14).

Since Negritude is often taken to mean the revalorization of African and black values, it is not surprising to find that its primary apostle, Leopold Senghor, soon took up this call persistently and systematically. His championing of the African past per se seems to date from a 1937 speech, "Le Problème culturel en A.O.F.," in which he stated that "the intellectuals have the mission of restoring the *black values* in their truth and excellence, to awaken their people to the taste of bread and wit, by which we are *Men*.

Especially through our writing. There is no civilization without a literature that expresses and illustrates its values, as a jeweller the jewels of a crown" (19*). In 1950 his words had more of an edge. He wrote:

> I want to be still more precise. I have known Negro intellectuals who preached the Negro values only to make them known to the white world. No, to know the civilization of your fathers is not enough, you must know it yourself, sympathetically. You have to live it, or rather relive it. Not in dreams, but in words, in everyday deeds. ("Le Problème de la culture," 94-95*)

Peter Abrahams illustrated a feeling for the African past when he said in 1952, "It seems to me that two things are indispensable to the writer who would serve Africa's deepest needs today. First, he must have a sense of history" ("African Writers," 11). V. C. Nchami had similar advice for writers the same year and said, "It is realised that *creative* writing, more than anything else, will do much to preserve for the coming generations the past and present culture of West Africa" (809). Cyprian Ekwensi's advice, four years later, was that "the African writer must first look back on his own heritage. Then he must look around at what is available to him" ("The Dilemma," 701).

In 1957 Paul Mushiete also addressed himself to the African writer: "The writers or those who will be called upon to build an African culture must not always feel themselves for or against Europe. They will find in their past and tradition a proper base capable of being fruitfully exploited, without referencing necessarily to the West" ("Notes," 620*). The Malagasay poet Jacques Rabemananjara noted the imposition of the colonial cultures and their effect on the African past, saying to his fellow writers, "Our task is therefore clear: the putting in order again of our values, the restoration of the plundered patrimony, the restoration of pages torn either brutally or surreptitiously from our family album" ("Les Fondements," 79*). Paulin Joachim saw a similar duty: "In writing for our people, we are certain to assure them an internal equilibrium and to start them marching again, to interrupt the dead period of colonialism. And, having been renewed, thanks to us, with their past and traditions, they will cease to be consumers and become in turn producers of culture" ("L'Ecueil," 7*).

One manifestation of the use of the African past has been the culture-conflict novel, of which Achebe's *Things Fall Apart* may be called the prototype. Others less realistic, more romantic, such as Laye's *L'Enfant noir*, may also be said to belong in this category. Laye talked about his view of the African past at the Freetown conference in 1963, when he said, "It is by starting from the knowledge of what we have been that we can fertilize the present and the future" ("The Black Lion," 128).

Achebe's attitude was somewhat different. He said in an interview the same year, "I cannot . . . understand this nostalgia for the Golden Age that one finds in Senghor, Mongo Beti or Camara Laye, whom I love nevertheless, especially in his second book. Here in Nigeria one does not pretend that in former times life was sweet and easy" ("Entretien avec Chinua Achebe," 42*). However, Achebe dealt positively with the past in a lecture given to the Nigerian Library Association, in which he saw the examination of the past as "The Role of the Writer in a New Nation." To the claim put forward, primarily by the enthusiasts for *engagement*, that the writer must deal with current, topical themes, colonialism in particular, Achebe countered by saying there is another theme that must take precedence: "that African peoples did not hear of culture for the first time from Europeans; that their societies were not mindless but frequently had a philosophy of great depth" ("The Role," 157). But Achebe also had definite ideas about the temptations awaiting the writer depicting the past. He said, "The credibility of the world he is attempting to recreate will be called to question and he will defeat his own purpose if he is suspected of glossing over inconvenient facts. We cannot pretend that our past was one long, technicolour idyll" ("The Role," 158). Of particular interest here is the connection Achebe draws between the importance of the artist's integrity and African reality, and what this means in terms of the African presence in the world. It is an indication of the deepseatedness of Achebe's attitude toward African reality.

The acuity Achebe called for, however, did not seem to be widely accepted, particularly not by French-speaking critics, who seemed to prefer a more Romantic stance. Charles Ngande, for example, said in 1963 of the African poets, "Let them sing our glorious, sorrowful, vitalising past; let them sing our efforts and our battles" (137). At the Dakar conference that same year, Mahanta Fall said, "The francophone African poet is also a poet who sings of Africa, the Africa of old as it was before the slave trading and colonization. It is about the Africa of great empires that saw the blooming of a brilliant civilization" (217*). Fall tempered this remark, however, by also saying, "But the African poet is not for all that confined to a contemplation of the grandeur of his past. If he sings of the African past, it is never at the expense of the present and future" (218*).

Two other francophone critics raised the importance of the African past above even that of *engagement*. Bernard Dadié said in 1963 that, even if *engagement* were somehow betrayed, "One thing shall remain: the link with the African Past" ("Folklore," 5). In 1964 Paulin Joachim went further, saying of African poetry, "Now that the colonial masters have left French Africa and independence has been regained, this poetry of combat and of bitterness has lost its *raison d'être*. The poets have a continuing duty, however, to delve into their cultural patrimony and the little-known values of their ancestors" ("Contemporary," 298).

Abiola Irele spoke of the African past to the younger anglophone writer when he cogently linked the Negritude poets to their own development:

> To dismiss the poetry of Negritude as romantic and out-of-date, and to uphold a new poetry in which the public tone is reduced, is to miss the very purpose of these poets, to lose sight of the necessary evolution which they prepared. Without the revalorisation of African cultural values which dictated their militant tone, without the self-conscious-ness of Senghor, Diop, Césaire and others, the new trend represented by Clark, Okigbo and Awoonor-Williams would hardly have been pos-sible. These poets are separated not only by language but by the years in which an acceptance of African values gradually became a matter of course. (Review of *Poems*, 276-77)

Lewis Nkosi remarked on the African past and in the process reminded his readers once again that the South African context demanded special at-tention and that generalizations about African literature often could not be applied to it. Nkosi noted that "certainly most Africans in South Africa react violently to Dr. Verwoerd's exhortations that Africans should go back to their tribal roots, to his assertion that they are unfit by nature to partici-pate in Western culture. Any talk of tribal roots smacks of apartheid" ("Con-temporary," 282). But he also recognized that the past, unperverted by poli-tics, ought to and could have value. He said:

> Only when African intellectuals are somehow finally integrated into the society, one feels, will they have enough courage to see beyond Dr. Verwoerd's nonsense about "Bantu culture" and be able to look back to their origins. Today they write with him staring over their shoulders. This severance from tradition has impoverished African writing to a certain extent. ("Contemporary," 283)

In his *Home and Exile* Nkosi explored the difficulties of recovering tradi-tion. He noted that the need to recover it arises only within the elite, whose "thin voice of nostalgia" must be distinguished from "traditional Africans" who "do not find the need nor the time to write books extolling the virtues of an African way of life. They are too busy living it" (46).

The African Past as a Critical Standard

Like the other concepts analyzed here, the use of the African past in Afri-can literature was discussed not only theoretically but in relation to specific literary works as well. The positive application of the African past as a criti-cal standard, like the positive theoretical statements about it, far outnumber the negative applications.

Leopold Senghor was one of the first to have applied this standard—as he was the first to take up so many other of the major concerns of African literary criticism. In the headnotes of his 1948 *Anthologie*, he explained, with obvious enthusiasm, why the Malagasay poet "[Flavien] Ranaivo freed himself from French influences as quickly as he had assimilated them. More than a discovery of Malgache poetry, there is in him a return to the sources" (207*). Several years later Senghor said of his fellow Senegalese Malick Fall and his *Reliefs*, "He renews himself here with the umbilical cord that binds him again to traditional Africa: to the stories, fables, and legends, by his mother, his grandmother and his ancestors, to the men, and especially to the women of his race" ("Malick Fall," 9-10*).

Other francophone critics followed Senghor's lead. Paul Mushiete also applied the standard in his description of Paul Lomami-Tshibamba's story *Ngando* (1948): "By the truth of its facts and the richness of its evocations, 'Ngando' is one of the first works that has described the depth of the soul of our people. This is a precious book, since it gives us an image of a disappearing world which needs to be fixed in the memory of man" (*La Littérature française africaine*, 34*). In the same place he said of Father Alexis Kagame that "he gave us more than a testimony. It is the richness of our world that he revealed to us. The ensemble of his work is a denial to the skeptics—black and white—who do not believe that values worthy of our interest could exist in the African tradition" (37-38*).

David Diop, very likely more unsympathetic than sympathetic toward the African past, preferring to attack colonialism more directly in his poetry and in his criticism as well, nevertheless tempered his commentary on Paulin Joachim's *Un Nègre raconte* (1954) in these terms: "I regret the overly idyllic description of our Africa of earlier ages opposed to a technologized Europe. But when one compares the violence of our epoch, is it forbidden to dream sometimes of a past that was no doubt less egoistic and cruel?" ("Poètes," 80*).

Bernard Fonlon and Peter Ogbonnaya applied the standard as well, soon after Achebe's *Things Fall Apart* appeared. They were pleased with the novel, saying, "The title of the novel has been fortunately chosen, because it refutes implicitly the prevailing idea that all was chaos in Africa before the coming of the white man. If the edifice collapses, it had to have maintained itself up to that point" (Fonlon and Ogbonnaya, 136). K. E. Senanu pondered the use of the past by Achebe and three other writers and concluded that "Ekwensi has yet to learn how very potent and useful traditional ways of grasping and interpreting experience can still be to a conscious artist, as has been shown in the cases of both Chinua Achebe and Camara Laye" ("The Literature," 184), and added that "only Achebe, Laye and Tutuola have yet attained, fully, a critical re-creation of traditional life and the values that it still holds" (184). Mbella Sonne Dipoko reflected a similar feeling in his review of Tutuola's *Feather Woman of the Jungle* (1962). He said, "The 'Africanness' of Tutuola's tall stories is of both ethnological and anthropological interest, reflecting to a certain extent the mentality of an age and the adventurous, dynamic and therefore creative nature of a life that blossomed in the heart of Africa before the colonizer's rifle barked and the talking drum announced surrender'' (Review of *Feather Woman*, 230).

Donatus Nwoga, on the other hand, while applying the same standard, was critical of Mongo Beti's *Mission terminée* because of Beti's cynical attitude toward traditional Africa. Nwoga noted that ''nobody, let alone an African, has looked at us with such impersonal disillusionment, no one has yet questioned the basis of traditional society with such conviction, and so definitely contradicted the spirit of Aimé Césaire's poem 'Hurrah for those who have invented nothing!' '' (''The Cynical Messenger,'' 52). He concluded his review saying, ''I would like to hope however that its cynicism is a temporary phase and that its author will, sooner or later, return to a positive attitude, an attitude which will admit the possibility of coordinating progress and tradition'' (52). Abiola Irele had similar negative feelings about Ezekiel Mphahlele:

> It is . . . very distressing to note the derogatory, patronising tone with which he writes of traditional African culture, for instance of the music and dances which still prove the vital pastime among the *vast majority* of Africans, but which he would rather confine to the museums and have replaced by the ephemeral escape music of the rootless urban communities. Mr. Mphahlele seems to think that the slightest consideration of traditional African life is not only a meaningless intellectual exercise but a foolish effort to arrest the development of African societies. (Review of *The African Image*, 233).

Chinua Achebe, whose own attitude toward the African past has been noted, applied the sense of those remarks to two other African writers. He thought Camara Laye's *The Dark Child* was ''a little too sweet'' and said, ''But I maintain that any serious African writer who wants to plead the cause of the past must not only be God's advocate; he must also do duty for the devil. . . . This is one of the things Wole Soyinka was saying in *A Dance of the Forests*'' (''The Role,'' 158).

The African Past: Reservations

Before examining the statements of critics taking a negative view of the African past, it must be said that there was a small number of critics who, while neither endorsing nor attacking it, seemed willing to support its use in African literature with reservations. The general trend of these remarks was that the African past should not be overly glorified or sought merely for its own sake but should be considered primarily for whatever light it could shed on the present. It was also pointed out that the colonial period was as much a part of Africa's past as the pre-colonial.

Ezekiel Mphahlele, though more often negative about the past than not, was perhaps one of the earliest critics to articulate this ambivalent point of view toward Africa's past. Mphahlele, en route from Great Britain to Nigeria on one of his many journeys, visited the Paris offices of *Présence africaine* in November 1959 and discussed some of the major differences—Negritude no doubt heading the list—that he felt with the journal's policies. He said of its staff,

> They admitted that while we try to re-establish our past, such a func-tion can only find proper focus if it is going to help us know ourselves better in the context of present-day cultural activity. When I am en-gaged in creative writing, for instance, my characters interest me as they are in a socially mixed society. What they were and what they did before the white man came interests me only as far as it throws light on their present behaviour and human relationships. (". . . Away into Ancestral Fields," 12)

In describing the activities of the Chemchemi Cultural Center in Nairobi, which he directed for some time, Mphahlele reiterated his attitude toward "tradition":

> It is not as if we in East Africa were being asked to dig up fossils of a culture to try to inject new life into them. Rather, there is, as in all of Africa, a solid thread of continuity in people's way of life in the hinter-land. So it is only a matter of establishing means of contact between urban and rural folk, of harmonising tribal idioms of music and dance towards a national culture. ("Chemchemi: Rediscovery," 42)

Abiola Irele expressed his ambivalence in these words:

> The black poet's descent into himself is an effort to disalienate his be-ing and to reestablish a concordance with a distinct essence. For this reason, he reconstitutes this essence as much as he can from the remains in him of the African heritage. Yet this march to an original past is coloured by a historical experience to which he has been submitted, imprinted in him indelibly. So that in the effort to achieve personality, there can be no question of a return to the past in its original form. ("A Defence," 11)

Wole Soyinka also tended to minimize the past by insisting on its integra-tion with the present. "Transition is *now*," he said,

> and is born of every experience, not buried in the stillness of antiquity. This freedom is the true legacy of the modern African, the freedom to reshape, to select and to reject, to build new forms around the image of the past, to reinterpret the ancient idioms through the uniqueness

of a personal, contemporary experience. For the new African, form is a movement that constantly supersedes itself. ("Nigeria," 4)

Edward C. Okwu took exception to Obiajunwa Wali's essay "The Dead End of African Literature" because of, among other things, what he considered an improper view of the past. Okwu said,

> I do not, for instance, agree with Mr. Wali that only writing in African languages would create and enrich a true culture of the African peoples. From the way he says these things one gets the impression that culture is a static thing and that expressing our culture in a foreign language will be too incongruous to be attempted. The new elements that have gone into our cultural stream during the past six or seven decades of our history are as much authentic aspects of our culture as such aspects of it that existed in our pre-colonial days. (290-91)

Chinua Achebe, commenting on Amos Tutuola and others in his foreword to *A Selection of African Prose* (1964), applied this blending of the past and present as a critical standard when he said,

> Folk tales, like folk songs, continue to be born and . . . new ones take account of all the new things surrounding life today. This syncretism is one of the chief attractions of Amos Tutuola, who is really a folk-writer. Syncretism is, of course, the despair of purists. . . . But any art which seeks to be up to date is at least alive; it has not yet ossified into a museum piece. (ix)

Anti-Past

There were also those critics—smaller in number—who were neither troubled by an ambivalence toward Africa's past nor exhibited any desire to rediscover or reevaluate it. They tended to see the past not as contributing to the present but as hindering it.

Although he elsewhere took a more moderate stance, Peter Abrahams was one of the first critics to take this position. While speaking primarily in political terms, it is clear that he did not hesitate, in 1954, to apply his thinking to literature as well. He said,

> To be truly democratic, the State must be founded on the underlying assumptions of Western culture. The tribal structure served the needs of tribal man. The moral codes of tribal man were adequate to his time. The needs of modern man, the conditions under which modern man lives, demand new structures and new values. The touching love of some anthropologists for the old ways should not blind us to their inadequacy for modern needs. Western culture is a world culture, not "reserved for Europeans only." ("The Conflict," 312)

Perhaps not surprisingly, Abrahams was joined in his general feeling by his fellow South African, Ezekiel Mphahlele. Writing in *Foreign Affairs* in 1964, Mphahlele described some actions of the South African government and their effect on black South Africans:

> The most recent laws that have serious consequences for cultural growth and self-realization in South Africa are the Bantu Authorities and Bantu Education Acts. The former provides the government with an instrument for splitting African communities into ethnic groups, and through the latter it has devised a system of education that trains the African to serve his ethnic group on the assumption that his people must not be given weapons whereby they can compete with the European. The perverted logic of it is that this provides an opportunity for the black man to live his own culture (meaning obviously tribal culture) and saves him years of frustration which lie before him if he tries to make a living in what has already been pegged as white man's territory, and in a society that disowns him. This of necessity means an inferior education and undermines the advance Africans have made in producing a considerable intellectual force that is now making itself felt in the politics of resistance. ("The Fabric," 619)

Elsewhere, in an interview in *Afrique*, Mphahlele said of Nigerian poetry,

> A poet can very easily return to his traditional roots one day, and distance himself the next. Poetry seems to me an artistic form so tied to the individual temperament that it would be foolish to tie a man to his traditional roots; the more because traditional Nigerian poetry treated subjects that no longer interest the people of today. ("Entretien avec Ezekiel Mphahlele," 57*)

Abrahams and Mphahlele were not alone in their thinking, nor was the distrust of the African past limited to South Africans. Michael Dei-Anang, a Ghanaian critic, saw an external and an internal danger facing the African artist standing "between two worlds." The internal danger, he said,

> stems from complacence with the past. This is sometimes the result of a certain inferiority complex which hates the exposure of weaknesses to new impulses and challenges and prefers to remain in the unchanging groves of traditionalism. The purists in language, traditionalists in music and art and the conservatists in dress all belong to this group. They kill progress and stultify advancement by their unyielding nature. ("A Writer's Outlook," 41)

Martin Tucker, an American critic, quarreled with what he called the "Headline Novels of Africa" because they were too topical and overly concerned with social situations, to the detriment of the development of character.

Responding to Tucker, the Society of Nigerian Authors indicated its feelings on the African past, saying,

> The great theme of today's Africa is the larger problem involving the whole continent and its leaders: the new statesmanship, the advent into the international scene, nation-building, the search for the right path in a world torn asunder by conflicting ideologies. Topical or not this is the theme of our generation. Has it occurred to Mr. Tucker that in its present mood Africa may not be interested in its past except in so far as it glorifies the present? (941)

In a 1963 letter to *West Africa*, Kunle Akande said, "I think it is shameful that an African should agree with the imperialists that he has no identity worth searching for" (1038). This brought the following reply from Yusifu Usman: "But do we have to search for an identity? Doesn't the need to search imply a lack of past traditions, with which we can identify ourselves? Surely any truly African writer has got enough background of culture and tradition, and need never go out looking for them" ("Cultural Colonialism," 1128).

Even two francophone critics questioned the value of the African past. Writing of the First World Festival of Negro Arts in 1966, Paulin Joachim asked, "Does Africa wish to enclose itself within its frontiers and to lean exclusively on its past as if to borrow a force it intends to use simply for its intellectual and spiritual promotion in the world" ("En Décembre," 23*)? Thomas Melone thought that the superior African writer "refuses the alternative offered him between the whimpering protest of anticolonialism and a certain mania for secularized folklore, which gives the illusion of a resurrection of great African myths with deafening tom-toms and tropical mysteries" ("New Voices," 67).

Anti-Past as a Critical Standard

The use of the African past was also applied negatively as a critical standard, although even less frequently than it was attacked theoretically. Nevertheless, the thrust of some of these statements is worth noting.

D.D.T. Jabavu was probably the first post-World War II critic to apply the standard negatively. In 1948 he commented on A. C. Jordan's Xhosa novel, *IngQumbo yemiNyanya*, and thought that "the novel is likely to remain unchallenged for a long time in Xhosa literature, for it reflects actual life to a detail and in a wholesome fashion, linking up the barbaric past to the romantic present with masterly judgement" (26). Aside from indicating Jabavu's preference for an African "reality" over the past, the language serves as a commentary on the distance African criticism has moved in four decades and the validity of the African past as a critical standard that developed since these words were written.

Another South African critic, Peter Abrahams, applied the same standard a few years later when he said of A. S. Mopeli-Paulus and Peter Lanham's novel, *Blanket Boy's Moon* (1953) that in spite of its faults, "the book still retains its validity as a serious attempt to throw light on what is, to my mind, the most pressing problem of Africa today: the problem of the African's transition from the tribal past into the technological present" ("The Conflict," 304). Abrahams's view of the past came out even more clearly when, reviewing Ekwensi's *People of the City*, he compared it to the work of Amos Tutuola in this way:

> Make no mistake about the importance of Mr. Ekwensi's book. It is the first *modern* novel by an African, charged with social meaningfulness, to come out of that part of Africa. Mr Ekwensi is thus a literary pioneer.
>
> True, we have already had Mr. Tutuola and his *Drinkard* wandering in the twilight world of the *Bush of Ghosts* among tribal monsters where we encounter telephone-voices but never enter the telephone world of the present. The word [world?] of the *Drinkard* is, to my mind, likely to appeal more to non-Africans than to Africans. For the literate African today lives, and is more interested in the real world of Mr. Ekwensi's Sango. Mr. Tutuola's *Drinkard* is as incapable of genuine development as is tribalism in the technological present. Mr. Ekwensi's Sango has a whole world of ideas ahead of him: the discovery of the uniqueness of human individuality, new and subtle ranges of feeling, and the mastery of the mechanical and technical skills. Mr. Ekwensi's inspiration is in the present and looks to the future and has only echoes from the past. It points a way and makes possible a contemporary literature for the future. ("A Literary Pioneer," 975)

Several years later Erisa Kironde had some objections to William Conton's novel, *The African*. One of them was that

> the hero's background cannot be authentic in East Africa today and must be less so in West Africa. Is it not time that our novelists based heroes on backgrounds that are other than those that have become stock in writing about Africa . . . the traditional tribal background? What about the background, bourgeois and Victorian, in which so many of us have grown in the twenties, thirties and forties of this century? (67)

Mphahlele, as we might expect, seemed to apply the past as a negative critical standard at least once. Surveying African literature in 1966, he said:

> Nigerians, generally speaking, are not haunted by ruins, ancestral faces or presences or music out of the past. Their poetry is more individualistic,

with a personally-felt immediacy. When they give lyrical expression to aspects of the black-white encounter, it is a personalization of the experience, such as we see in Gabriel Okara's *Piano and Drums*. ("African Literature for Beginners," 26)

Valerie D'Cruz liked John Munonye's novel *The Only Son* because Munonye had not fallen into certain pitfalls of the African novel; she said, "Nor is Munonye an escapist trying to defend adherence to his ancestral past; to a slight degree he romanticizes it but shows no inclination to move back" (45).

And finally, at least one francophone critic applied the African past negatively as a standard. Paulin Joachim, reviewing Jean Ikelle-Matiba's *Cette Afrique-là*, lamented the author's "Paradise Lost complex" and said,

It is impossible for us to follow Ikelle-Matiba along this dangerous path, because we think that one must live in one's time, that the old Africa no longer has its place in modern times, which have their own laws, that one must evolve in order to assure his place in the new world and that to choose a contrary course is to condemn oneself to stagnation and to allow oneself to be swallowed up by others. ("Les Lettres camerounaises," 39*)

CONCLUSION

Thus we can see that reality proved to be most elusive for African critics, as it has been elusive to all peoples and all times. Some Africans sought it through a preference for the tenets of Western Realism, while others seemed to find it through the techniques of Surrealism. For some Africans, reality lay uniquely in the present, while for others it resided in the past. Still others saw it in the relationship between the two.

I have used Western terms here merely for larger reference, with no desire to suggest that African literary criticism in its early years was tied—or felt itself tied—to non-African literary movements. Certainly some Africans have been more touched by Western influences than others, but few, if any, have succumbed so completely that they have lost all desire to discover, one way or another, the elusive African reality.

6 African Literature, *Littérature engagée*

THEORY

There is little question of the impact of Jean-Paul Sartre's essay "Orphée noir" on modern African literature. The Cameroun critic Jean-Paul Nyunaï referred to it as a "magistrale étude" (164), and seldom, if ever, has its importance been questioned. Ezekiel Mphahlele was disturbed by its influence, though primarily because he said it helped consolidate the vocabulary of the Negritude critics ("Postscript," 80-81). What has not been so thoroughly discussed is the importance of Sartre's other ideas on African literature—in particular, the concept of *engagement*, the view that literature should be *engagée*, or committed to the solving of the problems of the contemporary world, developed by Sartre in his essay *Qu'est-ce que la littérature* but explicated two years earlier in the initial issue of his *Les Temps modernes* ("Présentation").

Bernard Fonlon, the Cameroun editor of *Abbia*, was one of the few African critics to refer specifically to this aspect of "Orphée noir." In his Ph.D. dissertation at the National University of Ireland, he cited Sartre's statement that "black poetry in French is, today, the only great revolutionary poetry" (*La Poésie*, xii*).

One of the few Africans to consider the broader nature of Sartre's influence was Abiola Irele, though he was particularly interested in the European influence upon Negritude. Irele sketched the European context of this influence succinctly:

> The nature of literary activity in Europe has not been without consequences for the literature of *negritude*. The years preceding World War II saw the development of a literature of "causes," culminating in the outpouring provoked by the Spanish Civil War. This literature

committed to political causes was to receive a tremendous impetus
during the French Resistance; and after the war Jean-Paul Sartre developed the idea of *litèrature engagée* in a series of essays on the nature
of literature and on the relationship of the writer to society. The two
decades 1930-1950 were dominated by the literary figures of Louis
Aragon, Albert Camus, Paul Eluard, and Jacques Prévert. It was inevitable that the black writers should have been strongly influenced by
them, especially Sartre, who was the first European apostle of *negritude*, and others who were to have a direct hand in its formulation.

French writing thus had a marked social content in this period, and
the literature of *negritude* reflects the prevailing atmosphere in France.
("Negritude or Black Cultural Nationalism," 341)

Perhaps it was Sartre's interest in Negritude, in "Orphée noir," that paved
the way for the influence of his concept of *engagement*; perhaps the influence was due to the fact that Negritude itself was at that time more *engagée*,
more revolutionary, than it was to be in later years; or perhaps the concept
of *engagement* is inherent in African culture in a way that it is not in the
West, thus assuring an affinity with the Western form of it. Irele suggested
something of the latter in his review of the first four volumes of the Oxford
Library of African Literature, when he noted that

> the relationship that exists between traditional forms and written liter-
> ature, either in African languages or in modern European languages,
> has been obscured by the new social dimension of contemporary Afri-
> can literature. Demands that the experience of the African in the period
> of contact with Europe be expressed in literature have overridden any
> other considerations, with the result pointed out by Professor White-
> ley. . . : "one does notice tendencies towards a documentary rather
> than an imaginative treatment of events, and an interest in the impact
> of situation rather than in the individual personality." It might be re-
> marked of course that this is totally in keeping with the social concep-
> tion of literature in African societies. (Review of *A Selection*, 466)

Other Africans made this same point. Leopold Senghor said of traditional
African art, "It is created by everyone and for everyone," and "Because
they are functional and collective, African-Negro literature and art are committed" ("African-Negro Aesthetics," 28), to which he added, "A work of
[African] art is perishable. If one preserves the spirit and style one can readily duplicate an early work by modernizing it as soon as it becomes dated or
destroyed. In other words, in Negro Africa, 'art for art's sake' does not exist. All art is social" (29).

In the same vein, Lewis Nkosi, commenting on the artist's relationship to
society, noted some fundamental differences between modern and traditional
African society:

The idea of an artist as someone who stands apart and questions his society is admittedly a foreign one in Africa. Before we can meaningfully talk about the role of the poet in the present-day African society we must draw a contrast between what is accepted as the role of the artist in Western society and that achieved for the artist in the traditional African society. There was no recognized or readily ascertainable conflict between the poet and his community in traditional Africa. The poet's ideals and his social goals were not seen to be necessarily separable from and in conflict with those of the rest of the community. The function of the poet as an obsessed, even mad individual, a vertiginous rebel threatening the status quo, is essentially alien to the traditional African concept of the poet's role.

In this community the poet or the artist in general is there to *celebrate* his own or his society's sense of being (which, by the way, is not the same thing as celebrating its well-being) and not there to subvert its social values or moral order. (*Home and Exile*, 102)

But Nkosi did not advocate a return to traditional values in toto, nor did he deny the relevance of Sartre's *engagement*. He said,

In the traditional African society, for instance, the Sartre thesis would not only seem irrelevant, as I have indicated, but foolish and not worthy of a rebuttal. Yet we must admit that in many areas of Africa the destruction of traditional African values by European imperialism and the concomitant Christianisation of Africans has drastically reversed the role of the poet or artist in the community. (*Home and Exile*, 104)

But rather than search at length for the reasons behind Sartre's influence, let us proceed to determine its acceptance—largely implicit—by African critics.

Conferences

Beginning with the First International Congress of Negro Writers and Artists, held in Paris in 1956, and through the First World Festival of Negro Arts, held in Dakar ten years later, there were several occasions on which African writers and critics assembled. At the conclusion of these gatherings the practice was to issue resolutions that reflected the sentiments of the group. Several of these resolutions made reference in some way to the concept of *engagement*. These statements are in a way more significant than statements by individual critics, for they reflect the thinking of rather large groups of people, and they indicate those elements upon which the participants were willing to agree publicly.

The first of these, written at the First International Congress of Negro Writers and Artists, included among its "Final Resolutions" the following:

This Conference invites all Negro intellectuals to unite their efforts in securing effective respect for the rights of Man, whatever his color may be, and for all peoples and nations whatsoever.

This Conference urges Negro intellectuals and all justice-loving men to struggle to create the practical conditions for the revival and the growth of Negro cultures.

Paying tribute to the cultures of all lands and with due appreciation of their several contributions to the progress of civilization, the Conference urges all Negro intellectuals to defend, illustrate and publicize throughout the world the national values of their own peoples. ("Final Resolutions," 364)

The Conference of Tashkent, held in the Uzbek capital in October 1958 and uniting Asian and African writers at a time when most of Africa was still under colonial rule, issued this appeal: "Our conviction is that the purpose of literature is indefectibly tied to the destinies of our people, that the true flowering of literature can occur only in liberty, independence and the people's sovereignty; that the destruction of colonialism and racism is the condition for the entire development of literature" ("Conférence de Tachkent," 135*). Six months later, the Second Congress of Negro Writers and Artists, held in Rome in March 1959, also passed a resolution. This one mentioned *engagement* specifically, under "the responsibilities of the black writer to his people":

(b) the true expression of the reality of his people, long obscured, deformed or denied during the period of colonization.

This expression is so necessary in today's conditions that it implies for the black artist or writer the specific notion of engagement. The black writer can only participate in a spontaneous and total manner in the movement outlined above. Having been given the sense of his struggle at the outset, how could he refuse it? ("Résolution," 389*)

Although the First World Festival of Negro Arts did not draw up a formal statement or set of resolutions in 1966, *Présence africaine* (whose editor, Alioune Diop, was, after Senghor, probably the most ardent organizer of the festival) took it upon itself to counter the claim that Negro art had now become primarily aesthetic in the Western sense. Of African objets d'art at the festival, the journal editorialized that

these objects have not just an aesthetic value; *even today* they are still full of diverse meanings and, in living societies, have functions which do not concern aesthetics alone or are used in circumstances where aesthetics is not even dominant.

The Festival's sole purpose was not to reveal aesthetic forms; it was also intended to awaken a new consciousness in the Negro people (and not only among the elites). (P.A. [*Présence africaine*], "Language of the Heart," 6-7)

Mohamadou Kane reviewed the results of these various conferences and said,

> At these different congresses, our writers showed their readiness to become fully *engaged*—a readiness which was to affect the orientation of African literature since the writers wished to avoid all gratuitousness in art and were ready to fight colonialism in all its forms until it would be wiped out for good as far as their country was concerned. ("The African Writer," 10-11)

The *engagement* of African literature, then, became well established through the actions of various groups. Let us examine the extent to which the doctrine was held by individual critics.

Aesthetics can probably never be totally factored out of a work of art. Justine Cordwell made this point in her study of Yoruba and Benin cultures (244). And the African view of Western literary aesthetics has been perhaps overstated in this respect (after all, Sartre is a European, not without his European admirers), though it is the differences in emphasis and degree that interest us here—and these certainly exist. Let us proceed, then, to examine the various statements on *engagement* by African critics. Their forcefulness and near unanimity suggest an overall aesthetic viewpoint quite different from that of the West.

Francophone Critics

It was no accident, surely, that Leopold Senghor's *Anthologie* was introduced by Sartre's "Orphée noir," an essay still accepted as one of the more cogent statements on Negritude. Sartre was no doubt interested in "the only great revolutionary poetry," and Senghor no doubt had his good reasons for accepting an essay by a co-founder of *Présence africaine* and a leading European intellectual. It is not at all surprising, therefore, to find Senghor as one of the leading defenders of *engagement*. What is more surprising is that Senghor's *engagement* may have pre-dated Sartre's. Well before Sartre emerged from the crucible of the French Resistance, Senghor expounded something akin to what Sartre would call, several years later, *la littérature engagée*. In a 1937 speech before the Foyer France-Sénégal, Senghor said, "The intellectuals have the mission of restoring the *black values* in their truth and excellence, to awaken their people to the taste of bread and wit, by which we are *Men*. Especially through our writing" ("Le Problème culturel," 19*). Discussing the characteristics of Negro-African art in 1947, he said, "The Negro sings, dances and sculpts only what is *essential*. Neither the flower nor the dew nor even the eyes constitute 'objects,' but only the true realities of soul and person. There is no 'art for art's sake' " ("L'Afrique noire," 175*).

In an exchange during the First Congress of Negro Artists and Writers in 1956, Senghor suggested another influence on his belief in the importance of a *littérature engagée*: "Mao Tse-tung tells us we must write for the people. We agree. I have shown you that in Africa literature was made *by* everyone. Mao Tse-tung tells us we must write, we must speak *to the people* about *their* concerns" ("Débats," 71*). At the Second Congress, three years later, Senghor continued more specifically on the role of artists in society: "The writers and artists must play a major role in the fight for *decolonization*. It behooves them to remind the politicians that politics, the administration of the city, is simply an aspect of culture, and that the culture of colonialism, in the form of assimilation, was the worst of all" ("Eléments constructifs," 279*).

In opening the Dakar Conference on African Literature and the Universities in 1963, Senghor broadened his concept of *engagement* considerably to include all culture. He said, "To say that *Negro art*—and literature is art— is *reactionary* or *revolutionary*, as some have done, is to delight in confusion. All culture is revolutionary in the sense that it is, in space and time, the integration of Man in the world and the world in Man" ("Negritude et Civilisation," 10-11*). In the American fashion magazine *Vogue*, Senghor reiterated an earlier thought:

> Because the Black African artisan-poet is committed, unlike the European, he is not worried about producing for all eternity. A work of art is perishable. The moment an earlier work passes from fashion or is destroyed, it is promptly replaced, and although spirit and style are preserved, it is updated. This is one way of saying that in Black Africa "Art for art's sake" does not exist. All art is social. ("Hidden Force," 276)

Senghor was certainly the leading advocate of *engagement* among the francophone critics, but he was by no means the only one. His fellow countryman and poet, David Diop, perhaps one of the most virulent exponents of literary militancy, put forth his position during a "debate on national poetry" in *Présence africaine* in 1956. He said,

> We know that some people want to see us abandon militant poetry (a term that makes "purists" sneer) in favor of stylistic exercises and discussions of form. Their hopes will be disappointed because for us poetry does not amount to taming the beast of language but to reflecting on the world and maintaining the memory of Africa. ("Contribution," 115*)

Writing in 1958, two years before most African countries became independent, Hadj El Mukrane noted that "in France, generally, the romantic clientele is hostile toward a so-called political literature" and that the African writer, if he wanted to be published in France, "must first avoid like the plague a committed literature" (238*). However, Mukrane went on to predict, rather accurately, that

> it would be unfortunate for the jokers to shamefully create their nonsense in the sole and undeniable hope of gaining favor (illusory or real) with the colonialists. From now on, we will promise to cry out against the colonial oppression which rages in Black Africa. Or we will hold our tongues. It will no longer be possible now to juggle reality.
>
> The novel of Africa will be militant and strictly anti-imperialist. This is clear. (239*)

Another early call for *engagement* came from Madagascar in 1959. The poet Jacques Rabemananjara wrote that year, "The black poet buckles under the weight of a double fate, his own and that of his race, and he is the only poet who is refused the luxury of absenting himself *ad libitum* from the great affairs of his people" (*Nationalisme*, 99*).

In 1960 Bernard Fonlon submitted his National University of Ireland Ph.D. dissertation, a study of the role of poetry in helping to bring about Africa's pre-independence *prise de conscience.* In it he said,

> In effect, in the black poet, the black world has finally found its authentic and loyal voice. And he, the poet, took the solemn vow not to be silent to the song, "split the eardrums of those who will not listen and snap like the blows of a whip on the egoisms and conformities of the day." ("La Poésie," 2*)

In a telling remark in 1961, the Ivory Coast writer Joseph Miezan Bognini, being interviewed by *Afrique*, said, "When I was in primary school I already loved the texts for the simple pleasure of the words." The interviewer then asked, "Art for art's sake?" and Bognini replied, "Oh no! That is impossible for an African" ("Entretien," 57*).

In 1962 the defense and illustration of *engagement* was taken up by the francophones in earnest. It may be easier to follow the development here as it occurred in various countries and in various individual critics.

Several Senegalese followed Senghor's lead in championing literary *engagement*, the earliest of them being Alioune Diop, the editor of *Présence africaine*. Addressing the U.S. National Commission for UNESCO, he made a distinction between Africa and the West:

> The West distinguishes clearly between the responsibilities of its culture and those of its politics. To such an extent that in some upper spheres of society politics are treated with a sort of disdain or repugnance. There, it is fashionable to ignore politics, and there, culture is a kind of haven or salvation where the best of man is cultivated and invented, sheltered from an political aggression or intervention.

On the contrary, in the Emergent World, cultural concern is the germ from which profound political initiative evolves. ("Political and Cultural," 65)

Lamine Diakhaté, Senegalese poet-critic and a member of Senghor's cabinet, tied *engagement* to Negritude when he spoke of Senghor in these colorful terms:

Ambassador of Negritude? Why not? There have been soldier-poets. The Crusaders themselves—what were they if not soldiers of the spirit? To go forth as ambassador for Negritude is like going on crusade, like a witnessing and affirmation; a wish to actively participate in the edification of a world which could not be universal without the contribution of Africa. ("Contribution," 59-60*)

Mahanta Fall indicated his preference for a committed literature at the Dakar conference of 1963, although he concluded with a recognition of artistic considerations as well:

The African poet is not a poet enclosed in his ivory tower. But he wants to be an actor who assumes an important role in the great drama Africa is playing in at the moment. Even if the African poet belongs to an independent state his poetry will always remain a poetry of combat, because it is bound up not only with his other African brothers who are still fighting for their independence, but with other Blacks scattered throughout the world who are victims of injustice. Isn't the African poet, in effect, their interpreter, their spokesman, their voice, their trumpet who proclaims their political liberation? This means that poetry and politics mix intimately.

It must be added that *engagement*, this intrusion of politics in the domain of literature, steals nothing from the literary value of African poetry in French, because in marking his work with the stamp of Negritude, of Africanness, that distinctive mark which identifies it as an authentic African work, the great African poet never loses sight of the requirements of poetry, of Art. (218*)

Another Senegalese to draw a connection between *engagement* and Negritude was Alioune Sène. Unlike Fall, however, who thought black literature "was born with the fight for the independence of Saint Domingo" (211*), Sène had a different date in mind. Writing of Europe in the 1930s and 1940s, he said,

It was in this epoch when war and racism menaced Europe. Nazism was at its height, and Mussolini's fascism directed itself aggressively against Ethiopia, independent since the millennium. It is in the midst of this deadened Europe, tormented by racial hatred, and moving dangerously toward a confrontation of forces, toward violence, that the tortured cry of Negritude was flung, of the need for Justice and Dignity for the Negro race and its civilization.

From then on, Negro-African literature became a literature of combat, a literature *engagée*, a revolutionary literature. (99-100*)

Bernard Dadié was perhaps the most vocal supporter of *engagement* in the Ivory Coast. In an interview in *Afrique* he drew a clear line between "traditional" and contemporary poetry in these terms:

In our current situation, recently independent, this traditional poetry that sings of the joy of living, the sweetness of life, is not the one for going forward, for giving courage and strength, the ideals necessary to overcome all our present difficulties. Current African poems must be a cry, an encouragement to surmount our problems. The poets will be allowed to sing of the sweetness of life only when it truly arrives again, when the economic difficulties are resolved. (Hossman, 60*)

At least three Cameroun critics favored *engagement* in their writings. In addition to Bernard Fonlon was Thomas Melone, whose *De la négritude dans la littérature négro-africaine* appeared in 1962. He said of African art, "It has become the expression of the movements of conscience, it has finished by identifying the human condition. Art is uneasiness" (14*). Further on, Melone contrasted two forms of *engagement*—that of Senghor and that of Tolen Aron, the latter speaking before the Afro-Asian Committee of Writers and Intellectuals meeting in Tokyo in 1960. He noted that Senghor would have the African elite be "not the head of the people but certainly their mouth and trumpet" (108*), while "Mr. Tolen thinks not, that one doesn't liberate a people in a day, and that independence is a constant battle and that writing must participate—and in the avant-garde of this battle" (109n*). Melone made it clear that he preferred Tolen's concept of *engagement*, for he said, "The writer's role is not, then, to orchestrate but to be both he who asks questions and who gives answers, 'mouth and head' of the Negro" (109*).

A Third Camerounian, Charles Ngande, said in 1963 that "our poetry should espouse our times, our struggles, our labours and our march forward. The poets have a mission: they should lend an attentive ear to Africa which is in the process of being born" (137). He added, "We cannot permit ourselves the luxury of poets who are strangers in their narcissism, in their monologues. We would be mocking our people if we presented them with a bourgeois poetry, a poetry of the drawing room" (137).

Anglophone Critics

If Senghor and Ezekiel Mphahlele disagreed adamantly over Negritude, they agreed with equal certainty that African literature must be committed

to the causes of the African people. But whereas Senghor saw such commitment as constituting Negritude, at least in part, Mphahlele denied the connection. Mphahlele was nevertheless as articulate on the subject of commitment as Senghor, though in articulating his position he was the foremost
among African critics to illustrate the cultural differences between South
Africa and the rest of the continent. Writing in the *New Statesman* in 1960
he said, "Ours is a fugitive culture: borrowing here, incorporating there,
retaining this, rejecting that. But it is a virile culture. The clamour of it is
going to keep beating on the walls surrounding the already fragmented culture of the whites until they crumble" ("Black and White," 346).

At the Makerere Conference in 1962, Mphahlele made the contrast between
South and West Africa in these terms: "Needless to say, the West African
writer will yet find material for social criticism outside the modern-tradi-
tional encounter that he is portraying today, much closer to individual experience. On the other hand, the South African writer must continue in a
stage of commitment to the revolution that must come" ("Critic's Time,"
1). In an introduction to a collection of Nigerian writing, Mphahlele indicated the dangers of excessive commitment that led to a lowering of literary
quality: "The prose is largely still documenting the outline features, albeit
with care. The time will come when the writers will fill in the details, and
social criticism will take its rightful place within this framework without
necessarily bringing down literary standards" ("Preface," 13). At the Dakar
conference in 1963, after his belief in the importance of *engagement* had
been challenged, he said:

> An image of Africa that only glorifies our ancestors and celebrates our
> "purity" and "innocence" is an image of a continent lying in state.
> When I asked at the Accra Congress of Africanists last December [1962]
> how long our poets are going to continue to bleat like goats in the act
> of giving birth, I was suggesting that Ghanaian poets should start
> looking inward, into themselves. Now I am being accused of encour-
> aging "artistic purity" by asking writers to cease protesting against a
> colonial boss that has left their country. What is "artistic purity"?
> Am I being asked to lay the ghost of *l'art pour l'art*? Surely meaning-
> ful art has social significance or relevance and this very fact implies so-
> cial criticism—protest in the broadest sense of the word. ("A Reply,"
> 24)

Mphahlele was concerned that *engagement* and Negritude not be confused.
He named some writers and works he felt were "*engagées*" and yet not "bul-
lied by negritude" ("A Reply," 24).

Writing several years before Mphahlele, Cyprian Ekwensi was an early
proponent of *engagement* as a critical principle. In 1952 he wrote,

It is said that Dickens' Christmas Carol did more good to mankind than all the sermons ever preached since the birth of Christ. In the same way, a writer can do more good for his society than all the politicians since Disraeli. . . . The cinema does more to condition individual behaviour than is sometimes realised: in the same way, a good novel can help us "put our house in order." ("Challenge," 255)

In 1956 Ekwensi set down what he saw as six "functions of the fiction writer in society." Numbers 3, 4, and 5 indicated his continuing interest in a committed literature:

3. The African writer can, if he wishes, state a political or philosophical idea in his story or play—and state it safely, thus using his special medium as an instrument of propaganda.
4. He can be a powerful educator.
5. He can control codes of conduct, refine feelings, make the African more acutely aware of his place among his fellow men and in the world at large. In short, he can make for a more nationalistic (as opposed to tribalistic) outlook. ("The Dilemma," 701)

Chinua Achebe expressed his support of *engagement* throughout the 1960s. In speaking of the denigration of black people, he said in 1964, "This presents the African writer with a great challenge. It is inconceivable to me that a serious writer could stand aside from this debate, or be indifferent to this argument which calls his full humanity in question" ("The Role," 157). Achebe also saw the use of the African past as a means of "committing" literature:

I would be quite satisfied if my novels (especially the ones I set in the past) did no more than teach my readers that their past—with all its imperfections—was not one long night of savagery from which the first Europeans acting on God's behalf delivered them. Perhaps what I write is applied art as distinct from pure. But who cares? Art is important but so is education of the kind that I have in mind. And I don't see that the two need be mutually exclusive. ("The Novelist," 162)

In 1966 Achebe asked that the African writer's commitment change according to the situation:

Most of Africa is today politically free; there are thirty-six independent African States managing their own affairs—sometimes very badly. A new situation has thus arisen. One of the writer's main functions has always been to expose and attack injustice. Should we keep at the old theme of racial injustice (sore as it still is) when new injustices have sprouted all around us? I think not. ("The Black Writer's Burden," 138)

Wole Soyinka was another Nigerian profoundly *engagé*, to the point of being imprisoned for his alleged actions. In a 1966 interview Soyinka was asked, "How far do you consider yourself a committed writer?" He replied,

> I react to my social situation. Since I live in a certain social context . . . I am sensitive. I don't think of myself as a committed writer. I respond to things. I respond to events whether they are a personal experience or a social experience. It does not matter what. I do not sieve any aspect of my experience because it is politically inconvenient. I am not committed to any ideology. (Akaraogun, 17)

To another question, "Do you think writers, as sensitive and articulate members of society have any special role to play in politics?" he answered, "That is a question of individual choice and concern. The only thing which makes me sick is the suggestion that any group of people should not be involved in politics" (Akaraogun, 19).

Other Nigerians also defended *engagement*. Mokwugo Okoye said that literature must "promote the revolutionary transformation of society and the improvement of the lot of man. It should not merely portray 'life as it is' but also probe the problems life poses and help us to solve them" (74-75).

An American critic, Martin Tucker, accused West African writers of being "a servant of the social rather than the aesthetic spirit" (829). Robert Okara responded, wondering "whether any sincere writer can be purely aesthetic and write only for art's sake without any emotional link with the society and environment of his time. Perhaps it is the ability to harmonise realism and aesthetics without discord that marks the artist" (1050).

Dr. W. E. Abraham was one of several Ghanaian critics to defend *engagement*. His view of the relationship between *engagement* and the African past differed, however, from Achebe's. He said,

> There are African writers who imagine what must have been the past of Africa; and because they are not competent to dish out, as historians or anthropologists, they think that they will get away by putting these things in the form of novels, or plays, or poems. Present African writers must realize that they live in Africa today and should produce critiques of African society as things exist now. (Nkosi, "Some Conversations," 16)

Another Ghanaian, Frank Parkes, in a review of three poetry anthologies, felt that "certainly the poet has not to lose the right to social protest just because he happens to be a poet" (755). Michael Dei-Anang, with Yaw Warren, said in a note preceding a volume of their poems, "We are no politicians, but we are strong defenders of the ideals for which our beloved Ghana struggles. Patriotism requires us to express our feelings to the outside world, so that onlookers can appreciate the depth of the sentiments of our people and the force of our unity" (Dei-Anang and Warren, n.p.).

Mphahlele was certainly the major critical voice from South Africa on commitment, but his was not the only one. As early as 1946, Woodroffe Mbete said, "We need a literature by Non-Europeans endowed with a feeling for the sufferings of their people . . . Non-European authors to write on Indian, Cape Coloured, Malay and Bantu life . . . artists who could vividly depict the life of suffering humanity in South Africa . . . intellectuals to create an impression on the contemporary world" (14).

Lewis Nkosi, after Mphahlele the most prolific South African critic, summarized the feeling of several South Africans attending the Makerere conference in 1962 in these terms:

> What South Africans like Bloke Modisane, Arthur Maimane, and Ezekiel Mphahlele immediately noticed was that West African literature tended, at times, to be too idyllic and pastoral, as though it lacked the energy for social criticism. With the exception of books like Chinua Achebe's "No Longer at Ease", this literature had declined to come to grips with corruption, slum life, the social flaccidity of the Nigerian bourgeois class and all the other social ills of the new urban society. ("Press Report," 2)

Nkosi commented on Soyinka in another place, saying,

> When Wole Soyinka was queried in London recently about the obscurity of the message in his play *A Dance of the Forests*, the young playwright ignored the question and explained that his only responsibility to the public was to provide them with good theater. This sharp separation between literature as an art form and its content has resulted in a kind of poetry and drama that seems to shy away from social criticism.
>
> One day, perhaps, West African writers will turn their satire to the moral flabbiness near at home. ("Contemporary," 295)

Another South African, Alex Chima, made his position very clear:

> *In the new nations, as well as the areas still under alien domination, the artist and writer has the historic task of witnessing and communicating the new African culture emerging from the liberation struggles.*
>
> He is the instrument of the people's liberation spirit and through him art and literature can become powerful weapons in the struggle of the oppressed people to restore their identity, dignity, and freedom. (29)

East Africa had its share of committed critics as well. The Reverend John S. Mbiti saw an "engaged" role for literature when he told the Second Congress of Negro Writers and Artists in 1959 that "we cannot aspire for any unity—political, social, religious, economic or cultural—if we still have no literature which binds a country and a people together" (261).

Seven years later Rajat Neogy, the editor of *Transition*, was concerned about "the lack of a sense of crisis" in East Africa when he said:

> There is a lack of urgency in having to define our reasons for existence, however pompous this sounds. This is something East Africa does face. It is very complacent in this area. I think intellectuals, writers or whatever we call ourselves, have a special responsibility for being constantly provocative in an effort to erase this complacency. (Mphahlele et al., "The Literary Drought," 14)

Two East African writers, John Nagenda and James Ngugi, had an interesting discussion of commitment in an interview published in *Cultural Events in Africa*. Nagenda broached the subject first, saying to Ngugi,

> We really have to build and . . . with a lot of what we are going to build we have almost to start afresh because so much of it has been ruined. And when I feel like this then I really look on my other side almost as a traitor—as a sort of dilettante inconsequential figure. But then when I get to the other—the poetic side of me, you might say—then I don't have any apologies. For me, the time comes when I see something—it may be about society or it may not. It's just a moment that I experience—somebody walking or it might be a sunset. But superficial though it may sound, to me this is as important to society (perhaps not in the material sense, but certainly in the spiritual sense). ("A Discussion Between," iii)

Ngugi replied,

> Speaking to the writer as a citizen, I think he ought to be committed as an individual because what your vision is as an individual affects even your poetic mood. I would say that as far as I am concerned there is no question of art for art's sake. I'm concerned with the social and political problems as they are in Africa now—I want to see a change in Africa now. (iii)

Peter Nazareth, another East African critic, initiated an interesting discussion on commitment in the pages of *Transition* in 1965. He said,

> Of course certain areas of human experience are personal and individual and, in order to explore them, the artist should remain committed only to the truth of his vision and sensibility. But when writing about individuals in a changing present-day society, the African writer cannot but be committed; that is to say, unless he is perfectly satisfied with the *status quo*, unless he thinks the new society is ordered in the best possible way and change is not desirable. The writer who feels that the social system is basically wrong—or is changing to a new order

which is basically wrong—and must therefore be improved is committed, whether explicitly or implicitly. ("The African Writer," 6)

Nazareth continued with a broader view of commitment, which, at the same time, would carefully protect the freedom of the individual writer. He said, "All art is propaganda in that it seeks to persuade us, though not all propaganda is art. There is no such thing as the uncommitted writer; there is only good art and bad art" ("The African Writer," 7). And after a rebuttal by T.E.W. Rickford, Nazareth concluded the argument in a later issue:

> I think we are all agreed that for a creative writer to be dogmatic, or to write to justify dogma he may not believe in, is thoroughly undesireable. Much of our distrust of the Socialist-Realism movement in Russian writing stems from our belief that this movement is the result of writers working along lines laid down by the Soviet Government. ("Commitment," 7)

Unlike the schism over Negritude, which occurred more or less along ex-colonial lines, English- and French-speaking Africans are for the most part unified in wanting a committed literature.

ENGAGEMENT AS A CRITICAL STANDARD

Francophone Critics

Was *engagement* merely espoused or was it actually applied as a critical principle? The answer is clearly in the affirmative. Critics from many parts of Africa—francophone and anglophone alike—used *engagement* as a means of judging literary merit. In fact the application of *engagement* as a critical standard received a tremendous impetus—if not a beginning—from one of African literature's most celebrated causes—which might be called "the Laye affair."

"The Laye affair" began with the publication of Camara Laye's first novel, *L'Enfant noir*, in 1953. It is interesting to speculate why this book—and its author—became such a cause célèbre. One possible answer might lie in the fact that, like Amos Tutuola's *The Palm-Wine Drinkard*, this was a "first"—the first African novel in French since World War II. And as I have demonstrated, the African sensitivity as to the projection of an African presence into the world was widespread. True, the Zairian writer Paul Lomami-Tshibamba had published *Ngando* in 1948, but perhaps because of its generically greater proximity to folklore, the timing was not right for its reception in either Europe or Africa. It is possible also that the spectacular reception accorded only the year before to Tutuola's book was an important factor in the climate in which the French-speaking Africans awaited their first postwar novel. And possibly the unique character of Tutuola's book had an effect. Whatever the reasons, Laye's book was bitterly attacked, and the stage was set for a prolonged debate, most of which centered around the question of *engagement*.

The debate began with a review of *L'Enfant noir* by Alexandre Biyidi (Mongo Beti), in which Biyidi charged Laye for not writing in a "committed" manner. Biyidi said,

> Those of you who have read the moving "Black Boy" of R. Wright and for whom the comparison will occur: it is especially to you that the monstrous absence of breadth and depth of the Guinean's book will be manifest. All you who, finally, believe that this century requires the writer, as a categorical imperative, to resist gratuitous literature, art for art's sake. (A. B., "L'Enfant noir," 419*)

Further on Biyidi said, more specifically, "This Guinean, of my generation, who was, if we believe him, a very active boy—has he seen nothing other than a peaceful, beautiful, maternal Africa? Is it possible that not even once did Laye witness a single small extortion by the colonial administration" ("L'Enfant noir," 420*)?

The vigor of the attack, no doubt, as well as its content, brought a quick defense from Senghor, who noted the tendency of

> our fretful spirits to spread themselves about injuriously against the young writer and to reproach him in the name of Africa and a certain clumsy verbosity, for not having attacked Colonialism. Strange critic, truly, who asks of the artist not to make a work of art but a polemic. As if the French and foreign critic had not given, in its day, the same reception to the poems of Aimé Césaire, an authentic revolutionary. ("Laye Camara et Lamine Diakhaté," 1*)

In concluding his review, Senghor struck a middle road between *engagement* and art for art's sake, a position many critics took later. He said, "For me, I salute with joy my two juniors, and I propose them as examples to young French-speaking Negro-African writers. They have understood that art does not belong to a party nor is it necessarily apolitical" (3).

Laye's second novel, *Le Regard du roi*, followed a year later. Senghor took the initiative this time and reviewed it along with Lamine Niang's poem "Feu de brousse." Senghor said, "What interests me in *Le Regard du roi*, as in Lamine Niang's poem . . . is that they pose a certain number of questions which have been for several years at the center of the *engagement* debate among the young writers" ("Laye Camara et Lamine Niang," 3*). Having established Laye's *engagement* to his own satisfaction, Senghor went on to say, "[I hope] that the African elite do not rush to condemn Laye Camara again, under the pretext that his novel is not 'anticolonialist'. There are many ways to fight Colonialism. The path of *engagement* can not be the same for the writer as for the politician" (3*).

Senghor's plea was to little avail, however, for Biyidi's review of *Le Regard du roi* was even more virulent than his earlier one. Biyidi preceded his review with an article on "Afrique noire, littérature rose," in which he mentioned first some examples of his kind of poet: "There are those who are excellent poets: A. Césaire, D. Diop, Paul Niger, J. Roumain, etc. . . . They are found especially among men of color, I mean the colonized. They are generally very conscientious, sincere, and consequently incapable of any compromise with the colonial order" (134*). In the review that followed, Biyidi made it clear that he liked Laye's second book even less than the first. He concluded, "It remains that his work will never find a place on the shelf of black literature" ("Le Regard du roi," 144*).

A Cameroun critic, Mbella Sonne Dipoko, seemed to agree with Biyidi's assessment when, reviewing Gerald Moore's *Seven African Writers*, he said of Laye, "His portrayal of tribal life is charming—amusing by the very fact that it is sincere and naive. But it is a sincerity and naivete forged on the anvil of 'art for art's sake' " (31).

Laye's third book, *Dramouss*, generated two 1966 reviews by Olympe Bhely-Quenum and Paulin Joachim, both of which, in their way, indicated their interest in *engagement*. Bhely-Quenum said of Laye, implying in the process a form of agreement with Biyidi's earlier reviews while nevertheless arriving at a positive conclusion, "We will not reproach him, as in the time of 'L'Enfant noir,' for not having cared about African political problems. With 'Dramouss,' we enter directly into Guinean politics" ("*Dramouss*," 49*). He concluded his review saying, "The Black Child has grown up; he has become aware of his surroundings, and speaks to us of them with simplicity, even when one feels revolt screaming in him. This is a writer" (50*). Joachim praised Laye for his *engagement*, saying, "In this present book, Camara Laye seems to wake up little by little to the burning problems which the young independent nations of Africa face. It happens that he even begins to look like a political animal" ("Dramouss," 55*).

Another critic also chose to defend Laye in 1966, although not, like Bhely-Quenum, because Laye had now become more committed than in his first two novels, but by suggesting, along with Senghor, that the earlier critics, notably Biyidi, had failed to understand Laye's *engagement* in the first place. Christophe Gudijiga wrote,

> Laye is a shrewd soul and has a patient heart that questions itself and takes a position before its existence with the constant uncertainty of a wise man. Read and understand his point of view on the colonial question in "L'Enfant noir" and "Le Regard du roi." Laye is neither naive,

nor a fool in these situations; he does not try, as someone said, to ignore the conflict of cultures and civilizations. (147*)

What was most significant in "The Laye affair" was that no African critic
chose to defend Laye on the grounds that he need not have been *engagé* in
order to write a good novel. This is yet another indication of the strength of
engagement as a standard of African literary criticism.

Laye was by no means the only African writer to be judged by his *engagement* or lack thereof. Senghor weighed other writers according to the concept.
He was moved to write a preface to William J. F. Syad's poems, *Khamsine*,
in part because "Syad is not an entertainer. He is a poet. That is to say he is
committed" ("Préface," 8*). In another preface, Senghor said of the French
translation of Peter Abrahams' novel, "*Une Couronne pour Udomo* is certainly a 'political' novel; it is more than that: a human novel, the novel of
Man" ("Peter Abrahams," 425*). Senghor continued:

> Yes, *political novel* in the most noble meaning of the word. . . . This
> is the dilemma that confronts the African political leaders, the contra-
> dictions that Michael Udomo must attack in order to resolve them. I
> do not know a novelist who has exposed them with more force. (426*)

Along with Biyidi, David Diop wrote some trenchant reviews based on
the concept of *engagement*. Coming as they did between 1955 and 1957,
when African literature was germinating in both French and English, they
no doubt affected the directions that African literature and criticism would
take. The first of these was a review of four collections of poetry published
in the years 1954-1955. Of *Esanzo*, by the Zairian poet A.-R. Bolamba, Diop
said,

> Rare are those whose inspiration is not strongly marked by the colonial
> drama, whether this be to regret "the primitive freshness of the black
> country" or to sing of an Africa yearning toward progress and liberty.
>   But there are some poets for whom those problems are not the dom-
> inant element of the creativity and who are content to listen to the chants
> and legends of Africa to speak of its sunlit countryside, its dizzying
> dances.
>   Thus A. R. Bolambo, poet of the Belgian Congo. Is it prudence (we
> know the particular . . . severity of the royal administration) that en-
> courages Bolamba to distance himself from themes too dangerous? Be-
> cause it is impossible that he saw his country only as he describes it.
> ("Poètes africains," 79*)

Diop preferred Francis N'Dsitouna's *Fleurs de latérite* (1954), of which he
said,

With Francis N'Dsitouna the tone becomes brutal and the quality of the emotion changes. . . . We enter with both feet an Africa taken up with the contradictions of a cruel world, an Africa of the whip and injustice but which does not despair of its future. Perhaps one will not find in N'Dsitouna what the esthetes call the "breath of pure poetry" (isn't this, in fact, the real "pure poetry"?). ("Poètes africains," 80*)

In 1957 Diop praised Ferdinand Oyono's novels, *Une Vie de Boy* and *Le Vieux nègre et la médaille* (both 1956) because "in these accounts, we see the slow growth of conscience in two Africans facing the colonial reality" (Review of *Une Vie*, 125*). He liked Benjamin Matip's *Afrique nous t'ignorons* (1956) because Sam, its hero, had a "passionate need to assert himself through his actions" and because it somehow exhibited the principle that

the essential thing is first the disappearance of all forms of servile admiration or resignation before the official conformity. The youth that Benjamin Matip describes for us no longer lives in this oasis of exotic and reassuring charm so dear to another kind of literature, but in a world of struggle and strife. (Review of *Climbié*, 152*)

Also in 1957, in an ironic twist that no doubt delighted those who felt Mongo Beti had been unfair to Camara Laye, Diop reviewed Beti's novel *Mission terminée* unfavorably because of what he considered a lack of *engagement*. He very clearly preferred Beti's *Ville cruelle* (see Eza Boto) because of its greater commitment:

"At last, an African novel that does not have a hidden political meaning . . ." an editor's note tells us. If we understand by that that "Mission Terminée" does not at any time address the problem of the relationship between the colonizer and the colonized, such an opinion would seem correct. But must we rejoice in it?

We already have the admirable "Ville Cruelle," a short incisive novel that threw much light on the bloody underside of colonialism in Cameroun. . . . Everything in this novel made it a weapon against the colonial situation, the tense style, the dialogues in which the characters project themselves little by little, the unpitying relationship of the events.

Should we be surprised that such a testimony left us with a more lasting impression than "Mission Terminée"?

Some will surely accuse us of having an "anti-colonial obsession." "What?" they will cry, "an African novelist, in order to gain our praise, must systematically attack colonialism?"

Certainly not.

Two hundred pages of noble indignation does not necessarily make a good novel or achieve its goals. But may one not ask us to be satisfied without reservations with a book which, having been read, leaves us with a vague smile? (Review of *Mission*, 187*)

In concluding his review, Diop made it clear that it was Beti's *engagement*, and not his talent, that displeased him:

But does all that carry weight when all around us in Africa so many major events solicit our attention? We do not think it unreasonable to ask our novelists to be the active witnesses of these events.

This is why we think of Mongo Beti's latest novel as a pleasant vacation.

The short vacation of an author whom we appreciate and who has many other missions to terminate. (Review of *Mission*, 187*)

Another Senegalese, Lamine Diakhaté, was critical of Sembène Ousmane's first novel, *Le Docker noir*. Diakhaté spelled out the message of *engagement* he found lacking in the novel:

The unexpected thing here is not, as some have said, the fact that a Negro stevedore has written a book, but the fact that the promised and expected message has not been expressed.

A minority lives in France under atrocious conditions. This minority has problems. It struggles in an atmosphere that borders on despair. Its only support, its pride; its only weapon, its labor; its only morale, its steadfastness. This minority of Negro laborers in France do not market their pain. They fight to triumph over the bad faith of their bosses. . . . Their message is of brotherhood in their stumbling. This minority asks neither for pity nor favor. It proclaims its right to live. All its ideas, its virtues, its "tribulations" merit respect rather than sympathy.

What the world expected of Sembène Ousmane was the rigorous expression of this message. (Review, 154*)

In 1958 Diallo Siafoulaye said in a preface to Emile Cissé's *Faralako; roman d'un petit village africain* that "the author raises a whole series of serious political, economic, social, and cultural problems that impose themselves with acuity on our times in all colonial or non-independent countries" (9*). Also in 1958 Hadj El Mukrane admired the French translation of Peter Abrahams' *A Wreath for Udomo* because, he said, "Here is a work of importance that we must assuredly add to the notebook of anti-colonialism" (239*). And in the same year Bakary Traoré gave a good account of the early dramatic activities in the 1930s of the William Ponty school in Dakar in his *The Black African Theatre and Its Social Functions*. Traoré was critical of the direction this theatre often took and said that "the African theatre should fulfill new needs and create new values. Like its successor, the William Ponty theatre failed to do this" (105). He added, "The first immediate preoccupation of a modern Negro-African threatre *is to identify itself with the struggle for the emancipation of Black Africa*" (105).

Two years later an Ivory Coast critic, Bachir Touré, implicitly criticized the Ponty school for its lack of *engagement* while commenting on a production at the Theatre of Nations in Paris. He said,

> The comedy of M. Coffi-Gadeau, director of the Ivory Coast Ensemble, is no more and no less the decadent expression of the theatre of the William Ponty school. This French African theatre, you recall, was especially aimed at the amusement of the European administration of the colony—the teaching staff in particular. These primitive farces can in no way, today, reflect the thoughts and aspirations of Africans who have much better riches to exploit than the mother-in-law stories in the style of M. Coffi-Gadeau. ("Les Ensembles," 12*)

In 1962 the Guinean critic Condotto Nenekhaly-Camara attacked what he saw as Senghor's lack of *engagement*. He asked, "Of what does Senghor sing?" and answered by saying, "Sweet and evanescent impressions, the refusal of daily combat, the shade [*les ombres*, a reference to Senghor's *Chants d'ombre*], in short, themes belonging to a retarded romanticism" (13*). The critic then commented on a specific Senghor poem that he thought reflected such tendencies: "I would add that the writer sweetens his poem by feminizing the most male themes. Through his pen, the evocation of Chaka loses all its virile character: the epic of the brave Zulu warrior becomes a starlit romance" (13*). However, Nenekhaly-Camara, applying the same standard, gave good marks to Bernard Dadié: "But even in the intimacy of his interior universe, however it appears, Dadié refuses a gratuitous literature" (14*).

In addition to their comments on Camara Laye, Paulin Joachim and Olympe Bhely-Quenum on occasion used *engagement* to judge other writers as well. In 1963 Joachim, for example, found fault with Leonard Sainville's *Anthologie de la littérature négro-africaine: romanciers et conteurs* because it overlooked Paul Hazoumé's *Doguicimi*. One should not overlook this book, said Joachim, because it "remains one of the very first documents of the rising consciousness of Negro-African values" ("Anthologie," 61*). In the same year Bhely-Quenum liked Seydou Badian's *Sous l'orage* because "the author courageously confronts the problems of contemporary Africa, which, in love, in politics as in the reorganization of its traditions, is, in effect 'in the storm' " ("Sous l'orage," 36*).

Also in that year, a Cameroun critic, Marcien Towa, saw a faulty *engagement* in Jean Ikelle-Matiba's novel *Cette Afrique-là* because "the author himself sees his book especially as a record. And certainly the documentation is serious; but it teaches us very little, it seems, of what the German colonization really was, but a lot of the naive representation was able and still can be made of a mystified Camerounian'' (185-86*).

Whereas Nenekhaly-Camara criticized Senghor's lack of *engagement*, Octave Ugirashebuja was quite obviously enthusiastic about it. He said,

> Senghor's poetry is a poetry *"engagée."* Do not imagine his to be an empty calling to rhyme or to please. His goal is clearly defined: to sing of Negritude, to dazzle the Africans with their own riches and to enrich humanity with this new expression of beauty. (334*)

M. S. Eno Belinga, after quoting several poems and naming several novels in a 1966 article, concluded his discussion of African literature by cataloging some of the more committed works:

> These examples suffice to show that the Negro-African novel is no less engaged than the poetry: The Dakar-Niger railroad workers strike in 1947-1948 inspired Sembène Ousmane's *Les Bouts de bois de Dieu*; one also finds the evocation of the unionists' and African nationalists' battles in Bernard Dadié's *Climbié*; both the *chef-d'oeuvre* and the classic of the genre is Peter Abrahams' *A Wreath for Udomo*, the "Richard Wright" of southern Africa who distinguished himself admirably in the sorrowful battle against apartheid (*Mine Boy*; *Tell Freedom*; *Path of Thunder*). On this same problem must also be mentioned such striking works as Noni Jabavu's novel, *Drawn in Colour*, and Ezekiel Mphahlele's autobiographical tale, *Down Second Avenue*. (87*)

Anglophone Critics

The English-speaking critics applied *engagement* as a critical standard with almost as much frequency as their francophone counterparts. One of the first to do so was Cyprian Ekwensi, who in 1952 spoke favorably of Peter Abrahams' works, saying, "Peter Abrahams is seeking, through his work, the unity of all coloured peoples" ("Challenge," 255). Two years later, Abrahams in turn said he liked Ekwensi's *People of the City* partly because

> Mr. Ekwensi's inspiration is in the present and looks to the future and has only echoes from the past. It points a way and makes possible a contemporary literature for the future. It is important too as social criticism and will, if not read by sufficiently large numbers of West Africans, help in the creation of a social consciousness which is of prime importance to the young, emerging West African states. ("A Literary Pioneer," 975)

Ezekiel Mphahlele often suggested that various writers were too committed; however, he was one of the earlier anglophone critics to apply *engagement* as a standard. In 1957 he commented on several South African writers he thought were not committed enough:

> Their works are gems for their own sake, "lying in state", as it were, or standing still like statuettes, if you like. They lack the dynamic force that hits all the planes of our experience—the emotional, physical, and intellectual; they are parochial; not because the writers lack force, but because they had to limit their literature to the school market dictated by "educationists" and missionaries, who are part of the ruling class. They do not tell the whole truth about life. ("What the," 173)

In a later essay Mphahlele singled out some African works for their commitment, because they had risen above his *bête noire*, Negritude. He said,

> Surely meaningful art has social significance or relevance and this very fact implies social criticism—protest in the broadest sense of the word. Gorky, Dostoevsky, Tolstoy, Dickens and so on did this, but they were no less Russian or English; *certainly* they were much more committed than *negritude* poets. They took in the whole man. Camara Laye's *Le Regard du roi*, Ferdinand Oyono's *Le Vieux nègre et al médaille* and Mongo Beti's *Le Pauvre Christ de Bomba* are not bullied by *negritude*. They are concerned in portraying the black-white encounter, and they do this, notwithstanding, with a devastating poetic sense of irony unmatched by any that one sees in the English novel by Africans. ("A Reply," 24)

In 1965 several critics began applying *engagement* as a standard. Peter Nazareth, an openly committed East African critic, referred to two African works in a letter to *Transition* in this way:

> I would suggest that James Ngugi's first novel *is* a committed novel. If it is not so in the manner of Alex La Guma's *A Walk in the Night*, this is not only because the sensibility and approach of the two authors is different but also because the *societies* the two deal with are unlike each other. ("The African Writer," 6)

The same year, in an article in which he found merit in both the "pure" poetry of Jean-Joseph Rabearivelo and the "applied" poetry of Dennis Brutus, the Nigerian critic Daniel Abasiekong considered first the success of Brutus's poetry, saying, "His work has re-affirmed that it is possible and valid to create good, perhaps great, poetry out of politics and history—to write living and intensely personal poetry whose meanings take hold on public affairs" (45). But compared to Brutus, the critic felt that "Jean-Joseph Rabearivelo of Madagascar makes interesting reading for entirely different reasons. French African creative writing is so heavily committed to direct nationalist protest against imperialist subjugation and the depreciation of black African culture, that a French-African poet whose concern is *not* art as socio-political propaganda seems very different" (47-48).

Sunday A. Anozie was somewhat ambivalent about Gabriel Okara's novel *The Voice*, seeing in it two levels of commitment:

> An allegorical poem in which alienation and solitude are extolled and direct commitment rejected, Okara's first novel, *The Voice*, has this unchallengeable merit, though: that in its moral didacticism it under-lines its author's genuine belief in the virtues of the individual's moral courage, nobility and stoicism in an African society the direction of whose development and sophistication is increasingly towards rejecting these fundamental moral values. ("Theme," 66)

Lewis Nkosi, in reporting on the Makerere conference of 1962, described in his *Home and Exile* the criticisms that Bloke Modisane, Mphahlele, and Arthur Maimane had of West African literature for its lack of social criticism: "With the exception of books like Chinue Achebe's *No Longer at Ease*, this literature had declined to come to grips with corruption, slum life, the social flaccidity of the Nigerian bourgeois class and all the other social ills of the new urban society" (118).

The year 1966 saw a plethora of critiques that applied the measure of *engagement* to a wide variety of literary works. Wole Soyinka applied the standard to several specific works in his essay "And after the Narcissist?" Generally, Soyinka considered the African writers' narcissism to be dangerous because they might mistake it for real action, for *engagement*. But narcissism, he said, is the opposite of meaningful action. He cited an example: "By some strange retrogressive process, Chinue Achebe's latest novel, *Arrow of God*, reverts to this crippling process from which much of African writing has now begun to emerge" (55). He added that

> Achebe's method does not lie in celebration, as in Mongo Beti and Camara Laye, so the minutiae of living, trivial or profound, do not manifest a secondary innate quality of animation. In spite of its action, *Things Fall Apart* remains a genuinely contemplative novel, yet at its most preoccupied it never betrays the incipient narcissism that—if we accept this pattern of evolution in African writing—makes *Arrow of God* seem an earlier novel than *Things Fall Apart*. (55)

However, the bulk of Soyinka's attack was reserved for Senghor's poem "Chaka" (in *Ethiopiques*). He disliked Senghor's piece because it "implies a contradiction between the poet and the 'politician,' and this immediately arouses speculation of similar kinds of dissections, which, misdirected, become the poet's excuse for narcissistic indulgence" (55-56). He liked Laye's novel because "it is *The Dark Child*, however, which quietly proves that animist introspection need not involve narcissistic inflation'' (56). Soyinka wrote unfavorably of Gabriel Okara's *The Voice*:

> Certainly, there is no communication of the psychic drive which sets a man on a course of single minded enquiry into the heart of matter or existence; it is only an occasion for the hero's narcissistic passivity. His will to motion can hardly be calculated in terms of his effect on the community. Okolo is too set a set-piece; the catalytic effect of his quest on the external world is more expected than fulfilled. Okolo has lost himself in an animism of nothingness, the ultimate self-delusion of the narcissist. (62)

On the other hand, Soyinka in the same essay praised Alex La Guma's *A Walk in the Night* in these terms: "The politician is at his most sensitive when he responds to the physical interference of his own environment, and this is antithetical to the apostate contemplation of the navel, which is evasion. Alex La Guma is a politician, yet from the inner heart of physical trivia he forges an insurgent weapon of accusation" (61).

Soyinka's own work drew this comment from James Ngugi in a 1966 interview:

> I don't know the political sentiments of every individual African artist. But in their work, people like Wole Soyinka and Chinua Achebe have exposed corruption and social injustices in Nigeria. In his last novel, *A Man of the People*, Chinua Achebe has made a brilliant analysis of the character and workings of the present African regime. In South Africa artists and writers like Ezekiel Mphahlele, Alex La Guma, Dennis Brutus have been exiled, shot, or imprisoned. ("James Ngugi Interviewed," iv-v)

K. William Kgositsile, a South African critic, had serious doubts, along with Soyinka, about the commitment of Senghor's poetry:

> Because of Senghor's inconsistency and his constant pleas for reconciliation with Europe while claiming to champion the Black man's cause, we wonder if his *negritude* is just a poetic stance. We expect this to be reflected in his aesthetics if he pursues some art form. When a Black poet claims to be committed to his people and he embraces Europe we become suspicious. (9)

ANTI-ENGAGEMENT

Compared to the number of committed African critics, there were very few who made statements that could be interpreted as anti-*engagement*. This may or may not be an indication of the early combined weight of Senghor and Sartre. What is interesting to note, however, and which might suggest that those two figures indeed helped shape the first two decades of African literary criticism, is the fact that, with almost no exceptions, the critics who took a critical stand against *engagement* were English-speaking.

Francophone Critics

Of the few francophone attempts to challenge literary *engagement*, perhaps the clearest was that by a Camerounian, Jacques Muriel Nzouankeu. In a debate on whether the African was typically optimistic or pessimistic, he said, "I consider for my part that we should stop asking of literature a solution to today's political problems. I detest what one currently calls committed literature. I would even like literature to be the counterbalance of Africa's social and political ideas" ("L'Africain," 189*).

Paulin Joachim, in connecting *engagement* with his conception of Negritude, saw *engagement* as a passing phase. Reviewing *Présence africaine*'s anthology, "Nouvelle somme de poésie du monde noir," he said in 1966 of the poets therein, "One is not shocked that they chose a poetry of combat, but this form will become passe very quickly. Negritude is already becoming passe" ("Nouvelle somme," 61*). Gilbert Ilboudo agreed, saying of the committed quality of African literature, "While Africa certainly rejoices at having found such champions in her struggle for freedom, this militant aspect of African literature must unavoidably fade away with decolonisation" (31).

The Senegalese critic Mohamadou Kane made an interesting distinction between African and Western *engagement*, while pointing out some of the dangers inherent in the Western form of it:

> The notion of engagement, as inherited from the West, is almost always fatal to the work which remains within the dimensions of a stroke of luck. The form of engagement, moreover, is to a certain extent a cause for division because the work only represents a tendency or a group. Engagement in traditional literature is total, with the whole community taking part, and treating it as a part of life in all its aspects. ("African Writer," 29)

Anglophone Critics

The English-speaking opponents of *engagement* were far more numerous. In some cases, they were the same as those who, in other instances, supported it. It must be remembered, however, that we are here less interested in labeling critics than in identifying the major early strains of thought among African critics. It has already been seen that many of the critics who supported *engagement* in principle either did not support it without reservation or were not willing to apply it completely in any given instance. Similarly, there were those who, while not taking a stand completely in favor of art for art's sake, nevertheless preferred that position to an outright espousal of *engagement* or would perhaps apply a literary judgment based on "pure" aesthetic considerations in those cases where they felt *engagement* had gone so far as to impair artistic quality—a quite different consideration from denying any and all validity to *engagement*. Thus it will not seem altogether contradictory to find a handful of critics questioning *engagement* who have already been quoted in support of it.

If one had to decide upon any one critic as "the" African opponent of *engagement littéraire*, it would probably be the Nigerian poet-playwright John Pepper Clark, who on several occasions took pains to state his position. Writing in a *Transition* article in 1965 about whom he obviously considered West Africa's better poets, he said,

> Public gestures, programs, and matters of political propaganda and slogan do not seem to preoccupy their minds, excepting some mostly from Ghana where things, art not excluded, are of course more organized. Quite evident too is an awareness of the conditions of human existence as known to each personally. Perhaps, following from this, is their tacit acceptance, whether in pride or in humility, of the fact that a poem summoned to life by a committee of citizens, however revolutionary, is more likely to be the hotch-potch and doggerel that many national anthems are than a genuine work of art. ("Poetry in Africa," 24)

As for the claim that the traditional African arts are *engagées*, and therefore modern African literature, in being committed, is merely following tradition, Clark said of the song-poems of the Urhobo people of the Niger Delta that "the *Udje* is straight entertainment. That is, it is all art and little or no ritual and religion" ("Poetry of the Urhobo," 283).

After Clark might come another Nigerian poet, Christopher Okigbo, who died as an officer in the Biafran army. Okigbo is reported to have said at the Makerere conference of 1962, "I don't read my poetry to non-poets!" (Nkosi, "Press Report," 1). It would be difficult to imagine a more aesthetically, less committed statement. Okigbo reiterated his position in a 1965 interview. He was asked if he thought a poet should give society a "definite message," to which he replied, "It just happens that there might be some political tinge in their ["Heavensgate" and "Limits"] message, or the message of the Silent Sisters—but the message has nothing to do with me nor has it anything to do with my invention" ("Christopher Okigbo Interviewed," iii-iv).

In his doctoral dissertation, Romanus Nnagbo Egudu indicated a preference for aesthetic rather than social, economic, or political considerations in poetry. After citing the poets Abioseh Nicol, J.V.B. Danquah, and Dennis Osadebay, Egudu said, "The West African poets of the colonial period cannot be considered as poets in any serious sense. There is little or no aesthetic quality in their poetry. They seem to be concerned with putting their ideas across to the audience rather than with poetry as an art'' (59).

Eldred Jones was also less than enthusiastic about *engagement*. He said, ''The writer must of course be free from national theories of literature. Literature written to a prescription seldom succeeds,'' and ''It is to be hoped that writers in Africa will be undeterred by such narrow nationalistic theories of literature as the best writers elsewhere have been; otherwise our writers will produce not literature but propaganda'' (''Nationalism,'' 155).

Chinua Achebe had reservations about *engagement* if it limited the freedom of the artist. In an interview in *Afrique*, he was asked, ''Do you think a novel must be essentially social? realistic?'' He replied no, and added, ''A writer must not be limited'' (''Entretien avec Chinua Achebe,'' 42*). The Malawi critic David Rubadiri suggested a similar danger: ''One can only search for the African personality, and society demands this from its artists, much more from its writers. The literature of 'assertion' and 'protest' could easily be a negative factor in a society that teems with so much life and creative spirit'' (42).

Peter Abrahams on occasion sounded unsympathetic to *engagement*. In 1952, in the same place he praised Ekwensi's *People of the City* for its *engagement*, he said of the African writer that ''he must have a strong love of literature for its own sake, and an understanding of the age-old tradition of humanity that literature has served throughout the ages'' (''Challenge,'' 387). Lewis Nkosi occasionally sounded more aesthetically than socially concerned with the texts he discussed. After wavering for a time over the question of *engagement* in his *Home and Exile*, he concluded, ''It seems to me that in the overheated atmosphere of change and power-acquisition in which the masses of the people may even be compelled to do certain things, the pre-eminent duty of literature is still to proclaim the primal value of Life over the Idea'' (107).

Anti-*Engagement* as a Critical Standard

If very few African critics expressed a non-committed point of view, even fewer seemed to apply it as a critical standard. The few who did were English-speaking. Of these, Ezekiel Mphahlele was perhaps the most consistent. In his preface to a volume of Nigerian writing, he implied that the writers were too committed and looked forward to the day when the ''social criticism will take its rightful place within this framework without necessarily bringing down literary standards'' (''Preface,'' 13). After excepting the work of the Ghanaian poet Efua Sutherland, he said of another body of poetry, ''For the rest, Ghanaian poetry is all declamatory stuff breathing nationalism and Africanism through and through but to little purpose. And its theme is not helping the reader to understand the inner life of the Ghanaian'' (''Ghana,'' 12).

Mabel Aig-Imoukhuede reviewed Cyprian Ekwensi's two children's books, *The Drummer Boy* and *The Passport of Mallam Ilia*, unfavorably because she thought he was too didactic in them: "One might therefore say that Mr. Ekwensi should confine himself to straight-forward adventure in future and leave pathos and preaching to missionaries and writers of documentary films" (89).

Finally, Ugandan critic Taban Lo Liyong was critical of James Ngugi's *Weep Not, Child* because, he said, "Ngugi commits many technical sins, probably because he is more engrossed in espousing his ideas and ideals than in adhering to artistic precepts" (Review, 43).

CONCLUSION

Engagement, then, was not unanimously held by Africans as a critical principle, nor was it unanimously applied as a critical standard; however, it was the view that seemed to prevail among a large majority of African critics and was, in fact, one of the clearest single tenets of African literary criticism in its early years. Whether this was due to historical events or political conditions, or to the early impact of Jean-Paul Sartre's "Orphée noir," or due to a committedness inherent in traditional African culture is open to speculation. Whatever influence came from the extra-literary factors, and from Sartre, can be expected to fade or to be modified in time. The effect of traditional culture on modern African literature will no doubt be more lasting.

The larger question for the Western critic is the acceptance of the fact that Africans were choosing a standard they did not widely hold. Westerners have repeatedly asked why Africans continue to use *engagement* as a critical standard. Such a question is legitimate, of course; it is important, however, to make clear on which level the question is being asked. If one is interested, academically, in the divergencies of African and Western literary theory and practice, that is one thing; if one is attempting to impose Western standards upon African critics, that is another—in which case the African is well within his rights to merely refer the Westerner to Senghor's discussion of the "Civilization of the Universal." The Westerner, though he may not like it, can only accept the fact that African critics have been choosing and will continue to choose their own standards and that, in the case of *engagement*, they have chosen a standard that, while it may have enjoyed a certain currency in the wake of World War II and Sartre's *Qu'est-ce que la littérature?*, has since been in decline in the West. Any inquiry addressed to the divergencies of African and Western literary criticism should be made carefully—on the academic level of comparative literature. *Engagement* may take a different position in the African scheme of things as time goes on, but that is a matter that will be decided by Africans. The ongoing decision will be of interest, of course, to Westerners, but only, as it were, after the fact.

7 Negritude and the Critics

PRO-NEGRITUDE

As a francophone critic, Gilbert Ilboudo, put it, "It would certainly not be an idle task to try and determine what is really original in the substance of African literature" (30). However, Ilboudo's suggestion was not as simple as it might seem. By "original" did he mean what is *essentially* African in the literature? Did he mean Negritude? It would not be an idle task, certainly, to determine what Negritude is. Such a task is well beyond the scope of this study, of course, just as this chapter suggests it was beyond the scope of the African critics themselves in the early years of their criticism. Nevertheless, Negritude has been an important theme in African literary criticism—theoretical and applied—since Leopold Senghor began explicating the term in the 1930s.

More has been written on Negritude, perhaps, than on any other single concept concerning African literature. In the first two decades after World War II it was easily the most controversial issue among the critics themselves, and generated the most heated debate in journals and at the various conferences at which African critics gathered over the years. It has often been thought of as the dividing line between French-speaking and English-speaking African critics, though this chapter will indicate that this line was by no means rigid—exceptions being found on both sides of it.

No attempt will be made here to define Negritude, but rather an attempt will be made to show that, whatever it is, it has been of central concern to African critics. It will also be seen that, while the large part of the discussion of it has been theoretical, Negritude has also been applied as a critical standard.

The early story of literary Negritude is largely a story of two critics: Leopold Senghor and Ezekiel Mphahlele, with other critics rallying around one of the two main camps.

Senghor and the Definition of Negritude

It will be helpful to begin this inquiry with a review of the position of the one continental African co-coiner of the term "Negritude," Leopold Senghor, who, along with Aimé Césaire and Léon Damas, invented the term in the early 1930s while a student in Paris. Senghor said of those days,

> Early on we had become aware within ourselves that assimilation was a failure; we could assimilate mathematics or the French language, but we could never strip off our black skins nor root out our black souls. And so we set out on a fervent quest for the Holy Grail: our *Collective Soul.* And we came upon it. ("What Is," 1211)

The Holy Grail was of course Negritude, and Senghor almost singlehandedly undertook the task of defining the term. The definition most often repeated may be the one he gave in 1961: "Negritude is *the whole complex of civilised values—cultural, economic, social and political—which characterise the black peoples*, or, more precisely, the Negro-African world" ("What Is," 1211). Let us consider especially those values that apply to literature.

Earlier, Senghor mentioned a *"style nègre"* at least as early as 1939, and said *"Emotion is negro, as reason is Greek"* ("Ce que," 295*). Central to this *style nègre* was a surreal way of looking at the world that characterized the Negro: "What the Negro has is the ability to perceive the supernatural in the natural, the sense of the transcendent and the lively abandon that goes with it, the abandon of love" ("Ce que," 298-99*), which he saw as fundamentally different from the European world view. Senghor distinguished between the two by comparing the African to the European surrealist:

> I fear that the surrealists themselves had, for the Negro, an always discreet sympathy, that is, enlightened. How could it have been otherwise in a world enslaved by matter and reason, or where one denounced reason only to proclaim the primacy of matter. Because it was just that which caused the decadence of art in the 19th century; and the manifestoes "for French Art" that the review *Les Beaux Arts* published are significant. Realism and Impressionism are only two sides of the same error. It is the adoration of the real that leads to photographic art. ("Ce que," 307-308*)

In a 1947 essay he connected surrealism and Negritude even more clearly, saying, ". . . the Negro is defined, essentially, by his *ability to be moved . . .*" ("L'Afrique noire, 165*), and added that "But what moves the Black is not the exterior aspect of the object, it is the reality or, better—since "realism" has become sensuality—its surreality. Water moves him not because it washes, but because it purifies . . ." ("L'Afrique noire," 166*). Five years later, in 1952, he said, "The Surrealist Revolution, you know, would have permitted our poets to express Negritude only in French. In breaking down our vision, and then the sentence, by the elimination of linking words, in achieving the derangement of the dictionary by the citizenry's acceptance of technical and 'barbaric' words" ("L'Apport," 142*).

In 1954 he reiterated his distinctions "between European surrealism, which is uniquely empirical, and Negro-African surrealism, which is equally metaphysical, which is *supernatural*" ("Langage," 154*). In 1956 he clarified somewhat his claim that "emotion is Negro, as reason is Greek." He said,

> This is not to say that the Negro is traditionally devoid of reason, as one would have me believe. But this reason is not discursive; it is synthetic. It is not antagonistic, but sympathetic. This is another path to knowledge. Negro reason does not impoverish things. It does not mold them into rigid categories, eliminating the juices and the sap; it flows into the arteries of things, espouses all their contours and comes to rest in the living core of the real. White reason is analytical through use. Negro reason is intuitive through participation. ("African-Negro Aesthetics," 24)

The other facet of Senghor's early Negritude, along with emotion, was rhythm. Going back again to 1939, Senghor said then that "It is in the domain of rhythm that the Negro contribution has been the most important, the most uncontested" ("Ce que," 312*). In 1947 he asked what the principles of African poetry were. His answer was that "In its essence, in all that I have been able to study in Senegal, it rests on what is the most Negro: on *rhythm*, on precisely that which unifies word, music and dance" ("L'Afrique noire," 220*). In 1952 he called it "the common denominator of all Negro art" ("L'Apport," 144*), and the next year he connected it with the statement regarding Negro emotion and reason: "The Negro does not reason first. He does not separate himself from the object, he does not hold it at a distance. He feels it" ("La Contribution," 145*). He said further that "It is through the subjectivity . . . intimately mixed in his body and soul, 'open to all the breezes of the world,' that he discovers the other in its essential reality—rhythm" (145*). He then went on to define "rhythm" more specifically:

> I will first define rhythm, as the European does, as movement or, in the same time interval, the reoccurring of an accented note, syllable or gesture: In this interval, there are not necessarily the same number of notes, syllables or gestures. From which the unity in diversity comes by which we can also define rhythm. It is the only talent that no one will contest, that the man on the street identifies as Negritude. Whereas the Europeans confine rhythm to music, poetry and dance, the Negroes are so obsessed with it that they deify it so as to make it the essence of

being of their art as in sculpture, painting, tales and theatre. ("La contribution," 145-146*)

More specifically of rhythm in poetry, he said in 1956 that "it is the poem that best instructs us on the nature of African-Negro rhythm. Rhythm is not born of the alternations of long and short syllables; it is created solely by the alternations of stressed and weak syllables, by the alternations of quick and slow tempos" ("African-Negro Aesthetics," 33). He went further, saying rhythm was Africa's unique gift to the world: "Nowhere else [outside Black Africa] has rhythm reigned as despotically. Nature planned things well in seeing to it that every people, every race, every continent would cultivate with special pleasure certain of man's virtues" ("African-Negro Aesthetics," 37).

In the same essay Senghor said that "Imagery and rhythm are the two fundamental characteristics of the African-negro style" (30), and four years earlier, in 1952, he had said that "After the griots, our troubadors, the Negro French-speaking poets have received, as their primary talent, imagery" ("L'Apport," 143*). In a 1957 essay he spoke of "the virtues of Negritude" as being "first *emotion*, from which come *imagery* and *rhythm*" ("Le réalisme," 8*).

There were still other Senghorian aspects of Negritude. In 1953 Senghor said that "the first gift of the Negro-African is love" ("La contribution," 145*). In 1956 he spoke of rhythm "and humor, the other face of Negritude" ("Comme les lamantins," 116*). Still another facet was mentioned in connection with another poet, Malick Fall: "Third trait of Negritude: *music*, I mean the imitative harmony in some lines of poetry, which already have rhythm" ("Malick Fall," 13*).

In his "Orphée noir," Sartre referred to Negritude as an "antiracist racism" (xiv). Senghor suggested a broader definition:

Negritude is essentially this human warmth that is *awareness of life* in the world. It is an existentialism, to speak like you, rooted in mother earth, blooming in the sun of faith. This presence in the world is the subject's participation in the object, participation of Man in cosmic forces, *communion* of Man with other men and, through that, with all existing things from a pebble to God. ("Sorbonne," 317*)

And when some anglophone Africans accused him of racism, he responded in various ways. In the "Introduction" to his *Liberté I* he seemed to confuse the issue when he more or less fell back on Sartre's statement: "Negritude is what the anglophones call 'African personality.' It is only a matter of understanding the words. Because why would they have fought for 'independence' if not to recover, defend and illustrate their African personality" (8*)? To which he added, "*Negritude is therefore the collective Negro-African* *personality*. It is amusing to hear some accuse us of *racism*, who preach and emulate the 'Greco-Roman civilization,' the 'Anglo-Saxon civilization,' the 'European civilization' " (8*). He concluded, "Negritude is therefore not *racism*. If it became racist at first, it was antiracist, as Jean-Paul Sartre remarked in *Orphee noir*" (8*).

He responded more specifically in a 1966 essay, saying that "During the last thirty or so years that we have been proclaiming negritude, it has become customary, especially among English-speaking critics, to accuse us of racialism" ("Negritude: A Humanism," 1). He continued,

> Mphahleles have been sent about the world saying: "Negritude is an inferiority complex"; but the same word cannot mean both "racialism" and "inferiority complex" without contradiction. The most recent attack comes from Ghana, where the government has commissioned a poem entitled "I hate Negritude"—as if one could hate oneself, hate one's being, without ceasing to be.
>
> No negritude is none of these things. It is neither racialism nor self-abnegation. Yet it is not just affirmation: it is confirmation of one's *being*. (1)

He further added that "Negritude is nothing more or less than what some English speaking Africans have called the *African personality*. It is no different from the "black personality" discovered and proclaimed by the American New Negro movement" (1-2). In the same essay he repeated his most common definition: "It is obvious that peoples differ in their ideas and their languages, in their philosophies and their religions, in their customs and their institutions, in their literature and their art. Who would deny that Africans, too, have a certain way of conceiving life and of living it" (2)? His answer was, "Nobody, probably; for otherwise we would not have been talking about 'Negro Art' for the last 60 years and Africa would be the only continent today without its ethnologists and sociologists. What, then, is negritude? It is—as you can guess from what precedes—*the sum of the cultural values of the black world*; . . . ." (2).

It was small wonder, then, that Senghor saw Negritude as the moving force behind the First World Festival of Negro Arts in Dakar in 1966. And when he sensed among his fellow-Africans a difference of opinion on the matter he said:

> What has struck me and disappointed me is to realize, after the Festival, that some Negro intellectuals, writers and artists have looked at the values of Negritude with some contempt, simply to look good, to be in fashion; some have said that Negritude is *passé*; this is just as if the Arabs were to say that Arabness is *passé*, the Americans that Free Enterprise is *passé*, or the Soviets saying the same of communism.

That is, in my opinion, a form of inferiority complex. (Bhely-Quenum, "Une interview," 29*)

And finally, the following remark made in 1963 clarified that Senghor's concept of Negritude was a fluid one, rather than static. Speaking at the opening of the Dakar Conference of that year, he said, "I know, the word ['negritude'] alarms the delicate who fear air as much as germs, who confuse vulgarity and authenticity. As if literature was a cookbook and not the living expression of living men" ("Negritude et Civilisation," 10*).

So much, for the time being, for Senghor. For an update on him as literary critic, see Daniel Garrot's *Léopold Sédar Senghor; critique littéraire* (1978). To Senghor's credit, and no doubt at least in part because of his broad influence, there was a substantial cadre of critics anxious to take up the banner of Negritude behind him. Among the most consistent of these was Paulin Joachim, who attested as follows to the effect Senghor had on him:

> I discovered Senghor in Africa, around 1945 or 1946, at a time when I was looking feverishly to disintoxicate myself and eliminate from my heart and spirit all the theories that had caused me to hate being Negro, I mean a second class citizen, a being without past or future. Having never left the continent or made any overture toward the outside world, I could not believe that there existed, in the white man's—my master's— countries men of my race who were strong and powerful with no inferiority complex and capable of expressing themselves freely and with eloquence in the language of the Europeans. Senghor was the very first to give me pride of my race and showed me the spiritual powers in my blood. (" 'Nocturnes,' " 25*)

Others were not as explicit, but it seems reasonable to take Joachim's statement as an indication of a broader Senghorian influence upon a generation of writers and critics. The nature of the influence took several forms. Senghor himself suggested a double-edged interpretation of Negritude—reaction and quest—in his "Holy Grail" statement ("What Is Negritude?," 1211).

The Forms of Negritude

Negritude might be seen, then, as an historical phenomenon—a weapon with which to challenge the failure of assimilation, as well as the historical, political and human ramifications of the slave trade and colonialism; and at the same time something innate. Let us examine first the statements of a few critics who saw Negritude as a historical phenomenon.

Historical. Antoine-Roger Bolamba seemed to be one of the first Africans to express in print his acceptance of this aspect of Negritude. In 1954 he wrote, "Negritude is a tearing of the black soul at the moment when a civilization gave it new needs" (A.R.B., "Poésie bantoue," 204*). Alioune Diop spoke of a historical Negritude at the Second Congress of Negro Artists and Writers (Rome, 1959):

> Negritude—born in us by the feeling of having been denied, in the course of history, the joy of *creating* and being treated fairly—Negritude is nothing other than our humble and tenacious ambition to rehabilitate the victims and to show to the world precisely what one has specifically denied: the *dignity* of the black race. . . . Negritude therefore has the mission to restore its true dimensions to history. ("Le Sens," 42-43*)

In 1962 Thomas Diop saw several possible forms Negritude could take, the earliest of which was historical and political:

> In its early youth, the Negritude movement categorically denied, for a period of time, the white cultural values and held with a disarming assurance that only the Negro-Africans had a valuable message to give to the world. In sum, this double exaggeration was only the exact opposite of the excessive pretensions that their white interlocutors had formerly put forth in order to ensure their intellectual domination. Whatever one thought of this extreme attitude of the Negro-Africans, it at least had the merit of provoking in many white questioners a worthwhile psychological shock which led them to reexamine with increased vigor the judgment they had made up to that point of the cultural values of Black Africa and those of Europe. (133*)

Also in the same year Lamine Diakhaté, while seeing Negritude in a broader perspective, referred to its historical importance as well: "She is the daughter of history, geography, social context, politics, economics . . . the term itself served as a rallying point for the Senegalese and Caribbean intellectuals at a time of extreme tension, when they felt 'nothinged' by Europe" ("Contribution," 58*).

In 1964 Richard Rive saw Negritude as a temporary, historical phase—"a by product of French Colonial policy, an understandable reaction against being 'frenchified out of existence,' understandable but whether artistically condonable in terms of the diversity of Neo-African culture is another matter. It is an historical phase, and has an historical importance in terms of its assertion of African values" ("Images," 53-54). He added, "The role of Negritude as a socio-historical phase in the development of an important section of African poetry cannot be ignored. But it was essentially a transitional phase and can only be evaluated in terms of chronological perspective" (54).

Paulin Joachim seemed to agree, in his 1966 review of *Présence africaine*'s issue no. 57, "Nouvelle somme de poésie du monde noir." He said, "Negritude is already becoming *passé*" ("Nouvelle somme," 61*).

Metaphysical. More often than historical, Negritude was seen as innate—as the metaphysical quintessence of being black. This was seldom if ever defined by Africans, with the exception of Senghor's attempts, but it was often alluded to in various ways, and its existence was often taken for granted. This was as true within the domain of African literature as elsewhere. Such was the implication A. R. Bolamba made in 1953 when he said, "I would say that each art has its style. Read any poem written by a Black with a *black thought*, and you will find, beyond its personal form, the expression of a rhetoric typically African. The *Negro Genius* exists" ("Poésie négro-africaine et poètes noir," 303*). Bolamba reiterated this view in another essay in 1954, when he said, "The Negro is defined by *his ability to be moved*; he is stirred by the *great emotional warmth of his black blood*" (A.R.B., "Poésie bantoue," 204*).

Toussaint Viderot also invoked a very innate Negritude in the preface to his play, *Pour toi, Nègre, mon frère . . .*, saying, "It is in some ways the portrait of the Negro soul that I have made in this work. For this, I insist that what the book contains is not a dream, but the Negro reality in all its essence. Because, I, who wrote this portrait of Negritude, am myself an authentic Negro" (11*). Mustapha Bal took a similar view:

> It is not surprising to see that in its origins the Negro-African poetic movement, born of the colonial drama which was both its nourishment and its justification, exerted a negative function; the rehabilitation of the black race was only a part of it. Poetry will put into perspective the obvious qualities of the specific traits of the black world, the black soul, while also sanctioning a return to the sources. (19*)

Upon describing the performance of a Dahomean dance troupe in Paris, Olympe Bhely-Quenum suggested an innateness, saying, "Someone whispered behind me, 'It's splendid! They have been well trained.' But no! These men and women had never received a choreography lesson. All that is inherent in their nature, in our Dahomean nature, which drives us to create endlessly" ("A Paris," 36*). Paulin Joachim had this form in mind in 1964 when he wrote:

> Each African, on his arrival in this world, is imbued with the gift of poetry. It flows in his veins from morning to evening, infusing meaning into his every act—the greeting, the farewell, ritual ceremonies, and declarations of love to a woman. *L'homme noir* possesses incomparable emotional power; when his soul expresses itself, poetry gushes forth like a bubbling spring. ("Contemporary," 296)

Static or Fluid? Some discussion of Negritude centered around the question of whether it was static or fluid, whether it was, to use Jean-Paul Sartre's terms, essence or existence. Sartre began the debate in 1948 in "Orphée noir." Upon asking a double-edged series of questions, he concluded, "As all anthropological notions, Negritude is an iridescence of being and the duty to be; it makes you and you make it" (*Black Orpheus*, 59). Thomas Melone agreed with Sartre, some years later in 1962, when he said, "The Negro, a man who seeks and never finds himself. Negritude is an eternal race toward a purity that slips away" (*De la négritude*, 110*). In this same vein was Thomas Diop's observation that Negritude, if it was historical, was also much more:

> There were and still are a large number of Africans, young ones espe-
> cially, who maintain that Negritude has no more *raison d'être* and that
> its mission is finished. For us, their elders, who recall all the benefits
> we and our people owe to the fecundity of Negritude, and who see
> clearly the road opening before us, Negritude is real, dynamic, adapt-
> able to shifting realities of the existence of individuals and communi-
> ties. (136*)

In a cogent essay, Edris Makward in 1966 took up Sartre's question of the nature of Negritude, asking, "Is Negritude a *unique* and *static* ideology?" ("Negritude," 37). In support of his answer, Makward quoted Senghor's speech at the Congress of the Parti du rassemblement africain in 1959: "In order that our Negritude may be, instead of a curiosity for museums, the ef-ficient instrument of a liberation, we had to rid it of its scoria and insert it in the solidary movement of [the] contemporary world." Makward concluded that "Negritude is therefore not static, it is changing; yesterday it was seren-ity, today (that is during the struggle for independence) it is aggressiveness and grievousness and tomorrow it will be something else" (41).

Senghor himself expressed dismay that Negritude was considered by some to be passé in 1966. Shortly after the Dakar festival of that year, he said,

> It is obvious that in an earlier day the attitude of Negritude was one of
> revolt, confrontation, a somewhat crude attitude of affirmation of the
> values of Negritude; I think that we must now move on from this neg-
> ative phase to a positive one: Negro writers and artists especially must
> express and manifest Negritude, as if it was not challenged, all, more-
> over, in using techniques brought from Europe and even Asia. (Bhely-
> Quenum, "Une Interview," 29*)

Perhaps the most succinct outline of the various interpretations of Negri-tude is that which appeared in a *Présence africaine* editorial in 1966. The editorial led to another strain of interpretations—Negritude as a humanism:

> Those who consider that Negritude now belongs to the past of the black
> consciousness have forgotten that the two coincide for Césaire and
> Senghor. At the beginning, Negritude designated essentially the liter-
> ary gift of the negro poet aspiring to an originality comparable to that

of his European counterpart. Later on, it came to stand for politicocultural struggle for the dignity of the Negro peoples. Extending its
field of action, Negritude then took on the fight against colonization
and racism. Here, Negritude displayed an attitude with greater political overtones as its exigencies were deeply cultural. It then showed its
universalist ambition by questioning the very cultural foundations of
the Western world and this phase was the most exciting, the most dis-
puted and perhaps the most glorious. It was the period in which the figures of Senghor and Césaire as both poets and political leaders emerged
from darkness on to the international scene. It is from this angle particularly that the two Congresses of Negro Writers and Artists gave
food for spiritual and political thought to a new generation thirsting
for freedom and self-affirmation.

   Then another phase came into being with the announcement in 1960
of the World Festival of Negro Arts. Negritude now appeared as a humanism. (P.A., 5)

Negritude as a Humanism. Richard Dogbeh was among the first to see
Negritude as a humanism. In 1961 he said, "The problem of our liberation
having been resolved, *what will be the exact nature of Negritude? It seems
to us that it will be essentially cultural and humanist*" (31*). Alioune Sène
also saw Negritude in this way. He said in 1966, "Negritude is therefore for
the Black Man the condition of authenticity, the growth of consciousness in
the face of History, Culture and Destiny. But beyond that it is the Brotherhood of all men, it is Humanism" (95-96*).

   The First World Festival of Negro Arts was seen by several critics as a turning point for Negritude toward a more humanistic, less politically and socially
aggressive phase. Senghor saw this new direction as Africa's contribution to
the "Civilization of the Universal" and said, speaking of the festival, "At
last proof of the fact that negritude is a humanism of the 20th century is
provided by the welcome that has been accorded throughout the world to
the projected Festival of African Arts" ("Negritude: A Humanism," 7). He
concluded that

   this goes to show that the world—that is, the "Civilization of the Universal"—which has slowly been building itself up since the beginning of the
   century, on the ruins of racial hatreds and intercontinental wars, feels
   itself concerned. It feels itself concerned with good reason, for a number of its characteristics, as they are at present taking shape, would not
   be what they are without the fertilizing contributions of negritude. (7-8)

Pro-Negritude Anglophone Critics

With the exception of Richard Rive, the Africans who have been quoted
were all French speaking. However, Negritude was not espoused by all French-

speaking Africans, just as it was not unanimously attacked by all English-speaking ones. This is just another reminder of the complexity of the continent (and perhaps, therefore, of the danger inherent in such a term as *Negritude*). Let us examine the anglophone critics who defended Negritude.

The first to do so may have been Abioseh Nicol, who in 1960 said that "Negritude is to some African, West Indian and American Negro intellectuals what the Graeco-Roman-Christian ethos is to the European" (354). At the Third Annual Conference of the American Society of African Culture, also in 1960, T. O. Oruwairye, a Nigerian, sounded very much like Senghor when he said, "The tendency of Europeans is toward abstraction, and I think this is their primary difficulty in understanding African culture. Negritude is no more than a reminder that there is such a thing as experiencing life as a whole, a synthetic whole, without the necessity of splitting it up" (354).

Three years later, while reviewing Gerald Moore's critical study, *Seven African Writers*, the bilingual author-critic Mbella Sonne Dipoko quarreled with Moore's interpretation of Negritude and then, significantly, concluded his review with a favorable quotation from Moore, noting its historical phase:

> Gerald Moore considers the issue of negritude in terms of the question, "Is it a false and artificial movement?" His answer is that all literary movements involve a measure of artificiality and arbitrary selection. The chief danger of negritude is that it may degenerate into a racialism as intolerant and arrogant as any other. Moore concedes, nevertheless, that the movement "unlocked the talents of a very remarkable group of young Negroes; it gave them an attitude out of which they could create; it provided a vehicle for the passion, energy, and conviction of a whole generation." (Review of *Seven African Writers*, 31)

A year later, George Awoonor-Williams (Kofi Awoonor) made a similar comment:

> It was politically necessary to call attention to the negro situation, to sing about Africa and the glories of the past; these did serve an important purpose in the political emergence of Africa. It was necessary to create and reshape the African image; and this the *negritude* writers did. Some might have overdone it, but overdoing it is surely more welcome than neglecting to do it. (7)

Cyprian Ekwensi was still another anglophone critic to recognize at least the historical importance of Negritude. Responding to Wole Soyinka's famous comment, he said,

> Wole Soyinka has been quoted as saying that "a Tiger does not shout about its Tigritude." This may be true when it is not necessary for the Tiger to shout. But it must be remembered that twenty years ago when

negritude was first postulated by the Martinique poet, Aimé Césaire, it was necessary for the blackman to reassure himself of his pride in being black because blackness had become a shameful thing, an undignified state. There was in fact a "flight from blackness" and a yearning for becoming white. Thus negritude served as an affirmation of the African personality, the assertion of the human quality of the blackman. ("African Literature," 295)

Other critics responded to Soyinka's challenge as well. In a review, the Ghanaian poet Frank Parkes said the anti-Negritudinists "continue to be influenced by such arguments against Negritude as: 'A tiger does not have to proclaim his tigritude.' . . . [but] Africans have proved their ability to think in abstractions. And that is why they can, and the tiger cannot, proclaim their negritude" (755). Davidson Nicol wrote of Soyinka's comment, "One must observe however that if a tiger lived in a society dominated by lions, it would be understandable if it occasionally emitted a roar in defence or proclamation of its tigritudity" (*Africa*, 74). Donatus Nwoga said in 1965 that

in spite of the wariness of creative artists about the slogans carried by politicians, in this case the slogan about the African Personality, there is no denying that the atmosphere generated by these slogans influences the mind of the artist. In practical terms, the African is beginning to recognize himself as a person who does not require to declare that he is a person. ("West Africa," 14)

A. Bodurin, the same year, said,

Nowadays in Nigeria, pride in indigenous dress, food, music and sculpture is the new status symbol. Thirty, even fifteen, years ago such a pride was unthinkable. What is this pride if not Negritude?
　　Having said all this, I must acknowledge some valid criticisms levelled against "Negritude." One is that it risks becoming itself a black racialism. (36)

The previous remarks notwithstanding, one anglophone critic stood above all others in the defense of Negritude in the early years of African literary criticism. In reviews, a doctoral dissertation, and two long scholarly articles, Nigerian critic Abiola Irele was the primary defender of Negritude in English-speaking Africa. He began his defense in a 1962 review of Ezekiel Mphahlele's critical study, *The African Image*. He said,

The first three chapters of Mr. Mphahlele's latest book are in fact a development of his doubts and hesitations *vis-à-vis* the efforts of black intellectuals to provide a common base on a conscious level for the *undoubted* cultural bond which exists among the Negro people. Ironically

enough, his book falls squarely within the framework of a general movement of the reappraisal of Africa and its people which is at the basis of
Negritude, whose object in the long run is to project a healthy African
image against the dark and spiteful one which the white man has for
so long presented. (231)

Further on, Irele took delight in pointing out how Mphahlele, ironically,
illustrated his own Negritude:

That is why he can sneer at Senghor's famous phrase that "emotion is
at the heart of Negritude", and only six pages later comes out with
basically the same thing in different words by categorically asserting
the biological factor: "The black man is *naturally* demonstrative and
in the South he will look for the most *intensive* as well as the nearest
medium of expressing himself." (232)

Two years later, in 1964, Irele defended Senghor and the innateness of
Negritude in these terms:

This negro being is rooted in African tradition, which is unified by a
common philosophical conception, cultural variations notwithstanding: a common ontological outlook which governs the African psyche
and in which the negro in America can rightly be supposed to share.
This total African cosmology is what Senghor calls "the ensemble of
African values." ("A Defence," 10)

However, Irele remained as obscure on the specifics of Negritude as was
Senghor. He concluded:

Yet even in the absence of a formal analysis of the negro psyche, much
of the poetry of negritude seems to me to express something of a profound African consciousness and [Janheinz] Jahn is right in relating
Césaire's poetry to the work of Tutuola, and Senghor in making his
so often contested declaration that "the negritude of a poem is less in
the theme than in the manner." ("A Defence," 11)

And while he posited a certain essential quality of Negritude, Irele had at
least partial reservations as to how and if it might be discovered:

The black poet's descent into himself is an effort to disalienate his being and to reestablish a concordance with a distinct essence. For this
reason, he reconstructs this essence as much as he can from the remains
in him of the African heritage. Yet this march to an original past is
coloured by a historical experience to which he has been submitted, im-
printed on him indelibly. So that in the effort to achieve personality,
there can be no question of a return to the past in its original form. ("A
Defence," 11)

In 1965 Irele published two long studies on Negritude in the *Journal of Modern African Studies*. In the first of these, he indicated a move from the innate to the historical view: "I take negritude to mean not the philosophical idea of a Negro essence, which appears to me not only abstract but quite untenable—Senghor himself has moved far away from this point of view—but rather an historical phenomenon, a social and cultural movement closely related to African nationalism" ("Negritude or Black Cultural Nationalism," 322). He then traced its historical development through the Caribbean and the United States and concluded by saying, "The 1959 Congress in Rome was the last major public manifestation of *negritude* to date, and probably indicates the high water mark of the movement. . . . On the other hand, negritude has acquired a new orientation in ideas, due to the efforts of one man—Senghor" (347).

In the second article, Irele dealt with Negritude as the "cultural parallel" of Pan-Africanism and offered this caution regarding Senghor:

> Senghor's theory of *negritude* is not really a factual and scientific demonstration of African personality and social organization, but rather a personal interpretation. An element of speculation enters into his ideas, which lays them wide open to criticism. His more subtle formulations often have a specious character; besides, the most sympathetic reader of his theories cannot fail to be disturbed by his frequent confusion of race and culture, especially in his early writings. ("Negritude—Literature," 520)

Irele then commented on Negritude's impact on literary criticism:

> It is not suggested . . . that the romanticism of *negritude* was without its abuses. But this is a question for literary criticism, which must content itself with judging the aesthetic value of the finished product rather than legislating for the writer about his raw material. Besides, *negritude*, like any other literary school, has produced its uninspired writers, and like any other movement its lunatic fringe. (510n)

Negritude as a Critical Standard

Francophone Critics. Of particular interest here is not so much what Negritude is, or even what it meant to various African critics, but rather the fact that some critics used Negritude as a critical standard in their evaluations of specific literary works. It was not always clear what the critic meant by Negritude, but it was usually clear that the critic was aware of using this standard.

Just as African critics did not agree upon a definition of Negritude, let alone whether it was desirable to discuss it at all, they also were less than unanimous in their application of it as a standard. In some cases, the presence or absence of Negritude was seen as a positive factor and in others a negative one, illustrating the concern with Negritude as a critical tool and its importance in the minds of both its supporters and detractors.

The primary apostle of Negritude, Leopold Senghor, was one of the first to apply it, consistently, to particular works of African literature. In 1947 he said of Birago Diop's poems, "The reproach that one can make of them is that they are not 'Negro' enough" ("L'Afrique noire," 243*). In an introductory note in his *Anthologie* the next year, Senghor said of David Diop, "We do not doubt that, with age, David Diop will become milder. He will understand that a poem's Negritude is less theme than style, the emotional warmth which gives life to words, which transmutes the word into verb" ("David Diop," 173*).

A few years later Senghor entered the controversy surrounding Camara Laye. Senghor approved of *Le Regard du roi* in part because of its Negritude: "That Camara borrowed, in the beginning, the method of Kafka does not displease me. The symbolism comes from a Negro-African vein. What makes it Negro is precisely that he opens the door to hope, that he is a mystic" ("Laye Camara et Lamine Niang," 3*). In his preface to Tchicaya U Tam'si's *Epitome*, Senghor said, "Tchicaya is a witness whose only goal here is to manifest *Negritude*" ("De la," 10*). In another preface (the major form Senghor's practical criticism has taken) Senghor wrote of a Senegalese poet that "to turn the back on white civilization is, especially, to return to the sources of *Negritude*, to Nature. As in Claude McKay, the Jamaican poet, one will see, in Lamine Niang, the identifying *Trinity: Nature, Negritude, Africa*" ("Lamine Niang," 9*). And of yet another Senegalese, he said, "Like his elders, Malick Fall intends to assert himself, in expressing *'himself'* . . . while singing of *Negritude*" ("Malick Fall," 8*). And finally, reviewing the French translation of Peter Abrahams's *A Wreath for Udomo*, Senghor said that "there is a distance between the intellectual and the revolutionary [characters in the novel], between dream and act. What ties them together, in their diversity, is the Negritude" ("Peter Abrahams," 428*).

Senghor was not the only critic to apply Negritude as a standard. Zairian critic A. R. Bolamba, an early Senghor disciple, applied it in 1955 when he said approvingly of a line in Birago Diop's poetry that "the following extract reflects a philosophy authentically Negro" ("Birago Diop," 819*), and again when he said of another poet, "The great achievement of Flavien Ranaivo is that he remains true to the genius of his race while respecting French thought and technique" ("Flavien Ranaivo," 119*).

Another Zairois, Paul Mushiete, said openly that he used Negritude as a standard for selecting material for his anthology, *La Littérature française africaine*: "The authors were chosen according to two very precise criteria: their talent and their Negritude" ("Introduction," 3*). The effect of such an avowal in print can hardly be underestimated.

In 1960, E. Ralaimihoatra approved of his fellow Malagasay poet Jean-Joseph Rabearivelo because "he has put to the test what Senghor has called Negritude. Negritude is passion. It is fecundity. Rabearivelo lived a lifetime illustrating a work representing the Malagasay soul" (523*). In the same year another Malagasay critic, Gabriel Razafintsambaina, based his approval of Rabearivelo on the same ground, saying of his work, "It is, in sum, the whole movement of Negritude which is blooming in our time that he already had introduced" (635*).

For Paulin Joachim, writing in 1961, the *Nocturnes* of Senghor illustrated their author's philosophy. He said of the collection, "Senghor's song throws streams of light on the royal paths of Negritude. This is an explosive sacrament for all the militant supporters of Negritude" (" 'Nocturnes,' " 25*). Joachim also applied the standard to Seydou Badian's *Sous l'orage* when he said that "the author has known how to both keep and develop a profoundly African soul" ("Sous l'orage," 47*). Joachim said of Olympe Bhely-Quenum's novel, *Un Piège sans fin*, "It behooves every African and every man of culture to know this novel, premiere manifestation of the Negro soul" (Mercier and Battestini, 60*).

Bhely-Quenum, in his turn, also applied Negritude as a standard. He said of Tchicaya U Tam'si's *Epitome*,

> Tchicaya has clearly manifested his distrust of Negritude, under the pretext—pretext, by the way, very questionable for almost a decade—that it implied racism, [but] he is (by chance?) one of the most authentic representatives of this philosophy since one can, with no doubt, apply the concept of Negritude to more than one of the themes Tchicaya develops. (" 'Epitome,' " 42*)

Of the poetry of Jacques Rabemananjara, Bhely-Quenum said, "The themes raised by the poet and by the analysis of his works, all while keeping it in a context essentially malgache, do not dissociate it therefore from Negritude" ("Jacques Rabemananjara," 51*).

Anglophone Critics. Abiola Irele, no doubt the most sympathetic of the English-speaking Africans to the concept of Negritude, was very likely the only one to apply it as a standard positively. He was critical of Ulli Beier and Gerald Moore's anthology, *Modern Poetry from Africa*, because, he said,

> The point of course is that where the African poet is not simply making verse out of a borrowed rhetorical tradition, where his whole being is attuned to the particular atmosphere of his native origin, he must necessarily produce a poem that translates a definite African sensibility. It is in this sense that Negritude is a *vital* poetic message, the expression of a total African vision. (Review of *Poems*, 277)

In another review Irele praised the journal *Black Orpheus* for being open to, among other things, the early Negritude school of writing because

> it is in fact significant that the early numbers were devoted almost exclusively to the works of this group of writers, who were exposed to the formative influences of the western literary tradition, on which they were able to draw to compose an individual idiom, but from which the English-speaking African writers were cut off. ("Black Orpheus," 152)

In these examples, Negritude was used as a positive critical standard. We shall see that it was used negatively as well, which, rather than compromising its validity, indicates instead the concept's particular validity. Again, we are here more interested in identifying standards than in asking how the standards are applied in any given instance.

ANTI-NEGRITUDE

Anglophone Critics

As the expounding and championing of Negritude was to a large extent the work of one African, so the challenging of it was assumed for the most part by another. Ranged against the Negritude of Leopold Senghor, in almost perfect symmetry, was the rejection of it by South African critic Ezekiel Mphahlele.

Much theorizing has been done as to the causes of the split among Africans over Negritude. My purpose here is not to evaluate these comments but to bring them together in one place in the hope of seeing them perhaps more completely than has been possible in the past and to show that Negritude was used both negatively and positively as a critical standard.

Mphahlele first seemed to take an anti-Negritude stance in 1960. Writing in the *New Leader*, he said,

> To writers and artists in multi-racial communities like South Africa, of course, *negritude* is just so much intellectual and philosophic talk. What's so extraordinary about our African traits that there need be a slogan or battle cry about them? If my writing displays an intensity of feeling and *therefore* of style (Senghor says *negritude* has less to do with the theme than style), why should I imagine that I have a monopoly over such a trait simply because I am black—even granted that I am much more demonstrative and theatrical than the white man? ("The Importance," 11)

He added,

> I am a product of cultural cross-impacts, having lived with whites, Indians and colored people all my life in South Africa. These must exercise

a tremendous influence on my art. If there is any Negro-ness in it—as there is bound to be if my tone is not false—why should I get excited about it and formulate philosophic statements about the fact? Imagine a Chinaman waking up one morning and shouting in the streets that he has discovered something Chinese in his carving or painting or music! (11)

While at a conference called by the American Society of African Culture, in Philadelphia in 1960, Mphahlele said,

> You are very much excited by reading [J. Newton] Hill—you first recognize that the artist may express frequently with remarkable ability a sentiment of the race to which he belongs, but that this is not to subscribe to a philosophy regarding environmental influences on the artist, nor is this an admonition that the artist is inescapably controlled by ethnological factors. What we mean is that the artist, by the simple relationship that he bears to persons and things all about him, can seldom speak absolutely for himself as though he were a being in isolation. And there you are creating something. Still, where is negritude? ("Comments," 347-48)

Further on he commented on "The African Personality," saying that although it may exist, one must not be deluded into thinking it can be found:

> We keep looking for it all the time and it is the creative artist who keeps looking for it. It is elusive. We must not cheat ourselves into believing we have now caught the African Personality which we can describe in any tangible terms. We can only look for it, and that search for it is the very thing that makes the artist. The very conflict we're in the midst of makes the content of our art. ("Comments," 348)

Mphahlele had a great deal to say about Negritude at the Conference on African Literature and the University Curriculum (Freetown, 1963). He first made clear that his rejection of Negritude was not total when he asked, "Who can quarrel with negritude as a historical concept, a protest against political and cultural colonization, and a positive assertion of African values? It only concerns us here as a critical approach, since it has now been 'capped' as a principle of art" ("The Language of African Literature," discussion paper 13-14). He then admitted, though with reservations:

> Let us admit that negritude poetry brings the African experience to French poetry—a valid contribution. But we must also admit that as far as the attitude of mind it brings to poetry is concerned, it is wrong to pretend that it is doing something new, that 19th century European man has not been through all this revolt against machines and cannons. Again, negritude poetry has no right to set itself up as the monitor of

the African's poetic expression. ("The Language of African Literature," discussion paper 14-15)

Perhaps Mphahlele's strongest remarks on Negritude were given in a reply to another paper given at the Freetown conference, "Negritude and Its Enemies," by Wendell Jeanpierre. Mphahlele said,

> Who is so stupid as to deny the historical fact of *Negritude* as both a protest and a positive assertion of African cultural values? All this is valid. What I do not accept is the way in which too much of the poetry inspired by it romanticizes Africa—as a symbol of innocence, purity and artless primitiveness. I feel insulted when some people imply that Africa is not also a violent Continent. I am a violent person, and proud of it because it is often a healthy human state of mind; someday I'm going to plunder, rape, set things on fire; I'm going to cut someone's throat; I'm going to subvert a government; I'm going to organise a *coup d'etat*; yes, I'm going to oppress my own people; I'm going to hunt down the rich fat black men who bully the small, weak black men and destroy them; I'm going to become a capitalist, and woe to all who cross my path or who want to be my servants or chauffeurs and so on; I'm going to lead a breakaway church—there is money in it; I'm going to attack the black bourgeoisie while I cultivate a garden, rear dogs and parrots; listen to jazz and classics, read "culture" and so on. Yes, I'm also going to organise a strike. Don't you know that sometimes I kill to the rhythm of drums and cut the sinews of a baby to cure it of paralysis . . . ? This is only a dramatisation of what Africa can do and is doing. The image of Africa consists of all these and others. And *negritude* poetry pretends that they do not constitute the image and leaves them out. So we are told only half—often even a falsified half—of the story of Africa. Sheer romanticism that fails to see the large landscape of the personality of the African makes bad poetry. ("A Reply," 23-24)

Mphahlele was by no means alone; many other Africans joined with him in attacking Negritude. Not the least of these was Nigerian poet-playwright-critic Wole Soyinka, who reportedly said at the Makerere conference in 1962 that "a tiger does not have to proclaim his tigritude"—a remark on which much of the discussion of Negritude then turned. Soyinka did not write much on the subject—understandably, since to do so might have been seen as a proclamation of tigritude. In an interview he once balked, saying, "Certainly, I will not discuss negritude!" (Akaraogun, 18). But he was at other times willing to discuss the concept, as in this conversation with Bernard Fonlon:

> *Soyinka*: . . . Negritude seems to me to have bred a kind of . . . it has become a kind of summation, a kind of entity within itself. In other

words, the trend, the actual trend as demonstrated by the creative work, contradicts the theoretical principle which Senghor has clearly enunciated. In other words, Negritude is not an end. But it seems to me that the followers of Negritude, the poets who create in this idea . . . within this idea, have for too long a time rested, exploited this theme to [the] detriment of true artistic creativity.

Fonlon: There is a truth in what you say, because now in this a distinction must be made between the genuine Negritude that was felt at a time when the pressure . . . the condition of the Negro fully justified this type of poetry. Now . . . and at that time when Césaire and the rest were writing it was a real, genuine expression of what they really felt. But I do think that, as time went on, there crept in a kind of a sloganized version of this and I think that is to what you are referring.

Soyinka: Yes. (National Educational Television, "In French-Speaking Africa," 74)

In another interview, with Lewis Nkosi and Chinua Achebe, Soyinka made the following remark upon hearing Achebe's rationale behind the writing of *Things Fall Apart*:

Achebe: You see, I feel that this particular society had its good side. . . . But it had this cruel side to it and it is this that I think helped to bring down my hero.

Soyinka: Well, for a moment I was beginning to think that this sounded dangerously like the philosophy of negritude, or shall I say almost the myth of negritude, but I was relieved when you mentioned an extra dimension to it. (Nkosi, "Some Conversations," 19)

Soyinka and Mphahlele had their allies. Achebe, for one, voiced his opposition to Negritude in a 1963 interview, saying, "I am against slogans. I don't think, for example, that 'Negritude' has any meaning whatsoever. Panafricanism? Maybe. Negritude, no" ("Entretien avec Chinua Achebe," 42*).

In a 1963 letter to the editors of *West Africa*, Yusifu Usman made known his feelings about Negritude when he criticized the lack of publication of Muslim authors. He said, "The spaces that could have been given to these writers are filled with the trash of the Negritude poets whose roots anyway, are on the banks of the Seine rather than in the sands and jungles of Africa" ("Muslim Writers," 1243). In the same year Davidson Nicol was asked by *Afrique*, "When you write, do you consciously try to create in an authentic African style?" He replied, "No. What counts is what I think. When I write, I don't think at all about Negritude or of any other authentic African style" ("Entretien avec le Docteur," 50*).

In writing of the Berlin festival of 1964 and the Africans who attended it, Richard Rive sounded this anti-Negritude note, saying of African literature, "It cannot be judged in terms of its own yard-stick, or dictate its own terms of reference. This would imply 'writing to a march' of its own individual composition, a situation in Negritude rightly condemned by English-speaking writers" ("African Poets," 68).

Another South African critic, Lewis Nkosi, was also staunchly in the anti-Negritude fold. In 1965 he wrote, "There is no justification for bandying slogans like the 'African Personality' if its main function is not to increase for ourselves and those who come into contact with us an area of freedom and spontaneous action" (*Home and Exile*, 105). He agreed specifically with Mphahlele: "Mr. Mphahlele is right in his warning against the development of negritude as a cult—a dogma against which works by modern artists have to be tested. Self-conscious writing is bad enough, but self-righteous writing is intolerable," (124).

In his cogent essay, "The Background of Modern African Literature," Ben Obumselu questioned Negritude in these terms:

> It is, of course, possible to insist that the unique material of African literature is an enduring state of racial consciousness, quite as distinct from historical situations and the institutions which that consciousness enters and conditions. Such a conception is legitimate. Evidently something of the kind is implied in the theories of *negritude* and African personality. But these theories make questionable assumptions of first principles. To take one instance only, there is no justification to my mind for the belief that there are racial paradigms of experience which intervene between universal human nature (biological or imaginative) and the cultural discipline which distinguishes one society from another. When Senghor attempts to define *negritude*, he gives the impression sometimes that he is expounding a universal philosophy to which the ancient [sic] European wisdom of Pierre Teilhard de Chardin has contributed far more than have the Serer folk; at other times he is simply decribing the cultural and historical limitations of Negro experience. Senghor does not, I am afraid, discriminate sufficiently between the accidents of racial history, the supposed forms of the racial imagination, and his own philosopical ideals. (54-55)

Perhaps one of the most explicit attacks on Negritude was one by Taban Lo Liyong in 1966, done in his inimitable style: "Oh, Matthew Arnold. You said what literature of power is. You did not live long enough to say that Negritude is the literature of weakness. It is. Maintain the literature and you perpetuate the weakness" ("Negritude," 10-11). A few lines later he said,

> Ban, Ban, Ban, Caliban. What did Prospero teach Caliban? Language. What did Caliban do with it? Curse. A curse is a compressed prose, to

be hurled against one's enemy like a hand grenade. And language itself is the forged currency of communication. Beware of falling in love with the currency rather than the article of trade. There are things you must do but not give names. Name them, they die. That's what happened to Negritude. (11)

And he added,

Past conditions should not be congealed into a philosophy when conditions are changing rapidly. Unless one maintains the status quo in order to prove his point. To embrace Negritude is to shackle the mind, to be tethered to proved myths, religions and superstitions; it means to be inhibited and confined; it calls for respect for old useless ways, and that means fear. ("Negritude," 12)

Francophone Critics

Not all the attacks on Negritude came from English-speaking Africa. Just as some anglophone Africans supported Negritude, so there were French-speaking Africans who attacked it. Most of them were Senghor's own countrymen.

The first of these to question Negritude was, ironically, David Diop, considered by many to be one of the arch-poets of the movement. Diop, however, as early as 1956 realized the excesses to which literary Negritude could lead, and commented,

Originality at all costs is also a danger. In the pretext of being loyal to "Negritude," the African artist can let himself bloat his poems with terms borrowed from his mother tongue and to look systematically for a "typical" turn of phrase. Believing he is "reviving the great African myths" to the excessive beating of the tam-tam and tropical mysteries, he in effect gives back to the colonial bourgeoisie the reassuring image it wants to see. Which is the surest way to fabricate a "folklore" poetry by which the salons where one discusses "Negro art" will be amazed. ("Contribution," 115*)

Another Senegalese, Abdoulaye Sadji, writing in 1958, said,

Truth to say, there does not exist, to my knowledge, an authentic Negro-African culture characterized by modes of thought or proper expression among the diverse people that populate black Africa. Unless by "culture" we mean the ensemble of efforts to adapt to life that each of these peoples makes daily and has perhaps done so since the millennium to live and die without too much suffering. (71*)

Sembène Ousmane, also Senegalese, questioned Negritude at the 1963 Dakar conference, African Literature and the University Curriculum:

There was a time when *negritude* meant something positive. It was our breast plate against a culture that wanted at all costs to dominate us. But that is past history. In 1959 some of us who called ourselves writers, on the strength of having managed to get a book or a couple of short stories into print, were already opposing *negritude*. (56-57)

He added:

There are things that do truly characterise the black races, I agree, but no one has yet worked out exactly what they are, no really thorough study of *negritude* has ever been undertaken, because *negritude* neither feeds the hungry nor builds roads. (57)

At the same conference, another Senegalese writer, Cheikh Hamidou Kane, said of Negritude:

We must nevertheless give up trying to bring everything down to it, unless we wish to become completely hidebound. To act otherwise would itself, I think, be a new form of imperialism. Moreover, it would also be to split the solidarity that unites us with the rest of mankind. (Ousmane et al., 60)

Senegal was not the only bastion of anti-Negritude sentiment. It came from several other quarters as well. The Malagasay writer Jacques Rabemananjara questioned the racial aspect of Negritude with regard to literature, though not with regard to other areas. In his *Nationalisme et problèmes malgaches* (1959), he said, "The color of the skin will not, in any way, exercise the least mortgage on the birth or the value of a poetry. It is obvious that the conditions responsible for the new black poetry received nothing from the overly famous category of *negritude*" (108*).

Bachir Touré of the Ivory Coast asked in 1960 for an African theatre based on discipline rather that one relying solely on inspiration coming from one's race. Touré likened the study of acting to that of directing, saying of the African actor, "Many of my friends are too content to tell themselves they are born artists. A grand master once said, 'there is no great art without discipline and there is no discipline without sacrifice.' We must destroy the myth of the 'Negro-Artist' " ("Défense," 28*).

In 1966, Thomas Melone, although favorably disposed toward Negritude generally, was, like Mphahlele, aware of the contradictions that were apparent within the "African Personality": "The world dichotomy, or Manichaeism, between the criminal-white colonialist and the innocent-Negro colonized no longer allows a certain literary romanticism to survive in Africa. The Negro is not, of course, that innocent and pure; he can colonize his own people, exploit them, and fail to lead them to noble objectives" ("New Voices," 65). In that same year, Congo-Brazzaville poet Gerald-Felix Tchicaya U Tam'si was another doubter of sorts. In an interview with *Afrique*, he said,

Negritude is a matter of generation and also school. I am of another generation and another school, and I am a joker who can't resist the temptation to burst out laughing at each lesson someone wants to teach me. And besides, the world is too small for me to accept being cooped up in a ghetto. Give me space!'' ("Tchicaya U Tam'si,'' 43*)

Anti-Negritude as a Critical Standard

For the most part the above statements have been theoretical. The real test of a critical standard, however, is not whether it is expressed in theoretical terms but whether it is applied to specific literary works—whether in fact it is used in the literary judgment of *something*. And just as Negritude was applied as a positive standard in the early decades of African criticism, so was it also used negatively. Not very surprisingly, perhaps, Ezekiel Mphahlele was the most consistent and persistent critic to use Negritude to suggest that a literary work was bad—or not as good as another—or not as good as it might have been if it had not taken as its duty the expression of Negritude.

Mphahlele's first application of Negritude, or anti-Negritude, as a critical standard was apparently in 1961, in the pages of *Encounter*. He said of some of Senghor's poems,

> The original disciples of *negritude* must surely know that this pose or attitude they are striking flattens much of their verse by narrowing its boundaries and restricting its emotional range to what they think is ''proper'' or ''African'' to feel. Senghor's *Prayer to Masks* is another example of *negritude* verse that provides a narrow field of response and cannot (as I. A. Richards would say) stand ironic contemplation. Neither facile rejection nor facile acceptance makes good poetry.
>
> The imagery in his *New York* is most exciting at first reading, because its disparate elements of feeling provide a larger area of response than is found in the verse already referred to. ("The Cult,'' 50)

He added, ''And then you stop and think. You feel there is an ironic twist somewhere which escapes Senghor, and with which he would have been able to reinforce his image of New York if he were not preoccupied with waving a banner'' (51). He added commentary on two poems by Gabriel Okara: ''The mawkishness of his *negritude* poem, *You laughed and laughed and laughed*, is quite glaring'' (51), but he said, ''In contrast to this, Okara's poem, *Piano and Drums*, brings out a more convincing and meaningful image of the poet, and the true artist takes off where slogans and catchwords stop'' (51).

Mphahlele reiterated this comment on Okara in his *The African Image*, saying, ''The true poet in Okara appears not when he is asserting his negroness, which is only a fraction of his humanness, but when he exposes himself to disparate impacts, without trying to say which is the more or most valuable; as in his *Piano and Drums*" (195). Elsewhere in the book he had harsh words for William Conton's novel, *The African*, which he liked because it "is a beautifully written and highly polished book and it shows a keen sensitivity" (22), although he said it "is also a good example of how political slogans, if made a principle of art, can destroy the impact a work of art might have had" (22), and that "a number of experiences Mr. Conton's hero goes through in order to rediscover his Africa, to 'project the African Personality,' are contrived, and this is the stance that spoils the author's good writing" (23).

In a similar vein he said of a poem by Nigerian poet Mabel Segun,

There is venom enough in A SECOND OLYMPUS. . . . But it is in a public stance, and we do not know how the poet herself feels she has been violated. This is not necessarily a default: She can be part of the crowd. But it seems that two-dimensional protest seldom makes good poetry, i.e. the kind that seeks to evoke a single response to a single hurt. ("Preface," 12)

Elsewhere Mphahlele compared J. P. Clark's poem "The Year's First Rain" to Senghor's "Prayer to Masks" and said, "Clark's experience here is being given expression for what it is. It is self contained, and he mounts with the action of the rain, fusing its image with that of a pregnant mother. He never lets his subject diffuse its significance or dissipate itself. The emotion is compact," while in Senghor's poems he felt that

the individual is not important here, but the object of adoration as a broad symbol of what is often called "the African essence." At their worst, poets who write like this often remind me of Swinburne. An image is beautifully expressed, even powerfully, one suspects. And yet it is difficult to grasp its meaning because when one looks deeper into it, one realizes that the tangible experience wasn't there. ("African Literature," 227)

Other anglophone critics also applied the anti-Negritude standard. One was Eldred Jones, who said in a 1965 review of Chinua Achebe's *Arrow of God*, "His novel is a human novel. His success in bringing out the general humanity above the Africanness of his themes is what gives him a high place among African writers" ("Achebe's," 178). Jones also used the standard negatively when he said in his review of Christina Aidoo's play *Dilemma of a Ghost*, "The play has a hopeful end. Not the rather doubtful hope that black people, whatever their background, can always understand each other, but the more universal one that there is a common underlying essential humanity, which, given certain conditions can come to the surface" ("A Note," 38).

Soyinka's views on Negritude and narcissism came the next year. He disapproved of the inward-looking narcissist, seeing something akin to the search for innate Negritude:

> For, confounded by the hardened skin-patch on the navel, quite impenetrable, the poetic eye becomes glazed from hopeful concentration, turns its own mirror. From then on, all venturing ceases, only reiteration of totemic features, lineage by lineage, lineament for lineament, and a substitution of this for poetic vision. ("And After," 53)

More specificially, Soyinka said of Senghor's poem "Chaka,"

> To be a poet is presumably to be persuaded not only of the inexhaustible poetry of the self, but to presume the even more transcendentalist view that the poetic self is in itself inexhaustible. It would appear that Senghor's poetic mission is to exhaust both possibilities in the creation of a quasi-religious kingdom of black denomination. Not for him the world beneath the matter, the realities of the mystic kingdom in which other black writers are wont to explore lineaments of body or soul. He takes it instead to its furthest conceit, the pretense to activity within the existential kingdom of black poesy—the separation of action and sensitivity. This tendency remains a common inclination among the narcissistic writers, as if action is contradictory to poetry; but rarely is it made into such an overt declaration of faith as we find it in Senghor's *Chaka*. ("And After," 57-58)

Soyinka compared two other works as well. Speaking first of Camara Laye's *The Dark Child*, he said,

> Into this world the audience is seduced with patience, with no condenscension. The writer, the poet has not stopped to contemplate his own immersion; his wonder is gently felt, and the stranger is enchanted. Not so Okolo, the questing hero of Gabriel Okara's *The Voice*, whose self-conscious language is the device of the narcissist, a subterfuge within which the hero can contemplate his creator's navel while remaining himself impenetrable in the barrier of contrived language. . . . Okolo has lost himself in an animism of nothingness, the ultimate self-delusion of the narcissist. ("And After," 62)

Chinua Achebe was another to attack Negritude in its literary form, in particular when it was a response to white racism. Achebe said, "Black writers have used all kinds of arguments to reply to this racist clap trap. They have put forward counter-claims to an exclusive culture of black people—an essentially Negro, rhythmic, sensuous culture" ("The Black Writer's Burden," 136). He added, trenchantly,

If Equiano thought he was putting up a strong defence when he wrote that "we are almost a nation of dancers, musicians and poets," or Senghor when he wrote that ". . . we are men of the dance," the famous British explorer, R. F. Burton, had the perfect lion answer: "the removal of the Negro from Africa is like sending a boy to school; it is his only chance of learning that there is something more in life than drumming and dancing." (138)

CONCLUSION

The application of Negritude as a critical standard, then, whether positive or negative, was not as clear-cut as that of other standards, perhaps because of the difficulty of defining the concept. President Senghor was the only African to attempt a full-blown definition, and even his was elusive. However, it must be noted that whereas several francophone critics questioned the validity or usefulness of Negritude, I found no clear-cut example of a francophone critic's applying it negatively as a standard, which suggests a rather well-formed hegemony on that side of the language aisle. Perhaps all African literary criticism is an expression of Negritude—at least in the existential sense—as is perhaps all of African literature, and not just a part of it that is judged by someone, using some partially defined standard, to be more "negritudinal" than some other part. In this vein, it is perhaps fitting to close this chapter with a quotation from Ezekiel Mphahlele:

Only when people are involved in activities of self-expression can we begin to asses the Africanness in them or the lack of it—on the strength of what they actually produce . . . ("Chemchemi Creative Center," 117).

8 Conclusions

Modern African literature is a young literature. It began shortly after World War II, when the irony of being conscripted into the white man's armies to fight for the white man's liberation from a white oppressor was not lost on the Africans. It gave impetus to the drive for independence, which saw an independent Ghana by 1957 and culminated in the grand year of independence—1960—in which some seventeen former colonies became sovereign African nations. Like any young literature, it was concerned with problems of definition; and in the natural course of events, the burden of this definition fell on the shoulders of the critics—*African* critics, it should be emphasized—for the political and historical conditions from which modern African literature has emerged have been conditions largely caused and controlled by non-Africans.

Africans have had very little to say about the external control of their milieu since the late nineteenth century. But for independence, it is unlikely they would have had any more control over their literature, since Westerners have at times taken a proprietary attitude toward modern African culture. It was all the more important, then, that African critics take in hand this modern African culture and ask what it was and, more to the point, what it should be and what the critic's role should be in helping it to develop. This undertaking was difficult and complicated, fraught with traps of various kinds, but African critics accepted the task with pleasure.

In a sense, every literature is defined by its criticism. In the same sense, the process of definition is continual and never ending. Hence the early attempts to define African literature, at Makerere University in 1962 and again at the Université de Dakar and Fourah Bay College in Freetown in 1963, were no doubt premature. They were, however, valuable attempts to draw some basic ground rules. Was North Africa "African," for example? Was it possible that Sub-Saharan Africa had appropriated the term *African* in much the same fashion that the United States has appropriated the term *American*? Ezekiel Mphahlele thought that North Africa differed from that south of the Sahara by virtue of culture ("African Literature," 221). Such a division, however, seems to disenfranchise the several million Muslims, Negroid by race, living across West Africa from Senegal to the Sudan. And what of Janheinz Jahn's contention that style is the defining element of literature, who would therefore include all of the African diaspora in the Caribbean and South and North America? What also of the white South African writers? Was residence enough for membership? Did race exclude those in residence? What of Peter Abrahams, who had lived most of his adult life in London and Jamaica? If his novels were African because of their setting, then what of Joseph Conrad's *Heart of Darkness* and the "African" novels of Joyce Cary and Graham Greene? The problems were legion.

Christopher Okigbo felt in 1962 that the application of any defining factor other than geography was premature ("Transition Conference Questionnaire," 12). Perhaps Richard Rive was even closer to the truth when he said, following the Makerere conference in 1962, that "African literature" was "never defined because the answer *can* never be defined" ("No Common Factor," 55). Perhaps Cyprian Ekwensi's phrase, "writing which reveals the psychology of the African" ("Problems," 218), was the most acceptable because the defining element was as vague and indefinable as the thing it attempted to define.

American readers might best comprehend the complexity of such an undertaking if they set out to define "American literature." Would it include, as Ezekiel Mphahlele wondered, literature from Puerto Rico? the Somoan Islands? Would it include T. S. Eliot? Henry James? The "frenchmen" Stuart Merrill and Francis Viele-Griffin?

The shortcomings of the Creighton definition become clearer when it is rephrased to read "any work in which an [American] setting is authentically handled, or to which the experiences which originate in [America] are integral." Who is to say what is "authentically" American? The concept itself seems peculiarly un-American. Is Franz Kafka's *Amerika* a work of American literature? Who is to say it is not "authentic" simply because the author journeyed to that land only in his imagination?

And yet the urge toward self-definition proved inexorable for the African critics. In Chapter 2, "The Languages of African Literature," we saw that a few critics, led primarily by Obiajunwa Wali, contended that literatures are defined by the languages in which they are written—yet another attempt to define. A large number of critics disagreed. And while they tended almost unanimously to agree with Wali that it would be nice if African literature were written in African languages, the practical considerations of market and audience and the increased communication afforded within Africa made the choice of European languages a hard but inescapable reality.

Another group of critics insisted strongly that European languages could be used as media of expression for African literature, but only if the result were in some sense an "African English" or an "African French." Africans, they said, were not Europeans, nor need they speak European languages as if they were; English and French would be enriched by the fresh elements injected into them by Africans. Thus in this case "Africanness," whatever it was, came in part to define the literature through its effect on the European languages rather than being defined by them. It would not be difficult, for example, to define the "Africanness" of "African English," although the important point for the reader and critic of African literature is not to define it but to enjoy it. This is precisely what several African critics did, and it was an issue on which many expressed themselves. If the English, for example, was "African" enough, they appreciated it; if it was not, they did not. Hence, we may designate the "African" use of European languages as an important critical standard among African critics.

A further attempt at self-definition was seen in the critics cited in Chapter 3, "African Literature for Whom?" If African literature was written in European languages, it was directed largely at first toward a European audience. And if this was true, then the motivation for taking such a direction stemmed partially from a desire to explain oneself and, in explaining, to define. We saw the strong need felt by African critics to establish an African Presence in the world. There were personal, nationalistic reasons and historical reasons for wanting to do so. Reluctant as the West has been to admit it, the absence of African values from the world community has made world civilization in the twentieth century something less than universal—to use Senghor's term. Not only did the absence need to be redressed, but the West's militant and systematic exclusion of African values had to be recognized for what it was and be overcome.

This placed the African writer in a difficult—almost schizoid—position, for the African critic recognized, simultaneously, that no literature, if it was to have its own integrity, could design itself primarily as a response or reaction to another civilization, at least not for long—and hence the principle, widely held by critics and applied as a standard, that African literature needed to be written primarily for Africans, even though the dividends, material and psychological, of writing for non-Africans were also recognized. They did not hold that one had to write for Africans in a conscious manner but that one could *not* write consciously or primarily for Europeans. That this became a standard of criticism by which literary works were judged was a significant development because, as was the case with languages, the criticism was guided by external, extra-aesthetic factors. Just as the European languages were forced upon Africans, so were a European market and audience, not to mention the fact that the entire printing and publishing apparatus was also controlled by Westerners. This led the African critic to take refuge in an area unassailable by the West—Africanness. It was significant that this led to the sanctioning of an African audience, just as it led to a sanctioning of African forms of European languages.

There was a move toward the discovering and creating of an African literary tradition. *Discovery* is perhaps a term more appropriate in the African context than it is elsewhere in the world, for nowhere else in the world were the colonial powers of the nineteenth century quite so successful in eradicating indigenous cultures and values as they were in Africa. And although there was the feeling among many Africans that the contact with European culture was a very real and valid part of modern African culture, there was also the feeling that the "old" Africa must be rediscovered and made part of the "new." This was shown in Chapter 4, "The Making of a Literary Tradition," and it was apparent among those critics cited in the section on "The African Past" in Chapter 5. Critics, then, had to perform a balancing act in deciding how much validity to give the old, rediscovered traditions and how much to give the new traditions that had taken root in African soil as a result of the European domination of Africa.

More fundamental, however, was the African critics' determination to create their own literary tradition rather than allow it to be created by the indiscriminate and wholesale application of Western literary standards, aided and abetted by eager, however well-meaning, Western critics who would gladly explain to their African counterparts how to go about building a (albeit Western) literary tradition. Africans did not need this information, nor were they impressed by the general quality of the Western criticism of African literature. Their position in the face of this criticism was sensitive because, first, they were not so far removed in time to forget the colonial Africa in which they had been born and raised, and, second, they sensed an authoritarian tone in Western criticism that led them to suspect that many Western critics were looking upon African literature as the colonial administrators and so many missionaries had looked upon a "primitive" Africa in the early years of this century. That is, Western critics were approaching African literature as though from a position of authority and not, as should have been the case, as students of comparative literature. The Westerner's position was ambiguous perhaps because of the colonial hangovers that were dissipated less quickly in the arts than in politics. The fact that Africans wrote in Western languages and genres led some Westerners to argue that African literature in French and English were really sub-branches of French and English literatures. One wonders if such critics would approach Australian or Filipino literature in English with the same assuredness that they bring to the study of, say, Hemingway or Yeats. One wonders also if the Yeats scholar might not have some trepidation about making "authoritative" statements on, say, Alexander Pope or Jonathan Edwards. Clearly the study of any literature is to some extent comparative, and the further removed one is, in space and time, and culturally, from one's own milieu, the more one must carefully leaven one's aesthetic and intuitive responses with information of various kinds. To Africans it was apparent that many Westerners had not bothered to provide themselves with this information and had, in fact, operated on the assumption that their knowledge of French, British, and American literatures stood them in good stead to deal with African literature; there was, in effect, nothing in the literature of Africa that needed comparing with anything in their own. This position was unacceptable to African critics, who insisted that non-African critics, rather than bringing the French, British, and American elements to their reading of African literature, came rather to appreciate the African contributions to literature.

The Africans' task was complicated further by the fact that this "neo-African" culture (to use Jahn's phrase) had taken on non-African characteristics—non-African, that is, in relation to the "old" Africa—and that these "new" characteristics brought with them complicated ramifications. Primarily, the new art form was written; the old was oral. The functions of literature had also therefore changed. The old was informal, educational, often didactic, and a form of social, communal activity. The printed word is enjoyed, first, in the privacy of the mind and is only secondarily, if ever, shared with others. The printed word takes on a permanence that is more easily associated with the objet d'art. The reader is affected by the quality of paper, the quality of the print, the editing, not to mention the artistic form and content; whereas in the traditional context, the work itself may be remembered, but it is associated with a human being, the author or performer.

It was the absence of this human element that African critics had to reconcile in evaluating modern African literature. They were dealing with European art forms being handled in African ways by African authors, most of whom had had some contact with traditional African art forms. Not only had they had contact, but in some cases there were conscious attempts to graft the elements of the traditional African forms onto the European ones. Chinua Achebe's use of proverbs is but one example. The African critic had to judge not only what was grafted, but the grafting process as well. And although there was much discussion and little agreement on what constituted the African tradition, there was widespread agreement that it should be developed—preferably at the expense of any reliance upon Western tradition— and that African literature must both reflect and create its own tradition.

One cannot help but recall Ralph Waldo Emerson's words, "We have listened too long to the courtly muses of Europe," not to mention the whole American mid-nineteenth-century movement for an American literature in this respect. In fact, a comparison of the American and African declarations of literary independence would make an interesting study. In any case, the search for an African tradition was another attempt at self-definition, as a response to those who had discouraged any meaningful self-definition or self-realization.

Whereas tradition was a vague and complex matter for the critics, there was an everyday Africa that was readily accessible. Africans wanted to convey accurate information about Africa to the rest of the world in order to counter the partial or false information available to the non-African world. One function the African writer could undertake was to provide this sort of information.

There was, first, the argument over the best means by which to accomplish this goal. Was it realism? Or was it, as Senghor argued, that the African cosmology, being essentially surreal, could best be "realistically" presented in literature by way of surrealism? Beyond this, there was the question of accurate detail. If the "real" Africa had to be presented to the world, it had to be presented accurately. The near unanimity with which this position was taken by African critics placed a clear, if often limited, burden on the African writer. It meant that "realia" were to take precedence over imagination. Occasionally this led the writer into the trap of being too concerned with the realia, to the detriment of imagination. It led the writer at times to an excessive concern for anthropological or sociological detail.

These cases were significant because they represented one of the few points at which African literary criticism became noticeably concerned with aesthetic considerations over and above the extra-aesthetic factors, which generated such a large part of the early body of African literary criticism. This is not intended as a negative statement. Clearly the African situation in the world— the African experience—was and is like no other in the world today. There was no reason, therefore, to expect that Africa's literature should fall into any sort of Western mold; the same was equally true, if not more so, of its criticism. Africa has been determined and defined by others for a long time. It is not surprising to find its criticism first of all staking out its own territory, so to speak, and then defining—redefining—what had been defined by others. Certainly these were questions that took precedence over the fine aesthetic distinctions that have concerned both the West and East for some time and which led the West in the late nineteenth century to divorce art from everything around it and consider it entirely "for its own sake." The critical reaction to anthropological excesses, for example, suggests that African criticism might move more in aesthetic directions in the future, once the questions of definition are solved or have been accepted as being unsolvable. For the two decades following World War II, however, African criticism insisted in several ways that the literature be very clearly linked to the problems and realities of the world from which it grew.

One of these present realities concerned the past. What was the African past, and what should be its relationship to the present? In a sense, this question—asked though it was by many Africans—was a product of the West. In Africa the distinctions of past, present, and future are not as neat or as fundamental as they are in the West. Nowhere was this expressed better than in Birago Diop's poem, "Souffles," in the lines "Ceux qui sont mort ne sont jamais partis" ["those who have died have never parted"*] and "Les morts ne sont pas morts" ["the dead are not dead"*] (*Leurres et lueurs*, 64-66).

More compelling, perhaps, was the concern with the details of the past. What were they? Could, in fact, modern Africa in general, and African literature in particular, proceed with the creation of the present and future without knowing what they had been in the past? Here again was the crisis of self-identity—the double desire to create the new and discover the old, or, to use Sartrean terms, to create existence and discover essence. If African literary criticism concentrated more on the latter, it may be said that this was because essence—evanescent at best, in the most stable of conditions—in the case of Africa had been aggressively questioned, if not obliterated, by outside, non-African forces. Hence there was a greater urgency to recover it, leading naturally to the attempt to define Negritude and to other self-defining interests.

Two general tendencies of the criticism were indicated in Chapter 6, "African Literature, *Litterature engagée*," and Chapter 7, "Negritude and the Critics." The proclaiming of, as well as the search for, Negritude or the "African personality," was manifested in areas other than literature. It is not surprising, then, to find Negritude not so much manifested in literary works or criticism (for the manifestation of it is always open to interpretation) but to find it being searched for. As Ezekiel Mphahlele said, Negritude can never be "found" in any profound sense; it can only be searched for—continually. This search was conducted vigorously. Whether and to what extent Negritude was manifest in African literature can probably never be decided to everyone's satisfaction, but there can be little doubt that the search for it was indeed undertaken. It was a search primarily for essence, although the search itself was the existential half of Negritude.

Chapter 6 indicated the clearest expression of another general trend of the criticism. In insisting that African literature be *engagée*—tied very closely to the social, economic, political, and cultural problems of contemporary Africa—and that it attempt to contribute solutions to these problems, African criticism quite naturally emphasized the real over the imaginary and content over form.

To some extent, formal considerations may be seen in the advocating of Africanized styles of English and French; in the calling for a style tailored in such a way as to indicate the primacy of an African over a European audience; in encouraging the use of formal elements of the oral tradition whenever possible; as well as discouraging any wholesale acceptance of European literary traditions. Those critics encouraging Negritude might also be said to be more oriented toward form that content. Senghor himself discussed the concept in terms such as *rhythm, image* and *un style nègre* but very seldom, if ever, in terms of content: "What makes a poem's Negritude is less the theme than the style, the emotional warmth that gives life to words, that transmutes the word into verb" ("David Diop," 173*). The rudiments for a more aesthetic, more formal criticism were present, if somewhat latent, in early African criticism.

The other tendency in the criticism, however, the tendency toward a concern for the real Africa, its real problems and situation—over and above questions of how to re-create these realities in artistic forms—seems by comparison much more explicit and much more insistent. In Chapters 5 and 6 content was far more important than form, as it was in the section on "The African Presence" in Chapter 3. Further, there was a militancy in this criticism that, one senses, caused it to carry the day. The impact of Alexandre Biyidi's reviews of Camara Laye's first two novels alone cannot be discounted. The reviews themselves, of the earliest modern African novels in French, coupled with their being accepted for publication by one of the leading journals concerned with African culture, which was also and significantly a publisher, was no doubt a combination of facts not easily lost on an aspiring young African writer. There was no similar militancy in the opposite direction, toward more formal, more aesthetic considerations.

This overriding concern with extra-aesthetic considerations is perhaps, for the Westerner, the single most troublesome aspect of early African literary criticism. It is the point at which the mainstreams of African and Western criticism diverge most sharply. The divergence results from two important factors prevalent not only in the thinking of Africa's literary critics but in many aspects and levels of African life: the need for self-definition, stemming from the attempted obliteration of African culture and from the advent of self-determination; and the imminence of political questions prior to independence, coupled with the residual questions of Western economic and cultural dominance following independence. The divergence may stem also from a third factor: the fact that traditional African culture is inherently *engagée* in a way Western culture is not. It is communal and essentially social; while it is very appreciative of artistic beauty, it rarely creates beauty for its own sake.

It was not the purpose of this study to determine which—if any—of these factors was primarily responsible for the *engagement* in African literature and criticism; the purpose was to point out that *engagement* became a robust critical standard. It may be argued that this tendency was related to the relative infancy of African literature and that it was a natural enough part of the birth trauma of a new literature. The reader need only recall the self-defining crucible from which an American literature eventually emerged. Bernard Fonlon, in fact, drew a similar parallel between the beginnings of African literature and the Irish renaissance (*La Poésie*). It is possible that literatures undergo a form of evolutionary development, that they tend to move in similar directions, though at various times, and that African literature and criticism will develop in a direction that will make them resemble their Western counterparts more; and, further, that it is only a matter of time until Africans become more concerned with aesthetic considerations than they have been in the past. This is an interesting theory and one that ought to be kept in mind as African literature continues to grow. Much may be learned from the observation of a young literature, and it is not often that the world can bear witness to the beginnings of a new literature. African literature should be studied by Westerners if for no other reason than this.

The expounding of such a theory, however, has not been the purpose of this study, though the findings of this study might contribute to such an investigation. The purpose here has been to indicate how African criticism developed in the first two decades following World War II. Its implied purpose has also been to underscore the fact that any literature—certainly any new literature—requires a criticism furnished by its own critics, that is, by critics coming from the same milieu as the writers. Whatever others may think of this literature is secondary to the precept that every literature must have its own criticism. This is not to accept, incidentally, Joseph Okpaku's statement that "the Western critic's only valid job is to interpret African literature and the other arts to Western audiences. Except in a very unusual case, his views will at best be only 'interesting' to the African reader" ("Culture," 3-4). I prefer the position of the Senegalese critic Edris Makward:

> Though the resentment of several young African critics about the present situation of Modern African Literature, where paradoxically, the European critic remains so influential, is quite understandable, we cannot deny that the non-African critic's contribution may often be as invaluable—and even more so—to the African reader as the critical works on say, French literature by English, American, German critics, have been to native French readers themselves, and vice versa. For native readers often learn new truths about their own literature by seeing it sensitively assessed from the strong foothold of a different tradition. ("Is There," 10)

The difference in these two positions is primarily one of emphasis. Makward's position has the added merit, however, of mentioning explicitly the unique kind of contribution that can result from a comparative study of literature. This is the crux of the discussions that have taken place between African and Western critics: the Africans insist, pretty much unanimously, that Westerners approach African literature with the perspective of the "comparatist"; that they approach African literature with a sense of the distance between their own Western background and the object of their study—with all the humility and scholarly acumen they would bring to, say, Russian or Chinese literature. The Africans are asking only that theirs be treated as a literature among other literatures and not as a colonial domain. This is not to say that Westerners cannot contribute to the criticism of African literature; it is to say that the Africans will accept or reject Westerners' contributions on the basis of their experience; it is to say that it will be of interest, to Westerners and Africans alike, because it is *not* African, but that, being non-African, it must inevitably be offered—and accepted or rejected—in this light. It is to say that *for the Westerner the only valid approach to African literature is through the discipline of comparative literature.* Anything less is subject to the pitfalls of ethnocentrism.

Whether African and Western standards are similar is only part of the larger conflict often arising between African and Western critics. A more fundamental fact is that African critical standards, whether resembling Western standards or not, will be arrived at by and through the African critics themselves. Possibly Western critics have had and will have an influence on what standards are chosen by African critics; after all, many of the African critics have attended Western universities for varying lengths of time, with varying results. However, the influence the West will have on these Africans is a matter entirely in their hands. The influence, while it may be conscious or unconscious, cannot take on any validity unless or until it becomes manifest, explicitly or implicitly, in the critical behavior of the Africans. That manifestation is the point on which this study has attempted to focus.

As for the more concrete conclusions of this study, it may be said that at least six critical standards ran through, with varying degrees of unanimity, the body of African literary criticism between 1947 and 1966:

1. That, ideally, African writers would employ African languages as their literary media; failing this, for various practical reasons, it was both acceptable and desirable that they "do violence" to the standard forms of European languages as they were spoken in their motherlands in order to reflect the African world more accurately.

2. That African literature, while performing an important function in projecting an African presence heretofore lacking or distorted in the world, had nevertheless to be written primarily for an African audience and could not appear to be written primarily for a non-African audience.

3. That African writers needed to show discretion in their borrowings from Western literary traditions while reflecting, where possible, the form and content of the—primarily oral—African traditions.

4. That African literature could not falsify African realia, whether the writer chose realism or surrealism or some other literary technique to portray these realia, but that the information provided by these realia had to be transformed into art and not be presented simply for anthropological or sociological interest.

5. That African literature be *engagée*, addressing the problems facing Africa, and that it eschew the principle of art for art's sake.

6. That African literature be somehow African, whether one labeled this Africanness as Negritude or as something else, and without being African at the expense of being art.

Aside from attempting to arrive at the major trends of African literary criticism in its first two decades, it is hoped that a contribution has been made by suggesting that trends of literary criticism are validated as much or more through applied criticism as they are through theoretical statements and that, if anything, applied statements are the more revealing of the two types because of their essential concreteness. We can in fact learn much from criticism by studying it empirically, in its applied form.

It may be argued that the findings of this study produce no great surprises; that, in fact, one knew all these things already. I can only counter by saying that if these things were known, they were known intuitively, and that in documenting these intuitions I have given them added weight; second, and more important, the writer might ask that, if these things were already known, why has there been a long and sometimes acrimonious history of the question, "By what standards should African literature be judged?" My conclusion is that this question has continued to arise, be bandied about by Africans and Westerners separately and in concert, only to be abandoned and raised again, because it is the wrong question. The more proper question, or questions, are (1) "By what standards do (not *should*; the distinction is crucial) Africans judge African literature?" (2) "By what standards do Westerners judge African literature?" and (3) "How do these sets of standards agree and how do they differ—and why?"

The difficulty inherent in the question that is usually raised is twofold. First, there is the assumption that there is only one set of standards by which to judge this literature and, second, that this one set of standards should be used. The first assumption ignores distinctions between individual literatures and their incumbent bodies of criticism; the second assumption treats criticism as though it were essential rather than existential and that criticism can therefore be legislated. I reject both these assumptions, the first because, as Joseph Okpaku put it, "critical standards derive from aesthetics. Aesthetics are culture dependent. Therefore critical standards must derive from culture" ("Culture," 1). From this we may conclude that if cultures vary, then aesthetics and critical standards may also (although not necessarily in every case) vary. The second assumption—that criticism can be legislated—is no more acceptable than the proposition that literature can be legislated by criticism. Neither critical nor literary methods can be forced on anyone short of some form of police action by the state, such as the policy of social realism under which Soviet writers and critics have labored in varying degrees since 1917.

We have then been asking the wrong question. There are three questions, not one. This study has attempted to answer the first of these: "By which standards did Africans judge African literature during the two decades following World War II?" I feel strongly that Western critics must accept the sovereignty of the African critics and of the critical standards they choose to use. On the other hand, African critics must accept the sovereignty of the answers to the second question: "By what standards do Westerners judge African literature?" The Africans cannot expect Westerners to judge African literature by African standards, *even if they know them*. Westerners may or may not be well informed of the African context of the literature and therefore more or less able to interpret what happens in the literature, but they are capable of judging the literature only according to their own standards, which, again, to recall Okpaku's claim, derive from their own culture. Granting even that Western critics might be able to modify their own standards to some extent (keeping in mind also that these standards may be, but need not be, distinguishable in each and every case from those of their African counterparts), it is doubtful that their aesthetics could ever become more African than Western, or vice-versa. Africans can easily dismiss Western criticism based on misinformation and misconception. What they must be willing to recognize—if not accept—is Western criticism based on aesthetic precepts they do not share. When, for example, Westerners complain of the degree of *engagement* that the Africans require, the Africans must simply accept this as a cultural difference that no amount of debate is likely to resolve. When they distinguish carefully between these two types of Western criticism and recognize the sovereignty of the latter, and when the Westerners will do the same, then the answers to the third question—"How do these sets of standards agree and how do they differ, and why?"—will be well within our grasp.

Our grasp has been strengthened considerably by the criticism of the two decades since 1966. It has reiterated many of the same values that emerged in the earlier two decades, while the emphases have shifted. New names have appeared, new issues have arisen, writer-critic Wole Soyinka has won the Nobel Prize for literature, and thus African literature and criticism have in some way, through Soyinka's individual recognition, attained formal international acclaim for their contributions to what Leopold Sedar Senghor would no doubt fondly call the "Civilization of the Universal."

Since 1966, however, the volume of African literary criticism has increased many times over. A study of the nature and quality of this later criticism will require a work much more ambitious in its parameters than this one, but it is hoped that some worthwhile groundwork has here been laid and that the understanding of African literary criticism in its early years has been furthered.

Bibliography

CREATIVE WORKS

Abrahams, Peter. *Une Couronne pour Udomo*. Trans. Pierre Singer. Paris: Stock, 1958.

_____. *Mine Boy*. London: Crisp, 1946; London: Heinemann, 1963.

_____. *Path of Thunder*. New York: Harper & Bros., 1948.

_____. *Tell Freedom*. London: Faber & Faber; New York: Knopf, 1954.

Abruquah, Joseph Wilfred. *The Catechist*. London: Allen and Unwin, 1966.

Achebe, Chinua. *Arrow of God*. London: Heinemann, 1964.

_____. *A Man of the People*. New York: John Day, 1966.

_____. *No Longer at Ease*. London: Heinemann, 1960.

_____. *Things Fall Apart*. London: Heinemann, 1958.

Ademola, Francis, ed. *Reflections: Nigerian Prose and Verse*. Lagos: African Universities Press, 1962.

Aidoo, Christina. *The Dilemma of a Ghost*. Acrra, Ikeja: Longmans, 1965.

Aluko, Timothy Mofolorunso. *One Man, One Matchet*. London: Heinemann, 1964.

_____. *One Man, One Wife*. Lagos: Nigerian Printing & Pub. Co., 1959.

Amado, Jorge. *Gabriela, Clove and Cinnamon*. Trans. James L. Taylor and William L. Grossman. New York: Knopf, 1962.

Andrezejewski, B. W., and I. M. Lewis, eds. *Somali Poetry: An Introduction*. Oxford: Clarendon Press, 1964.

Badian, Seydou. *Sous l'orage*. Paris: Présence africaine, 1963.

Beti, Mongo. *Mission terminée*. Paris: Correa, 1957.

_____. *Mission to Kala*. Trans. Peter Green. London: Muller, 1958.

_____. *Le Pauvre Christ de Bomba*. Paris: Laffont, 1956.

Bhely-Quenum, Olympe. *Un Piège sans fin*. Paris: Stock, 1960.

Bolamba, Antoine-Roger. *Esanzo; chants pour mon pays*. Paris: Présence africaine, 1955.

Boto, Eza [Mongo Beti]. *Ville cruelle*. Paris: Présence africaine, 1971.

Cissé, Emile. *Faralako; roman d'un petit village africain*. Rennes: Imprimerie commerciale, 1958.

Clark, John Pepper. *A Reed in the Tide*. London: Longmans, 1966.

Conton, William. *The African*. London: Heinemann, 1960.

Cook, David, ed. *Origin East Africa: A Makerere Anthology*. London: Heinemann, 1965.

Dadié, Bernard. *Climbié*. Paris: Seghers, 1956.

———. *Légendes africaines*. Paris: Seghers, 1954.

———. *Un Nègre à Paris*. Paris: Présence africaine, 1959.

———. *Patron de New York*. Paris: Présence africaine, 1964.

Diakhaté, Lamine. *La Joie d'un continent*. Alès: Imprimerie de Pab, 1954.

Diop, Birago. *Les Contes d'Amadou Koumba*. Paris: Présence africaine, 1961.

———. *Contes et lavanes*. Paris: Présence africaine, 1963.

———. *Leurres et lueurs*. Paris: Présence africaine, 1960.

———. *Les Nouveaux contes d'Amadou Koumba*. Paris: Présence africaine, 1958.

Easmon, R. Sarif. *The New Patriots*. London: Longmans, 1965.

Ekwensi, Cyprian. *Burning Grass*. London: Heinemann, 1962.

———. *The Drummer Boy*. London: Cambridge University Press, 1960.

———. *Jagua Nana*. London: Hutchinson, 1961.

———. *The Passport of Mallam Ilia*. London: Cambridge University Press, 1960.

———. *People of the City*. London: Dakers, 1954.

Fall, Malick. *Reliefs*. Paris: Présence africaine, 1964.

Hazoumé, Paul. *Doguicimi*. Paris: Larose, 1938.

Henshaw, James Ene. *This Is Our Chance*. London: University of London Press, 1956.

Hughes, Langston, ed. *Poems from Black Africa*. Bloomington: Indiana University Press, 1963.

Ike, Chukwuemeka. *Toads for Supper*. London: Harvill, 1965.

Ikelle-Matiba, Jean. *Cette Afrique-là*. Paris: Présence africaine, 1963.

Jabavu, Noni. *Drawn in Colour; African Contrasts*. London: John Murray, 1960; New York: St. Martins, 1962.

Joachim, Paulin. *Un Nègre raconte*. Paris: Imprimerie des poètes, 1954.

Jordan, A. C. *IngQumbo yemiNyanya*. Lovedale: Lovedale Press, 1940.

Kagamé, Abbé Alexis. *La Divine pastorale*. 2 vols. Bruxelles: Editions du Marais, 1952-1955.

Kane, Cheikh Hamidou. *L'Aventure Ambiguë*. Paris: Julliard, 1961.

Komey, Ellis Ayitey, and Ezekiel Mphahlele, eds. *Modern African Stories*. London: Faber & Faber, 1964.

Ladipo, Duro. "Oba Koso." In *Three Yoruba Plays*. English adaptation by Ulli Beier. Ibadan: Mbari, 1964.

La Guma, Alex. *A Walk in the Night*. Ibadan: Mbari, 1962.

Laye, Camara. *The Dark Child*. Trans. James Kirkup, Ernest Jones, and Elaine Gottlieb. London: Collins, 1955.

———. *Dramouss*. Paris: Plon, 1966.

———. *L'Enfant noir*. Paris: Plon, 1953.

———. *Le Regard du roi*. Paris: Plon, 1954.

Lomami-Tshibamba, Paul. *Ngando*. Bruxelles: Deny, 1948.

Matip, Benjamin. *Afrique, nous t'ignorons*. Paris: Lacoste, 1956.

Maunick, Edouard. *Les Manèges de la mer*. Paris: Présence africaine, 1964.

Millin, Sarah Gertrude. *God's Stepchildren*. Johannesburg: Central News Agency, 1924.

Modisane, Bloke. *Blame Me on History*. London: Thames & Hudson, 1963.

Mofolo, Thomas. *Chaka*. Morija: Morija Sesuto Book Depot, 1925.

Moore, Gerald, and Ulli Beier, eds. *Modern Poetry from Africa*. Harmondsworth, Middlesex: Penguin, 1963.

Mopeli-Paulus, A. S., with Peter Lanham. *Blanket Boy's Moon*. London: Collins, 1953.

Morris, Henry F. *The Heroic Recitations of the Bahima of Ankole*. Oxford: Clarendon Press, 1964.

Mphahlele, Ezekiel. *Down Second Avenue*. London: Faber & Faber, 1965.

Munonye, John. *The Only Son*. London: Heinemann, 1966.

Mushiete, Paul, ed. *La Littérature française africaine*. Leverville: Bibliothèque de l'étoile, 1957.

Mutswairo, Solomon Matsva. *Feso*. Cape Town: Oxford University Press and Southern Rhodesia Literature Bureau, 1956.

Ndao, Cheik A. *L'Exil d'Albouri suivi de La Décision*. Paris: Pierre Jean Oswald, 1967.

N'Dsitouna, Francis. *Fleurs de latérite*. Monte Carlo: Regain, 1954.

Ngugi, James [Ngugi wa Thiong'o]. *The Black Hermit*. London: Heinemann, 1968.

_____. *The River Between*. London: Heinemann, 1965.

_____. *Weep Not, Child*. London: Heinemann, 1964.

Niang, Lamine. *Négristique*. Paris: Présence africaine, 1968.

Nokan, Charles. *Le Soleil noir point*. Paris: Présence africaine, 1962.

"Nouvelle somme de poésie du monde noir." *Présence africaine* 57 (1966).

Nwankwo, Nkem. *Danda*. London: Deutsch, 1964.

Nwanodi, Glory O. *Icheke and Other Poems*. Ibadan: Mbari, 1964.

Nzekwu, Onuora. *Blade among the Boys*. London: Heinemann, 1962.

_____. *Wand of Noble Wood*. London: Hutchinson, 1961.

Okara, Gabriel. *The Voice*. London: Deutsch, 1964.

Okigbo, Christopher. "Heavensgate," "Limits," and "Lament of the Silent Sisters." In his *Labyrinths with Path of Thunder*. New York: Africana Pub. Co., 1971.

Ousmane, Sembène. *Le Docker noir*. Paris: Debresse, 1956.

_____. *Les Bouts de bois de dieu*. Paris: Le Livre contemporain, 1960.

_____. *L'Harmattan*. Paris: Présence africaine, 1964.

Oyono, Ferdinand. *Houseboy*. Trans. John Reed. London: Heinemann, 1966.

_____. *Une Vie de boy*. Paris: Julliard, 1956.

_____. *Le Vieux nègre et la médaille*. Paris: Julliard, 1956.

Peters, Lenrie. *The Second Round*. London: Heinemann, 1965.

Plaatje, Solomon Tshekisho. *Mhudi*. Lovedale: Lovedale Press, 1930.

Quenum, Maximilien. *Au Pays des Fons*. Paris: Larose, 1938.

Rabearivelo, Jean-Joseph. *Poèmes; Presques Songes; Traduit de la nuit*. New ed. Tananarive: Les Amis de Rabearivelo, 1960.

_____. *Vielles chansons des pays d'Imerina*. Tananarive: Imprimerie officielle, 1937 [?], 1939 [?].

Rive, Richard. *Emergency*. London: Faber & Faber, 1964.

Sadji, Abdoulaye. *Maïmouna*. Paris: Présence africaine, 1958.

_____. *Nini*. Paris: Présence africaine, 1958.

_____. *Tounka*. Paris: Présence africaine, 1965.

Sainville, Leonard, ed. *Anthologie de la littérature négro-africaine: romanciers et conteurs*. Paris: Présence africaine, 1963.

Sellassie, Sahle. *Shinega's Village*. Trans. Wolf Leslau. Berkeley and Los Angeles: University of California Press, 1964.

Senghor, Léopold Sédar, ed. *Anthologie de la nouvelle poésie nègre et malgache d'expression française*. Paris: Presses universitaires de France, 1948.

_____. *Chants d'ombre*. Paris: Editions du Seuil, 1945.

_____. *Ethiopiques*. Paris: Editions du Seuil, 1956.

_____. *Nocturnes*. Paris: Editions du Seuil, 1961.

Sinda, Martial. *Premier chant du départ*. Paris: Seghers, 1955.

Soyinka, Wole. *A Dance of the Forests*. London: Oxford University Press, 1963.

_____. *The Lion and the Jewel*. London: Oxford University Press, 1963.

_____. *The Road*. London: Oxford University Press, 1965.

_____. "The Strong Breed." In *Three Short Plays*. London: Oxford University Press, 1969.

_____. "The Swamp Dwellers." In *Three Short Plays*. London: Oxford University Press, 1969.

_____. "The Trials of Brother Jero." In *Three Short Plays*. London: Oxford University Press, 1969.

Syad, William J. F. *Khamsine*. Paris: Présence africaine, 1959.

Tchicaya U Tam'si, Gérald-Félix. *Epitome. Les Mots de têtes pour la sommaire d'une passion*. Tunis: Société nationale d'éditions et de diffusion, 1962.

Tutuola, Amos. *Feather Woman of the Jungle*. London: Faber & Faber, 1962.

_____. *My Life in the Bush of Ghosts*. London: Faber & Faber; New York: Grove, 1954.

_____. *The Palm-Wine Drinkard and His Dead Palm-Wine Tapster in the Dead's Town*. London: Faber & Faber, 1952; New York: Grove, 1953.

Viderot, Toussaint. *Pour toi, Nègre, mon frère . . . "Un homme comme les autres."* Monte Carlo: Regain, 1960.

Vilakazi, Benedict Wallet. *Inkondlo kaZulu*. Johannesburg: Witwatersrand University Press, 1935.

Whiteley, W. H., comp. *A Selection of African Prose*. 2 vols. Oxford: Clarendon Press, 1964.

CRITICAL WORKS

A. B. [Alexandre Biyidi, Mongo Beti]. "Afrique noire, littérature rose." *Présence Africaine* n.s. 1-2 (1955): 133-40.

_____. "L'Enfant noir." *Présence africaine* 16 (1954): 419-20.

_____. "*Le Regard du roi* par Camara Laye." *Présence africaine* n.s. 1-2 (1955): 142-45.

A.R.B. [Antoine-Roger Bolamba]. "Birago Diop." *La Voix du congolais* 115 (1955): 818-20.

_____. "Poésie bantoue." *La Voix du congolais* 95 (1954): 204-7.

_____. "Le Poète martyr." *La Voix du congolais* 102 (1954): 689-91.

Abasiekong, Daniel. "Poetry Pure and Applied: Rabearivelo and Brutus." *Transition* 23 (1965): 45-48.

Abbia. "Note de la rédaction." *Abbia* 2 (1963): 101.

Abraham, W. E. *The Mind of Africa*. Chicago: University of Chicago Press, 1962.

Abrahams, Cecil. "Schweitzerism: The African Writer and the Western Critic." In *Language and Literature in Multicultural Contexts*, 1-10. Ed. Satendra Nandan. Suva, Fiji: University of the South Pacific, 1983.

Abrahams, Peter. "African Writers' Part in the Battle against Racial Prejudice: The Long View." *African World* (June 1952): 11-12.

_____. "Challenge to African Writers." Letter. *West African Review* 23 (1952): 387.

_____. "The Conflict of Culture in Africa." *International Affairs* 30 (1954): 304-12.

_____. "A Literary Pioneer." Review of *People of the City* by Cyprian Ekwensi. *West Africa*, October 16, 1954: 975.

Achebe, Chinua. "The Black Writer's Burden." *Présence africaine* 59 (Eng. ed. vol. 31) (1966): 135-40.

_____. "English and the African Writer." *Transition* 18 (1965): 27-30.

_____. Foreword to *A Selection of African Prose*, vii-x. Vol. 1. Comp. W. H. Whiteley. Oxford: Clarendon Press, 1964.

_____. *Morning Yet on Creation Day*. Garden City, N.Y.: Anchor Press, Doubleday, 1975.

_____. "The Novelist as Teacher." *New Statesman*, January 29, 1965: 161-62.

_____. "The Role of the Writer in a New Nation." *Nigeria Magazine* 81 (1964): 157-60.

_____. "Where Angels Fear to Tread." *Nigeria Magazine* 75 (1962): 61-62.

Adelugba, Dapo. "Nationalism and the Awakening National Theatre of Nigera." M.A. thesis, University of California at Los Angeles, 1964.

"The African Literary Scene." *AMSAC Newsletter* 5, no. 5 (January 1963): 2-3.

Agovi, J. K. "Towards a Formulation of Critical Standards for Modern African Literature." *Universitas* (Legon, Ghana) 3, no. 3 (1974): 128-33.

Aidoo, Christina. "New Directions?" Review of *Seven African Writers* by Gerald Moore. *Transition* 10 (1963): 45-46.

Aig-Imoukhuede, Mabel. Review of *The Drummer Boy* and *The Passport of Mallam Ilia* by Cyprian Ekwensi. *Nigeria Magazine* 68 (1961): 88-89.

Aire, Victor O. "African Literature and the Problem of Evaluation." *West African Journal of Modern Languages* 2 (1976): 35-44.

Akande, Kunle. "Cultural Colonialism." Letter. *West Africa*, September 14, 1963: 1038.

"Akanji." *Black Orpheus* 4 (1958): 63.

Akaraogun, Olu. "Wole Soyinka." *Spear* (Lagos) (May 1966): 15-19, 42.

Akinjogbin, I. Adeagbo. Letter. *West Africa*, June 5, 1954: 513.

Aluko, Timothy Mofolorunso. "Case for Fiction." *West African Review* 20 (1949): 1237, 1239.

Amadi-Tshiwala, Regina. "Critical Bearings in African Literature." *Présence africaine* 115 (1980): 148-55.

Anozie, Sunday O. "Negritude, Structuralism, Deconstruction." In *Black Literature and Literary Theory*, 105-25. Ed. Henry Louis Gates, Jr. New York: Methuen, 1984.

_____. "The Theme of Alienation and Commitment in Okara's 'The Voice.' " *Bulletin of the Association for African Literature in English* (Freetown) 3 (1965): 54-67.

Appiah, Anthony. "Strictures on Structures: The Prospects for a Structuralist Poetics of African Fiction." In *Black Literature and Literary Theory*, 127-50. Ed. Henry Louis Gates, Jr. New York: Methuen, 1984.

Armstrong, Robert P. "African Literature and European Critics." Paper presented at African Studies Association meeting, Chicago, 1964.

Atangana, G. Towo. "De l'Avenir des langues africaines." *Tam-Tam* 1-2 (1963): 19-22.

Attwell, David. "The British Legacy in Anglophone African Literary Criticism." *English in Africa* 11, no. 1 (1973): 79-106.

Awoonor-Williams, George. "Modern African Literature." *Eastern Horizon* 3, no. 8 (1964): 5-10.

Bâ, Sylvia Washington. *The Concept of Negritude in the Poetry of Leopold Sedar Senghor.* Princeton: Princeton University Press, 1973.

Bailly, Sery Z. "A Propos de la revalorisation de la forme chez les critiques africains." *Revue de littérature et d'esthétique négro-africaines* 3 (1981): 71-78.

Bal, Mustapha. "L'Homme noir dans la poésie." *La Pensée* 103 (1962): 18-29.

Belinga, M. S. Eno. "La Culture négro-africaine." *Démocratie nouvelle* 7-8 (1966): 73-88.

Beti, Mongo. *See* A. B.

Beuchat, P.-D. *Do the Bantu Have a Literature?* Johannesburg: Institute for the Study of Man in Africa, 1963.

Bhely-Quenum, Olympe. "A Paris l'ensemble national dahoméen a remporté un triomphe." *La Vie africaine* 27 (1962): 36-37.

_____. "*Dramouss* par Camara Laye." *L'Afrique actuelle* 12 (1966): 49-50.

_____. " 'Epitome' de Tchicaya U Tam'si." *La Vie africaine* 35 (1963): 42.

_____. " 'L'Harmattan' par Sembène Ousmane." *La Vie africaine* 49 (1964): 40.

_____. "Jacques Rabemananjara." *La Vie africaine* 51 (1964): 51.

_____. " 'Les Manèges de la mer' par Edouard J. Maunick." *La Vie africaine* 51 (1964): 51.

_____. "Sous l'orage—par Seydou Badian." *La Vie africaine* 40 (1963): 36.

_____. "Une Interview du Président Senghor." *L'Afrique actuelle* 10 (1966): 28-31.

Birame, Samba. "Sur le théâtre africain." *Présence africaine* 14 (1952): 304-6.

Bishop, Rand. "African Critics and the Western Literary Tradition." *Ba Shiru* 8, no. 1 (1977): 65-75.

_____. "African Literature for Whom: The Janus-like Function of African Literary Criticism." *Présence africaine* 101-2 (1977): 57-80.

_____. "A Bibliography of African Literary Criticism, 1947-1966." *Africana Library Journal* 4, no. 2 (1973): 2-31.

_____. "On Identifying a Standard of African Literary Criticism: Characterization in the Novel." In *New African Literature and the Arts,* 199-223. Ed. Joseph Okpaku. Vol. 3. New York: Third Press, 1973.

Biyidi, Alexandre. *See* A. B.

Blair, Dorothy. "African Literature in University Education." In *African Literature and the Universities*, 74-79. Ed. Gerald Moore. Ibadan: Ibadan University Press, 1965.

Bodunrin, A. "The First Festival of Negro Arts: A Preview." *African Statesman* 1, no. 2 (1966): 27, 29.

———. Review of *The Mind of Africa* by W. E. Abraham. *African Statesman* 1, no. 3 (1966): 45-47.

Bodurin, A. "What Is African Literature?" *African Statesman* 1, no. 1 (1965): 33-42.

Bognini, Joseph Miezan. Review of *Un Nègre à Paris* by Bernard Dadié. *Présence africaine* 36 (Eng. ed. vol. 8) (1961): 156-57.

Bohannon, Paul. "Artist and Critic in an African Society." In *The Artist in Tribal Society*, 85-94. Ed. Marian W. Smith. Glencoe, Ill.: Free Press, 1961.

Bolamba, Antoine-Roger. *See* A.R.B. and A. R. Bolamba.

Bolamba, A[ntoine]. R[oger]. "Flavien Ranaivo." *La Voix du congolais* 119 (1956): 118-19.

———. "Poésie négro-africaine." *Jeune Afrique* (Elisabethville) 20 (1953): 8-15.

———. "Poésie négro-africaine et poètes noirs d'expression française." *La Voix du congolais* 86 (1953): 300-19.

Bolarin-Williams, Adebayo. "Marxian Epistemology and the Criticism of African Literature." *Ufahamu* 13, no. 1 (1983): 84-104.

Bulane, Mofolo. "Cameroon! Cameroon!" Review of *Houseboy* by Ferdinand Oyono, trans. John Reed. *New African* 5, no. 10 (1966): 216-17.

———. "Raymond Mazisi Kunene: The New Voice in African Poetry." *New African* 5, no. 5 (1966): 111-12.

Chakaipa, Patrick F. "Vernacular Literature Now and in the Future." In *African Literature in Rhodesia*, 49-52. Ed. E. W. Krog. Gwelo, Rhodesia: Mambo Press, 1966.

Chima, Alex. "Culture and Politics in Africa." *Africa and the World* 2, no. 22 (1966): 29-31.

Chinweizu. "African Literary Criticism Today." *Okike* 9 (1975): 89-105.

———, Onwuchekwa Jemie, and Ihechukwu Madubuike. *Toward the Decolonization of African Literature*. Washington, D.C.: Howard University Press, 1983.

Christie, Phillipa. "Technique in the Writing of Poetry." In *African Literature in Rhodesia*, 70-78. Ed. E. W. Krog. Gwelo, Rhodesia: Mambo Press, 1966.

"Christopher Okigbo Interviewed by Robert Serumaga on His Recent Visit to London." *Cultural Events in Africa* 8 (1965): i-iv.

Clark, John Pepper. "Aspects of Nigerian Drama." *Nigeria Magazine* 89 (1966): 118-26.

———. "A Note on Nigerian Poetry." *Présence africaine* 58 (Eng. ed. vol. 30) (1966): 55-64.

———. "Our Literary Critics." *Nigeria Magazine* 74 (1962): 79-82.

———. "A Personal Note." In his *A Reed in the Tide*. London: Longmans, 1965. vii-viii.

———. "Poetry in Africa Today." *Transition* 18 (1965): 20-26.

———. "Poetry of the Urhobo Dance Udje." *Nigeria Magazine* 87 (1965): 282-87.

Collins, Harold. "Is the Criticism of African Literature Culture-bound?" *Compass* (Kutztown, Pa.) 5-6 (1974): 7-16.

Conde, Maryse. "The Impasse of African Criticism." In *Le Critique africain et son peuple comme producteur de civilisation*, 417-26. Paris: Présence africaine, 1977.

_____. "Non-spécificité de la critique littéraire 'africaine.' " *African Perspectives* (Leiden) 1 (1977): 35-41.

"Conférence de Tachkent (1er au 7 octobre 1958): Appel des écrivains des pays d'Asie et d'Afrique aux écrivains du monde entier." *Présence africaine* 22 (1958): 135-37.

Cordwell, Justine M. "Some Aesthetic Aspects of Yoruba and Benin Cultures." Ph.D. diss., Northwestern University, 1952.

Creighton, T.R.M. "An Attempt to Define African Literature." In *African Literature and the Universities*, 84-88. Ed. Gerald Moore. Ibadan: Ibadan University Press, 1965.

Cudjoe, Selwyn R. "Criticism and the Neo-African Writer." *Black World* 21, no. 2 (1971): 36-48.

Dabo, S. K. "African Literature and the African Critic." In *Le Critique africain et son peuple comme producteur de civilisation*, 352-82. Paris: Présence africaine, 1977.

Dadié, Bernard Binlin. "Folklore and Literature: Part I." *AMSAC Newsletter* (April 1963): 4-6; "Part II" (June 1963): 3-5.

_____. "Le Fond importe plus." *Présence africaine* n.s. 6 (1956): 116-18.

D'Cruz, Valerie. Review of *The Only Son* by John Munonye. *Nexus* 1, no. 1 (1966?): 43-45.

"Débats, 1er Congrès international des écrivains et artistes noirs." *Présence africaine* n.s. 8-9-10 (1956): 66-83.

Dei-Anang, Michael. "La Culture africaine comme base d'une manière d'écriture originale." *Présence africaine* n.s. 27-28 (1959): 5-10.

_____. *Ghana Resurgent.* Accra: Waterville, 1964.

_____. "Introduction: Poetry in Africa." In his *Africa Speaks*, ix-xii. Accra: Guinea Press, 1960.

_____. "A Writer's Outlook." *Okyeame* 1, no. 1 (1961): 40-43.

_____, and Yaw Warren. "Authors' Note." In their *Ghana Glory*. London: Nelson, 1965.

Diagne, Pathé. "La Critique littéraire africaine." In *Le Critique africain et son peuple comme producteur de civilisation*, 429-40. Paris: Présence africaine, 1977.

Diakhaté, Lamine. "Contribution sénégalaise à la défense et à l'illustration de la négritude." *La Revue française* 145 (1962): 58-60.

_____. Review of *Le Docker noir* by Sembène Ousmane. *Présence africaine* n.s. 13 (1957): 153-54.

Diop, Alioune. "Niam n'goura or *Présence africaine's* raison d'être." Trans. Richard Wright and Thomas Diop. Editorial. *Présence africaine* 1 (1947): 185-92.

_____. "Political and Cultural Solidarity in Africa." *Présence africaine* 41 (Eng. ed. vol. 13) (1962): 65-71.

_____. "Préface." In Bernard Dadié, *Légendes africaines*, 7-8. Paris: Seghers, 1954.

_____. "Remarks on African Personality and Negritude." In *Pan-Africanism Reconsidered*, 337-45. Ed. American Society of African Culture. Berkeley: University of California Press, 1962.

_____. "Le Sens de ce congrès." *Présence africaine* 24-25 (1959): 40-48.

_____. "The Spirit of 'Presence Africaine.' " Trans. C. L. Patterson. In *Proceedings of the First International Congress of Africanists*, 46-51. Eds. Lalage Bown and Michael Crowder. London: Longmans, 1964.

Diop, Cheikh Anta. *The Cultural Unity of Negro Africa*. Paris: Présence africaine, 1962.

_____. "Quand pourra-t-on parler d'une renaissance africaine?" *Le Musée vivant* (numéro special) (November 1948): 57-65.

Diop, David [Mandessi]. "Contribution au débat sur la poésie nationale." *Présence africaine* n.s. 6 (1956): 113-15.

_____. "Poètes africains." Reviews of *Esanzo; chants pour mon pays* by A. R. Bolamba, *Fleurs de latérite* by Francis N'Dsitouna, *Un Nègre raconte* by K. Paulin Joachim, and *Premier chant du départ* by Martial Sinda. *Présence africaine* n.s. 3 (1955): 79-80.

_____. Reviews of *Climbié* by Bernard Dadié, and *Afrique, nous t'ignorons* by Benjamin Matip. *Présence africaine* n.s. 13 (1957): 152-3.

_____. Review of *Mission terminée* by Mongo Beti. *Présence africaine* n.s. 16 (1957): 186-87.

_____. Reviews of *Une Vie de Boy* and *Le Vieux nègre et la médaille* by Ferdinand Oyono and *Le Pauvre Christ de Bomba* by Mongo Beti. *Présence africaine* n.s. 11 (December 1956-January 1957): 125-27.

Diop, Papa. "La Critique littéraire négro-africaine d'expression française: Situation et perspectives." *L'Afrique littéraire* 63-64 (1982): 9-23.

Diop, Thomas. "Le Mouvement de la négritude." *Documents pour l'action* 2, no. 9 (1962): 130-36.

Dipoko, Mbella Sonne. Review of *Seven African Writers* by Gerald Moore. *Africa Report* 8, no. 2 (1963): 30-31.

_____. Review of *Feather Woman of the Jungle* by Amos Tutuola. *Présence africaine* 44 (Eng. ed. vol. 16) (1962): 230.

"Discour du Président Senghor." *L'Afrique actuelle* 9 (1966): 20-21.

"A Discussion Between James Ngugi, Author of 'The River Between' (Heinemann), Who Is Studying at Leeds University, John Nagenda, a Writer from Uganda Who Has Just Spent Some Time in the United States of America and Is Now on His Way Back to Uganda, and Robert Serumaga from Uganda Who Is Studying at Trinity College, Dublin." *Cultural Events in Africa* 15 (1966): i-iii.

Dogbeh, Richard. "A Propos de l'article d'Ezekiel Mphahlele." Reply to letter by Mphahlele. *La Vie africaine* 14 (1961): 31.

Dogbeh, Yves-Emmanuel. "Critique littéraire et tendances critiques des littératures africaines." *L'Afrique littéraire et artistique* 50 (1978): 15-20.

Dramé, Kandioura. "French Criticism of African Literature: On the Present State." In *African Literature Studies: The Present State/L'Etat présent*, 275-83. Ed. Stephen H. Arnold. Washington, D.C.: Three Continents, 1985.

Dzeagu, S. A. "The Criticism of Modern African Literature." *Universitas* (Legon, Ghana) 3, no. 3 (1974): 134-40. Also in *Bulletin of the Association of African Universities* 1, no. 2 (1974): 91-96.

Echeruo, Michael J. C. "Incidental Fiction in Nigeria." *African Writer* 1, no. 1 (1962): 10-11, 18.

_____. "Traditional and Borrowed Elements in Nigerian Poetry." *Nigeria Magazine* 89 (1966): 142-55.

Egejuru, Phanuel Akubueze. *Towards African Literary Independence: A Dialogue with Contemporary African Writers*. Contributions in Afro-American and African Studies 53. Westport, Conn.: Greenwood Press, 1980.

Egudu, Romanus Nnagbo. "Criticism of Modern African Literature: The Question of Evaluation." *World Literature Written in English* 21, no. 1 (1982): 54-67.

―――. "The Matter and Manner of Modern West African Poetry in English: A Study of Okigbo, Clark, Awoonor-Williams and Peters." Ph.D. diss., Michigan State University, 1966.

Ekpenyong, J. O. "The Use of English in Nigeria." *In Commonwealth Literature: Unity and Diversity in a Common Culture*, 144-50. Ed. John Press. London: Heinemann, 1965.

Ekwensi, Cyprian. "African Literature." *Nigeria Magazine* 83 (1964): 294-99.

―――. "Challenge to West African Writers." *West African Review* 23 (1952): 255, 259.

―――. "The Dilemma of the African Writer." *West African Review* 27 (1956): 701-704, 708.

―――. Letter. *West African Review* 23 (1952): 607.

―――. "Literary Influences on a Young Nigerian." *Times Literary Supplement*, June 4, 1964: 475-76.

―――. "Outlook for African Writers." *West African Review* 21 (1950): 19.

―――. "Problems of Nigerian Writers." *Nigeria Magazine* 78 (1963): 217-19.

―――. "A Yoruba Fantasy." Review of *The Palm-Wine Drinkard* by Amos Tutuola. *West African Review* 23 (1952): 713, 715.

Emenyonu, Ernest. "African Literature Revisited: A Search for Critical Standards." *Revue de littérature comparée* 48 (1974): 387-97.

―――. "African Literature: What Does It Take to Be Its Critic?" *African Literature Today* 5 (1972): 1-11.

Ene, J. Chunwike. " 'No Longer at Ease' by Chinua Achebe." *Ibadan* 11 (1961): 43.

"Entretien." Interview with Bertene Juminer and Joseph Miezan Bognini. *Afrique* 2 (1961): 57.

"Entretien avec Camara Laye." *Afrique* 26 (1963): 54-57.

"Entretien avec Chinua Achebe." *Afrique* 27 (1963): 41-42.

"Entretien avec le Docteur S.W.H. Davidson Nicol, ou l'homme comblé de talents." *Afrique* 32 (1964): 46-50.

"Entretien avec Ezekiel Mphahlele." *Afrique* 17 (1962): 56-59.

Eze, Mark N. Review of *Reflections: Nigerian Prose and Verse*, ed. Frances Ademola. *Central African Examiner* 7, no. 8 (1964): 14.

Fall, Mahanta. "Sens et portée de la poésie africaine d'expression française." In *Actes du colloque sur la littérature africaine d'expression française, Dakar, 26-29 mars 1963*, 211-18. Université de Dakar, Publications de la Faculté des Lettres et Sciences Humaines, Langues et Littératures 14. Dakar: Université de Dakar, 1965.

Fayolle, Roger. "Quelle critique africaine?" *Présence africaine* 123 (1982): 103-10.

"Final Resolutions. 1er Congrès international des écrivains et artistes noirs." *Présence africaine* n.s. 8-9-10 (1956): 363-64.

Fonlon, Bernard. "African Writers Meet in Uganda." *Abbia* 1 (1963): 39-53.

―――. "La Poésie et le reveil de l'homme noir." Ph.D. diss., National University of Ireland, 1960.

―――. "A Word of Introduction." *Abbia* 14-15 (1966): 5-13.

―――, and Peter Ogbonnaya. Review of *Things Fall Apart* by Chinua Achebe. *Présence africaine* 23 (December 1958-January 1959): 135-38.

Garrot, Daniel. *Léopold Sédar Senghor; critique littéraire.* Dakar: Nouvelles éditions africaines, 1978.

Gates, Henry Louis, Jr. "Criticism in the Jungle." In *Black Literature and Literary Theory*, 1-24. Ed. Henry Louis Gates, Jr. New York: Methuen, 1984.

"General Discussion on Publishing African Literature." In *African Literature and the Universities*, 130-32. Ed. Gerald Moore. Ibadan: Ibadan University Press, 1965.

Graft, Joe de. Review of *The Catechist* by J. W. Abruquah. *Okyeame* 3, no. 1 (1966): 63-64.

Green, Robert. "African Literary Criticism: The Banality of Cannibalism." *Journal of Commonwealth Literature* 19, no. 1 (1984): 52-63.

_____. "Under the Mango Tree: Criticism of African Literature." *Journal of the New African Literature and the Arts* 3 (1967): 25-30.

Gudijiga, Christophe. "Quatre thèmes dans l'oeuvre de Camara Laye." *Congo-Afrique* 6, no. 3 (1966): 139-48.

Healy, Jack. "The Louvre, the Musée de l'Homme and the Criticism of African Literature." *ACLALS Bulletin* 5, no. 3 (1980): 13-25.

Hossman, Irmelin. "Bernard Dadié ou l'écrivain engagé." Interview. *Afrique* 43 (1965): 59-61.

Hutchinson, Alfred. "Quality and Less." Reviews of *One Man, One Matchet* by T. M. Aluko and *The Second Round* by Lenrie Peters. *New African* 4, no. 5 (1965): 114.

Ijomah, Chuma P. "La Littérature africaine: Renouveau romanesque et critique littéraire." *Présence francophone* 16 (1978): 11-18.

Ikiddeh, Ime. "Writers and Values: Aesthetic and Ethical Questions in the Criticism of African Literature." In *Le Critique africain et son peuple comme producteurs de civilisation.* 80-94. Paris. Présence africaine, 1977.

Ilboudo, Gilbert. "Modern Literature in French-Speaking Africa." Trans. Madeleine Hurel and Henri Evans. *Ibadan* 19 (1964): 28-31.

Irele, Abiola. *The African Experience in Literature and Ideology.* London: Heinemann, 1981.

_____. "Black Orpheus: A Journal of African and Afro-American Literature." *Journal of Modern African Studies* 3 (1965): 151-54.

_____. "A Defence of Negritude." *Transition* 13 (1964): 9-11.

_____. "Negritude or Black Cultural Nationalism." *Journal of Modern African Studies* 3 (1965): 321-48.

_____. "Negritude—Literature and Ideology." *Journal of Modern African Studies* 3 (1965): 499-526.

_____. Review of *The African Image* by Ezekiel Mphahlele. *Présence africaine* 44 (Eng. ed. vol. 16) (1962): 231-34.

_____. Reviews of *Arrow of God* by Chinua Achebe and *Weep Not, Child* by James Ngugi. *Présence africaine* 52 (Eng. ed. vol. 24) (1964): 234-37.

_____. Reviews of *Poems from Black Africa*, ed. Langston Hughes, and *Modern Poetry from Africa*, eds. Gerald Moore and Ulli Beier. *Présence africaine* 49 (Eng. ed. vol. 21) (1964): 275-78.

_____. Reviews of *A Selection of African Prose*, 2 vols., comp. W. H. Whiteley; *The Heroic Recitations of the Bahima of Ankole*, ed. Henry F. Morris; and *Somali Poetry* by B. W. Andrezejewski and I. M. Lewis. *Journal of Modern African Studies* 2 (1964): 464-68.

Iyasere, Solomon Ogbede. "Art, a Simulacrum of Reality—Problems in the Criticism of African Literature." *Journal of Modern African Studies* 11 (1973): 447-55.

_____. "African Critics on African Literature: A Study in Misplaced Hostility." *African Literature Today* 7 (1975): 20-27.

_____. "Cultural Formalism and the Criticism of Modern African Literature." *Journal of Modern African Studies* 14 (1976): 322-30.

Izevbaye, D. S. "Criticism and Literature in Africa." In *Perspectives on African Literature*, 25-30. Ed. Christopher Heywood. New York: Africana Publishing Corp., 1971.

_____. "Phrase and Paraphrase: Problems and Principles in African Criticism." *African Perspectives* (Leiden) 1 (1977): 25-34.

_____. "The State of Criticism in African Literature." *African Literature Today* 7 (1975): 1-19.

Jabavu, Davidson Den Tengo. *The Influence of English on Bantu Literature.* Lovedale: Lovedale Press, 1948.

Jabavu, Nontando. "Life in Nigeria." Review of *One Man, One Wife* by T. M. Aluko. *West Africa*, May 2, 1959: 421.

Jahn, Janheinz. Introduction to *A Bibliography of Neo-African Literature from Africa, America and the Caribbean.* Dusseldorf-Koln: Verlag; London: Deutsch, 1965.

_____, and Claus Peter Dressler. *Bibliography of Creative African Writing.* Nendeln: Kraus-Thomson, 1971.

"James Ngugi Interviewed by Fellow Students at Leeds University: Alan Marcuson, Mike Gonzalez, and Dave Williams." *Cultural Events in Africa* 31 (1967): i-v.

Joachim, Paulin. *See also* P. J.

_____. "Anthologie des romanciers et conteurs négro-africains par Leonard Sainville." *Bingo* 130 (1963): 61.

_____. "L'Aventure ambiguë par Kane Cheikh Hamidou." *Bingo* 103 (1961): 21, 75.

_____. "Contemporary African Poetry and Prose. 3. French-Speaking Africa's Poètes-Militants." In *A Handbook of African Affairs*, 296-300. Ed. Helen Kitchen. New York: Praeger, 1964.

_____. "Contes et Lavanes par Birago Diop." *Bingo* 125 (1963): 51.

_____. "Dramouss par Camara Laye." *Bingo* 166 (1966): 54-55.

_____. "L'Ecueil à éviter." Editorial. *Bingo* 105 (1961): 7.

_____. "En Décembre 1965 les artes nègres seront au rendez-vous de Dakar." *Bingo* 143 (1964): 22-24.

_____. "Les Lettres africaines sont bien parties: Sembène Ousmane." *Bingo* 161 (1966): 47.

_____. "Les Lettres camerounaises à l'honneur: Jean Ikelle-Matiba, 3e lauréat du prix de l'afrique noire d'expression française." Review of *Cette Afrique-là* by Jean Ikelle-Matiba. *Bingo* 127 (1963): 39.

_____. "Un Livre de Bernard Dadié." Review of *Patron de New York. Bingo* 142 (1964): 45.

_____. " 'Nocturnes' de Léopold Sédar Senghor (Des joyaux lumineux qui éclairent les voies royales de la négritude)." *Bingo* 105 (1961): 25.

_____. "Nouvelle somme de poésie du monde noir." Review of *Présence africaine* 57 (1966). *Bingo* 165 (1966): 61.

———. "Le Soleil noir point par Charles Nokan." *Bingo* 123 (1963): 58-59.

———. "Sous l'orage par Seydou Badian." *Bingo* 126 (1963): 47.

———. "Trois livres d'Abdoulaye Sadji." Reviews of *Maïmouna, Nini,* and *Tounka* by Abdoulaye Sadji. *Bingo* 153 (1965): 39.

———. "Un Piège sans fin par Olympe Bhely-Quenum, romancier dahoméen." *Bingo* 96 (1961): 41.

Johnson, Babasola. "The Books of Amos Tutuola." Letter. *West Africa*, April 10, 1954: 322.

Jolaoso, Mabel. Review of *My Life in the Bush of Ghosts* by Amos Tutuola. *Odu* 1 (1955): 42-43.

Jones, Eldred. "Achebe's Third Novel." Review of *Arrow of God* by Chinua Achebe. *Journal of Commonwealth Literature* 1 (1965): 176-78.

———. "Language and Theme in 'Things Fall Apart.' " *Review of English Literature* 5, no. 4 (1964): 39-43.

———. "Nationalism and the Writer." In *Commonwealth Literature: Unity and Diversity in a Common Culture*, 151-56. Ed. John Press. London: Heinemann, 1965.

———. "A Note on the Lagos Production of Christiana [*sic*] Aidoo's *Dilemma of a Ghost*." *Bulletin of the Association for African Literature in English* 2 (1965): 37-38.

———. "The Potentialities of Krio as a Literary Language." *Sierra Leone Studies* n.s. 9 (1957): 40-48.

———. "The Role of the African Critic." In *Le Critique africain et son peuple comme producteur de civilisation*, 189-96. Paris: Présence africaine, 1977.

———. "Turning Back the Pages III: Amos Tutuola—The Palm Wine Drinkard: Fourteen Years On." *Bulletin of the Association for African Literature in English* 4 (1966): 24-30.

Jones-Quartey, K.A.B. " 'The New Patriots.' " Review of "The New Patriots" by R. Sarif Easmon. *Legon Observer* 1, no. 9 (1966): 17-18.

———. "Our Language and Literature Problem." *Africana* (Newcastle) 1, no. 3 (1949): 23-24.

Joppa, Francis Anani. *L'Engagement des écrivains africains noir de langue française: Du témoignage au dépassement*. Etudes 35. Sherbrooke: Naaman, 1982.

Jordan, A. C. *Towards an African Literature: The Emergence of Literary Form in Xhosa*. Berkeley: University of California Press, 1973.

Kahari, G. "Oral and Written Literature in Shona: Contrasts and Continuities." In *African Languages in the Schools*, 97-102. Ed. G. Fortune. Salisbury: Department of African Languages, University College of Rhodesia and Nyasaland, 1964.

Kane, Mohamadou. "On the Criticism of Modern African Literature." In *Le Critique africain et son peuple comme producteur de civilisation*, 257-75. Paris: Présence africaine, 1977.

———. "The African Writer and His Public." *Présence africaine* 58 (Eng. ed. vol. 30) (1966): 10-32.

Karanja, J. "The Flies in Our Literary Soup." *Busara* 8, no. 1 (1976): 33-38.

Kesteloot, Lilyan. *See also* Lagneau-Kesteloot.

———. "Esthétique africaine et critique littéraire." In *Colloque sur littérature et esthétique négro-africaine*, 303-9. Dakar: Nouvelles éditions africaines, 1979.

Kgositsile, K. William. "Negritude: Stance or Ideology?" *Liberator* 6, no. 10 (1966): 8-9.

Killam, G. D. "Contexts of African Criticism." In *Neo-African Literature and Culture: Essays in Memory of Janheinz Jahn*, 296-310. Mainzer Afrika-Studien 1. Weisbaden: Heymann, 1976.

Kironde, Erisa. Review of *The African* by William Conton. *Black Orpheus* 10 (1963): 67-68.

Kisob, J. A. "A Live Language: Pidgin English." *Abbia* 1 (1963): 25-31.

Ki-Zerbo, Joseph. "The Crisis of African Culture." *WAY Forum* 26 (1957): 10-13.

Klima, Vladimir. "The Present-Day Criticism of African Writing." *Archiv Orientalni* 51, no. 2 (1983): 109-15.

Komey, Ellis Ayitey, and Ezekiel Mphahlele. Introduction to *Modern African Stories*, 9-12. Eds. Ellis Ayitey Komey and Ezekiel Mphahlele. London: Faber & Faber, 1964.

Koudou, Aiko. "Critique des littératures négro-africaines: A quel saint se vouer." *Revue de littérature & d'esthétique négro-africaines* 5 (1984): 5-14.

Kronenfeld, J. Z. "The 'Communalistic' African and the 'Individualistic' Westerner: Some Comments on Misleading Generalizations in Western Criticism of Soyinka and Achebe." *Research in African Literatures* 6, no. 2 (1975): 199-225.

Kwapong, A. A. "African Viewpoints." Review of *People of the City* by Cyprian Ekwensi. *Universitas* 1, no. 5 (1955): 24-5.

Lagneau-Kesteloot, Lilyan. *See also* Kesteloot.

————. "Problems of the Literary Critic in Africa." Trans. Kamala-Veloso. *Abbia* 8 (1965): 29-44.

Laye, Camara. "The Black Lion." In *African Literature and the Universities*, 124-29. Ed. Gerald Moore. Ibadan: Ibadan University Press, 1965.

————. "The Soul of Africa in Guinea." In *African Literature and the Universities*, 64-73. Ed. Gerald Moore. Ibadan: Ibadan University Press, 1965.

"Lecture by Thomas Melone of the Cameroon: 'African Literature of French Expression.' " *AMSAC Newsletter* 4, no. 2 (October 1963): 3-6.

Leshoai, Bob. "Theatre and the Common Man in Africa." *Transition* 19 (1965): 44-47.

Lindfors, Bernth. "The Blind Men and the Elephant." *African Literature Today* 7 (1975): 53-64.

Liyong, Taban Lo. "Can We Correct Literary Barrenness in East Africa?" *East Africa Journal* (December 1965): 5-13.

————. *The Last Word: Cultural Synthesism*. Nairobi: East Africa Publishing House, 1969.

————. "Negritude: Crying over Spilt Milk." *East Africa Journal* (November 1966): 7-14.

————. Reviews of *Weep Not, Child* by James Ngugi and *Origin East Africa*, ed. David Cook. *Africa Report* 10, no. 11 (1965): 42-44.

McDowell, Robert. "The Criticism of African Literatures." *Africa Today* 18, no. 3 (1971): 92-100.

Maduakor, Obiajuru. "Soyinka as Literary Critic." *Research in African Literatures* 17, no. 1 (1986): 1-38.

Makouta M'Boukou, J.-P. "Tâtonnements de la critique des littératures africaines." *L'Afrique littéraire et artistique* 50 (1978): 7-14.

Makward, Edris. "Is There an African Approach to African Literature?" Paper presented at the eleventh annual meeting, African Studies Association, Los Angeles, 1968.

———. "Negritude and the New African Novel in French." *Ibadan* 22 (1966): 37-45.

Mariko, N'Tji Idriss. "Le Critique africain et son peuple comme producteur de civilisation." In *Le Critique africain et son peuple comme producteur de civilisation*, 166-86. Paris: Présence Africaine, 1977.

Mateso, Locha. "Critique littéraire moderne en Afrique." *Zaïre-Afrique* 94 (1975): 233-45; 95 (1975): 293-307.

Mativo, Kyalo. "Criteria for the Criticism of African Literature." *Ufahamu* 13, no. 1 (1983): 65-83.

Maximin, Daniel. "Critique de l'activité critique dans le Tiers-Monde noir." In *Le Critique africain et son peuple comme producteur de civilisation*, 314-37. Paris: Présence africaine, 1977.

Mbete, Woodroffe. "Non-European Writers." *Trek* 10, no. 15 (1946): 14.

Mbiti, John S. "Reclaiming the Vernacular Literature of the Akamba Tribe." *Présence africaine* 24-25 (1959): 244-61.

Melone, Thomas. "La Critique littéraire et les problèmes du langage: Point de vue d'un Africain." *Présence africaine* 73 (1970): 3-19.

———. *De la Négritude dans la littérature négro-africaine.* Paris: Présence africaine, 1962.

———. "New Voices of African Poetry in French." *African Forum* 1, no. 4 (1966): 65-74.

———. "The Theme of Negritude and Its Literary Problems." *Présence africaine* 48 (Eng. ed. vol. 20) (1963): 166-81.

Mercier, R., and M. and S. Battestini. *Olympe Bhely-Quenum.* Paris: Nathan, 1964.

Midiohouan, Guy Ossito. "Littérature négro-africaine: Une critique de la critique." *Peuples noirs—peuples africains* 18 (1980): 75-88.

Modisane, Bloke. "Literary Scramble for Africa." *West Africa*, June 30, 1962: 716.

Moore, Gerald. "The Black Hermit." Letter. *Transition* 3, no. 8 (1963): 34.

———. *Seven African Writers.* London: Oxford University Press, 1962.

Mortty, G. Adali. Review of *Things Fall Apart* by Chinua Achebe. *Black Orpheus* 6 (1959): 48-50.

Mouralis, Bernard. "La Littérature négro-africaine: Quelle critique pour quelle littérature?" In *Interdisciplinary Dimensions of African Literature*, 27-34. Eds. Kofi Anyidoho, Daniel Racine and Janice Spleth. African Literature Association Annuals 8. Washington, D.C.: Three Continents, 1985.

Mphahlele, Ezekiel. *See also* Zeke Mphahlele.

———. "The African Critic Today: Toward a Definition." In *Criticism of African, Caribbean, and Black American Literature*, 13-19. Africana Studies and Research Center Monograph Series 4. Ed. Houston A. Baker, Jr. Ithaca: Cornell University Africana Studies and Research Center, 1976.

———. "African Culture Trends." In *African Independence*, 109-39. Ed. Peter Judd. New York: Dell, 1963.

———. *The African Image.* New York: Praeger, 1962.

———. "African Literature." In *The Proceedings of the First International Congress of Africanists*, 220-32. Eds. Lalage Bown and Michael Crowder. London: Longmans, 1964.

_____. "African Literature for Beginners." *Africa Today* 14, no. 1 (1966): 25-31.

_____. ". . . Away into Ancestral Fields?" *Fighting Talk* 14, no. 1 (1960): 11-12.

_____. "Black and White." *New Statesman*, September 10, 1960: 342-43, 346.

_____. "Chemchemi Creative Centre, Nairobi." *Journal of Modern African Studies* 3 (1965): 115-17.

_____. "Chemchemi: Rediscovery of the African Culture." *Africa and the World* 1, no. 2 (1964): 41-2.

_____. "Comments." In *Pan-Africanism Reconsidered*, 346-49. Ed. American Society of African Culture. Berkeley: University of California Press, 1962.

_____. "Critic's Time for the Novel." In *Conference of African Writers of English Expression*. [Paris]: [Congress for Cultural Freedom], [1962].

_____. "The Cult of Negritude." *Encounter* 16, no. 3 (1961): 50-52.

_____. "Ghana: On the Culture Front." *Fighting Talk* 16, no. 8 (October 1962): 12-13.

_____. "The Fabric of African Cultures." *Foreign Affairs* 42 (1964): 614-27.

_____. *A Guide to Creative Writing*. Nairobi: East African Literature Bureau, 1966.

_____. "The Importance of Being Black." *New Leader* 43, no. 41 (October 24, 1960): 10-11.

_____. "The Language of African Literature." Discussion paper, Conference on African Literature and the University Curriculum, Fourah Bay College, Freetown, Sierra Leone, April 3-8, 1963.

_____. "The Language of African Literature." In *Language and Learning*, 266-74. Eds. Janet A. Ewig et al. New York: Harcourt, Brace & World, 1964.

_____. Letter. *Transition* 3, no. 11 (1963): 7-9.

_____. "The Makerere Writers' Conference." *Africa Report* 7, no. 7 (1962): 7-8.

_____. "Out of Africa: A Negro Writer's Reply." *Encounter* 79 (1960): 61-63.

_____. "Postscript on Dakar." In *African Literature and the Universities*, 80-82. Ed. Gerald Moore. Ibadan: Ibadan University Press, 1965.

_____. Preface to *Reflections: Nigerian Prose and Verse*, 9-13. Ed. Frances Ademola. Lagos: African Universities Press, 1962.

_____. "A Reply." In *African Literature and the Universities*, 22-26. Ed. Gerald Moore. Ibadan: Ibadan University Press, 1965.

_____. *Voices in the Whirlwind and Other Essays*. New York: Hill and Wang, 1969.

_____. "What the South African Negro Reads and Writes." *Présence africaine* n.s. 16 (1957): 171-76.

Mphahlele, Ezekiel, Gerald Moore, Okot p'Bitek, and Rajat Neogy. "The Literary Drought: A Roundtable Discussion." *East Africa Journal* (March 1966): 11-15.

Mphahlele, Zeke. "Writers of Africa." *Fighting Talk* 16, no. 7 (1962): 12-13.

Mpondo, Simon. "Provisional Notes on Literature and Criticism in Africa." *Présence africaine* 78 (1971): 118-42.

Mukrane, Hadj El. Review of *Une Couronne pour Udomo* by Peter Abrahams, trans. Pierre Singer. *Présence africaine* 18-19 (1958): 238-39.

Munonye, John. "Book Business in Nigeria: Writing." *Nigerian Libraries* 2, no. 2 (1966): 77-79.

Mushiete, Paul. Introduction to *La Littérature française africaine*, 3-5. Ed. Paul Mushiete. Leverville: Bibliothèque de l'étoile, 1957.

_____. "La Littérature congolaise." *Flambeau* 43, nos. 3-4 (1960): 161-80.

_____, ed. *La Littérature française africaine.* Leverville: Bibliothèque de l'étoile, 1957.

_____. "Notes sur la littérature congolaise." *La Revue nouvelle* 25, no. 6 (June 15, 1957): 608-20.

Mveng, Engelbert. "Signification du premier Festival Mondial des Arts Nègres." *Abbia* 12-13 (1966): 7-11.

Nagenda, John. Review of *Weep Not, Child* by James Ngugi. *Makerere Journal* 10 (1964): 69-71.

Nata, Theophile. "Réflexion critique sur la littérature et la critique négro-africaines." In *Le Critique africain et son peuple comme producteur de civilisation,* 481-92. Paris: Présence africaine, 1977.

National Educational Television. "The African Writer in Search of His Audience." *Negro Digest* 15, no. 1 (November 1965): 10-17.

_____. "In French-Speaking Africa: The Literary Impact of Negritude." *Negro Digest* 14, no. 7 (May 1965): 70-74.

_____. "Modern African Writers: The Black Writer in Exile." *Negro Digest* 14, no. 2 (December 1964): 54-62.

Nazareth, Peter. *An African View of Literature.* Evanston: Northwestern University Press, 1974.

_____. "The African Writer and Commitment." Letter. *Transition* 19 (1965): 6-7.

_____. "Commitment and the African Writer." Letter. *Transition* 24 (1966): 6-8.

_____. *The Third World Writer: His Social Responsibility.* Nairobi: Kenya Literature Bureau, 1978.

_____. "Verse in 'The Black Hermit.' " Letter. *Transition* 9 (1963): 5.

Nchami, V. C. "Writing for a Living." *West African Review* 23 (1952): 809, 813.

N'Diaye, Papa Gueye. "La Littérature africaine et la critique." *Annales* (Université de Dakar, Faculté des lettres et sciences humaines) 2 (1972): 39-53.

Ndyanabo, Absalom. "Some Reviews of Nigerian Novels." Review of *Blade among the Boys* by Onuora Nzekwu. *Something* 5 (1966): 62-64.

"The Negro Theatre at the Theatre of the Nations." *World Theatre* 9, no. 4 (1960): 344-51.

Nenekhaly-Camara, Condotto. "Conscience nationale et poésie négro-africaine d'expression française." *La Pensée* 103 (1962): 7-17.

Ngande, Charles. "Cameroon Poetry." *Abbia* 2 (1963): 136-37.

Ngugi wa Thiong'o. *Homecoming: Essays on African and Caribbean Literature, Culture and Politics.* New York: Lawrence Hill, 1972.

Nicol, Abioseh. *See also* Davidson Nicol.

_____. "Negritude in West Africa." *New Statesman,* September 10, 1960: 353-54.

Nicol, Davidson. *See also* Abioseh Nicol.

_____. *Africa—A Subjective View.* London: Longmans, 1965.

_____. "Le Progrès industriel transformera la culture noire." *Preuves* 87 (1958): 38-9.

_____. "The Soft Pink Palms." *Présence africaine* n.s. 8-9-10 (1956): 108-21.

Niven, Alastair. "Wars, Skirmishes and Strategies in the Criticism of Modern African Literature." *World Literature Written in English* 19 (1980): 144-51.

Nkosi, Lewis. "The African Critic as a Creator of Values." In *Le Critique africain et son peuple comme producteur de civilisation,* 38-44. Paris: Présence africaine, 1977.

———. "Annals of Apartheid." Reviews of *Emergency* by Richard Rive; *Quartet*, ed. Richard Rive; *A Walk in the Night* by Alex La Guma; and *The Classic* 1, 1-3. *New Statesman*, January 29, 1965: 164-65.

———. "Contemporary African Poetry and Prose." In *A Handbook of African Affairs*, 275-95. Ed. Helen Kitchen. New York: Praeger, 1964.

———. "Fiction by Black South Africans." *Black Orpheus* 19 (1966): 48-54.

———. *Home and Exile.* London: Longman, 1965.

———. "Press Report." In *Conference of African Writers of English Expression*, 1-3. [Paris: Congress for Cultural Freedom, 1962].

———. "Some Conversations with African Writers." *Africa Report* 9, no. 7 (July 1964): 7-21.

———. "The Sting in the Adder's Tail." Review of *Blame Me on History* by Bloke Modisane. *Transition* 12 (1964): 54-55.

———. *Tasks and Masks: Themes and Styles of African Literature.* Harlow, Essex, U.K.: Longman, 1981.

———. "Where Does African Literature Go from Here?" *Africa Report* 9, no. 9 (December 1966): 7-11.

Nwoga, Donatus I. "The Cynical Messenger." Review of *Mission to Kala* by Mongo Beti, trans. Peter Green. *Transition* 16 (1964): 51-2.

———. "Ibo Village Life." Review of *Blade among the Boys* by Onuora Nzekwu. *West Africa*, July 28, 1962: 827.

———. "The Limitations of Universal Critical Criteria." *Dalhousie Review* 53 (1973-1974): 608-30.

———. "West Africa." *Journal of Commonwealth Literature* 1 (1965): 14-19.

Nyunaï, [Jean-Paul]. Review of *Schwarzer Orpheus* by Janheinz Jahn. *Présence africaine* n.s. 1-2 (1955): 164-65.

Nzekwu, Onuora. "An African on Africans." Reviews of *Things Fall Apart* by Chinua Achebe; *One Man, One Wife* by T. M. Aluko; and *Down Second Avenue* by Ezekiel Mphahlele. *Nigeria Magazine* 64 (1960): 105, 107.

Nzouankeu, Jacques Muriel. "L'Africain: pessimiste ou optimiste?" Letter. *Abbia* 3 (1963): 189-90.

———. "Réflexions sur la technique de la nouvelle suivi de 'Les oiseaux qui s'envolent.' " *Abbia* 11 (1965): 111-71; 14-15 (1966): 251-80.

Obiechina, Emmanuel. "Darkness and Light." Reviews of *The Voice* by Gabriel Okara and *Danda* by Nkem Nwankwo. *Nigeria Magazine* 84 (1965): 61-63.

Obumselu, Ben. "The Background of Modern African Literature." *Ibadan* 22 (1966): 46-59.

———. Review of *Things Fall Apart* by Chinua Achebe. *Ibadan* 5 (1959): 37-38.

Ogunba, Oyin. "Theatre in Nigeria." *Présence africaine* 58 (Eng. ed. vol. 30) (1966): 64-88.

Ogundipe, Phebean. "Three Views of 'The Swamp-Dwellers': For What Audience?" *Ibadan* 6 (1959): 29-30.

Ojo, S. Ade. "Subjectivity and Objectivity in the Criticism of Neo-African Literature." *African Perspectives* [Leiden] 1 (1977): 43-54.

Okai, Atukwei. "Literary Criticism and Culture." *West Africa*, July 14, 1980: 1282-85.

Okara, Gabriel. "African Speech . . . English Words." *Transition* 10 (1963): 15-16.

Okara, Robert. Letter. *West Africa*, September 22, 1962: 1050.

Okeke, Alex Chudi. "Ngugi Recounts the Ills of Colonialism." Review of *Weep Not, Child* by James Ngugi. *Record* (Nsukka), October 15, 1966: 4.

Okoye, Mokwugo. *The Rebel Line.* Onitsha: Etudo, Ltd., 1962.

Okpaku, Joseph O. "Culture and Criticism: African Critical Standards for African Literature and the Arts." Editorial. *Journal of the New African Literature and the Arts* 3 (1967): 1-7.

_____. "A Novel for the People." Review of *A Man of the People* by Chinua Achebe. *Journal of the New African Literature and the Arts* 2 (1966): 76-80.

_____. "The Philosophy of the New African Literature." Editorial. *Journal of the New African Literature and the Arts* 1 (1966): 1-2.

_____. "Tradition, Culture and Criticism." *Présence africaine* 70 (1969): 137-46.

Okwu, Edward C. "A Language of Expression for Nigeria." *Nigeria Magazine* 91 (1966): 282-92, 313-15.

Oruwariye, T. O. "Comments." In *Pan-Africanism Reconsidered*, 353-55. Ed. American Society of African Culture. Berkeley: University of California Press, 1962.

Osadebay, D. C., E. L. Lasebikan, and J. H. Nketia. "West African Voices." *African Affairs* (April 1949): 151-58; (July 1949): 242-49.

Osofisan, Femi. "Enter the Carthaginian Critic?" *Okike* 21 (July 1982): 38-44.

Otieno, George. "African Writers' Break Through." Review of *A Reed in the Tide* by J. P. Clark. *East Africa Journal* (December 1966): 43.

Ousmane, Sembène, Cheikh Hamidou Kane, Ousmane Socé, Gérald Félix Tchicaya U Tam'si, and Camara Laye. "The Writers Speak." In *African Literature and the Universities*, 56-73. Ed. Gerald Moore. Ibadan: Ibadan University Press, 1965.

P. A. [*Présence africaine*]. "Language of the Heart." Editorial. *Présence africaine* 58 (Eng. ed. vol. 30) (1966): 5-9.

P. J. *See also* Paulin Joachim.

_____. "Sous l'orage par Seydou Badian." *Bingo* 126 (1963): 47.

Pageard, Robert. "La Recherche de voies nouvelles et la critique de la littérature négro-africaine." *Les Lettres romanes* 32 (1979): 78-83.

Parkes, Frank. "Poetry and Politics." Reviews of *Modern Poetry from Africa*, eds. Gerald Moore and Ulli Beier; *Reflections: Nigerian Prose and Verse*, ed. Frances Ademola; and *Poetry from Black Africa*, ed. Langston Hughes. *West Africa* July 6, 1963: 755, 757.

Poku, O. K. "We Must Develop and Preserve Our Vernaculars." *West African Review* 19 (1948): 900-1.

Porter, Abioseh Michael. "Smohl No Bi Sik: A Preliminary Survey of Pidgin Literature in Cameroon." *Pacific Moana Quarterly* 6, nos. 3-4 (1981): 62-69.

Povey, John F. "Canons of Criticism for Neo-African Literature." In *Proceedings of a Conference on African Languages and Literature Held at Northwestern University April 28-30, 1966*, 73-91. Eds. Jack Berry, Robert Plant Armstrong, and John Povey. [Evanston]: Northwestern University, 1966.

_____. "The Criticism of African Literature: Options for Outsiders." *West African Journal of Modern Languages* 2 (1976): 27-33.

Présence africaine. *See* P. A.

Rabemananjara, Jacques. "Les Fondements de notre unité tirés de l'époque coloniale." *Présence africaine* 24-25 (1959): 66-81.

———. *Nationalisme et problèmes malgaches.* Paris: Présence africaine, 1959.

———. "Préface" to Jean-Joseph Rabearivelo. *Poèmes; Presques-Songes; Traduit de la nuit,* 9-25. New ed. Tananarive: Les Amis de Rabearivelo, 1960.

Ralaimihoatra, E. "J.-J. Rabearivelo (1901-1937)." *Bulletin de Madagascar* 169 (1960): 523-27.

Ramsaran, J. A. Introduction to *New Approaches to African Literature,* 1-4. Ibadan: Ibadan University Press, 1965.

Razafintsambaina, Gabriel. "Les Amis de Rabearivelo." *Bulletin de Madagascar* 170 (1960): 632-37.

"Résolution concernant la littérature." *Présence africaine* 24-25 (1959): 387-92.

Rickford, T. E. W. "Commitment and the Writer." Letter. *Transition* 22 (1965): 6-7.

Rive, Richard. "African Poets in Berlin." *Contrast* 3, no. 3 (1965): 66-9.

———. "Images of Drums and Tom-Toms." *Contrast* 3, no. 1 (1964): 48-54.

———. "No Common Factor." *Contrast* 2, no. 4 (1964): 52-56.

Rubadiri, David. "Why *African* Literature?" *Transition* 15 (1964): 39-42.

Sabor, Pete. "Palm-Wine and Drinkards: African Literature and Its Critics." *Ariel: A Review of International English Literature* 12, no. 3 (1981): 113-25.

Sadji, Abdoulaye. "Culture négro-africaine." *Démocratie nouvelle,* special no. (June 1958): 71-72.

Sartre, Jean-Paul. *Black Orpheus.* Trans. S. W. Allen. Paris: Présence africaine, 1963.

———. "Orphée noir." In *Anthologie de la nouvelle poésie nègre et malgache d'expression française,* ix-xliv. Ed. Léopold Sédar Senghor. Paris: Presses universitaires de France, 1948.

———. "Présentation." *Les Temps modernes* 1 (1945): 1-21.

———. *Qu'est-ce que la littérature?* Paris: Gallimard, 1948.

Schmidt, Nancy Jeanne. "An Anthropological Analysis of Nigerian Fiction." Ph.D. diss., Northwestern University, 1965.

Sebudani, Gaetan. "Perspectives d'une littérature noire d'expression française." *Etudes congolaises* 9, no. 3 (1966): 76-82.

Senanu, K. E. "The Literature of West Africa." In *The Commonwealth Pen: An Introduction to the Literature of the British Commonwealth,* 167-84. Ed. A. L. McLeod. Ithaca: Cornell University Press, 1961.

———. "A Rebel Manque." Review of *No Longer at Ease* by Chinua Achebe. *Universitas* 4, no. 5 (1961): 153.

Sène, Alioune. *Sur le chemin de la négritude.* Le Caire: n.p., 1966.

Senghor, Leopold Sedar. "African-Negro Aesthetics." Trans. Elaine P. Halperin. *Diogenes* 16 (1956): 23-38.

———. "L'Afrique noire." In *Les Plus beaux écrits de l'Union française et du Maghreb,* 163-262. Presented by Mohamed El Kholti, Leopold Cedar [*sic*] Senghor, Pierre Do Dinh, A. Rakoto Ratsimamanga, and E. Ralajmihiatra. Paris: La Colombe, 1947. Also in his *Liberté I.*

———. "L'Afrique s'interroge: Subir ou choisir?" *Présence africaine* 8-9-10 (1950): 437-43. Also in his *Liberté I.*

———. "L'Apport de la poésie nègre au demi-siècle." In his *Liberté I: Négritude et humanisme,* 133-46. Paris: Editions du Seuil, 1964. First appeared in *Témoignage sur la poésie du demi-siècle.* Bruxelles: Editions de la Maison du Poète, 1952.

_____. "Birago Diop." In *Anthologie de la nouvelle poésie nègre et malgache d'expression française*, 135. Ed. Léopold Sédar Senghor. Paris: Presses universitaires de France, 1948.

_____. "Ce que l'homme noir apporte." In S. E. Le Cardinal Verdier et al. *L'Homme de Couleur*, 292-314. Paris: Librarie Plon, 1939. Also in his *Liberté I*.

_____. "Comme les lamantins vont boire à la source." In his *Ethiopiques*, 103-23. Paris: Editions du Seuil, 1956. Also in his *Liberté I*.

_____. "La Contribution négro-africaine à l'édification d'une civilisation mondiale." *Liberté de l'esprit* (June-July 1953): 143-46.

_____. "David Diop." In *Anthologie de la nouvelle poésie nègre et malgache d'expression française*, 173. Ed. Léopold Sédar Senghor. Paris: Presses universitaires de France, 1948.

_____. "De la Poésie bantoue à la poésie négro-africaine." In Gérald-Félix Tchicaya U Tam'si, *Epitome*, 7-13. Tunis: Société nationale d'édition de diffusion, 1962. Also appears as "Tchicaya, ou de la poésie bantoue à la poésie négro-africaine" in his *Liberté I*.

_____. "Eléments constructifs d'une civilisation d'inspiration négro-africaine." *Présence africaine* 24-25 (1959): 249-79.

_____. "Flavien Ranaivo." In *Anthologie de la nouvelle poésie nègre et malgache d'expression française*, 207. Ed. Léopold Sédar Senghor. Paris: Presses universitaires de France, 1948.

_____. "Le Français, langue de culture." *Esprit* 30 (1962): 837-44. Also in his *Liberté I*.

_____. "Hidden Force of Black African Art." Trans. A. Foulke. *Vogue* 148 (December 1966): 236-39, 276-77.

_____. Introduction to *Anthologie de la nouvelle poésie nègre et malgache d'expression française*, 1-2. Ed. Léopold Sédar Senghor. Paris: Presses universitaires de France, 1948.

_____. Introduction to *Liberté I: Négritude et humanisme*, 7-9. Paris: Editions du Seuil, 1964.

_____. "Lamine Niang, poète de la 'Négristique.' " In Lamine Niang, *Négristique*, 7-12. Paris: Présence africaine, 1968. Also in his *Liberté I*, which dates this volume 1963.

_____. "Langage et poésie négro-africaine." *Babel* 7 (1961): 151-59. Also in his *Liberté I*.

_____. "Laye Camara et Lamine Niang ou l'art doit être incarné." *La Condition humaine*, April 22, 1955: 3. Also in his *Liberté I*.

_____. "Laye Camara et Lamine Diakhaté ou l'art n'est pas d'un parti." *La Condition humaine*, July 29, 1954: 1, 3. Also in his *Liberté I*.

_____. "Malick Fall ou une poésie à hauteur d'homme." In Malick Fall, *Reliefs*, 7-14. Paris: Présence africaine, 1964.

_____. "Negritude: A Humanism of the 20th Century." Trans. Clive Wake. *Optima* 16, no. 1 (1966): 1-8.

_____. "Négritude et Civilisation de l'Universel." *Présence africaine* 46 (1963): 8-13. Also appears as "La Littérature africaine d'expression française" in his *Liberté I*.

_____. "Peter Abrahams ou le classique de la négritude." In his *Liberté I: Négritude et humanisme*, 425-30. Paris: Editions du Seuil, 1964. First appeared as preface to Peter Abrahams, *Une Couronne pour Udomo*. Trans. Pierre Singer. Paris: Club bibliophile de France, 1963.

―――. "La Poésie de Pierre Soulages." *Les Cahiers du musée de poche* (January 1960): 15-23. Also in his *Liberté I*.

―――. Préface to Antoine-Roger Bolamba, *Esanzo; chants pour mon pays*, 9-11. Paris: Présence africaine, 1955. Also appears in his *Liberté I* as "Bolamba."

―――. Préface to Birago Diop, *Les Nouveaux contes d'Amadou-Koumba*, 7-23. 3d ed. Paris: Présence africaine, 1958. Also appears in his *Liberté I* as "D'Amadou-Koumba à Birago Diop."

―――. Préface to William J. F. Syad, *Khamsine*, 7-8. Paris: Présence africaine, 1959.

―――. "Le Problème culturel en A.O.F." In his *Liberté I: Négritude et humanisme*, 11-21. Paris: Editions du Seuil, 1964. Speech given at Dakar Chamber of Commerce for the Foyer France-Senegal, September 10, 1937.

―――. "Le Problème de la culture." In his *Liberté I: Négritude et humanisme*, 93-97. Paris: Editions du Seuil, 1964. First appeared in *Journées d'études des indépendants d'outre-mer* (July 1950).

―――. "Le Réalisme d'Amadou Koumba." In Roland Colin, *Les Contes noirs de l'Ouest Africain*, 7-16. Paris: Présence africaine, 1957. Also in his *Liberté I*.

―――. "Sorbonne et négritude." In his *Liberté I: Négritude et humanisme*, 315-19. Paris: Editions du Seuil, 1964. Speech given at Sorbonne, April 21, 1961.

―――. "Les Voix et voie de l'Afrique noire." In Colloque culturel Occident-Afrique noire, *Cultures de l'Afrique noire et de l'Occident*, 49-59. Rome, 1960.

―――. "What Is Negritude?" *West Africa*, November 4, 1961: 1211.

Senghor, Sonar. "Situation du théâtre sénégalaise." *Afrique* (supplémentaire) (1966): 56-58.

Serumaga, Robert. "*The Road* by Wole Soyinka." *Cultural Events in Africa* 11 (1965): i-ii.

Shelton, Austin J. "Critical Criteria for the Study of African Literature." *Literature East & West* 12 (1968): 1-21.

Siafoulaye, Diallo. "En guise de Préface." In Emile Cissé, *Faralako, roman d'un petit village africain*, 9-10. Rennes: Imprimerie commerciale, 1958.

Signaté, Ibrahima. "Sembène Ousmane: Un Jeune écrivain ne doit jamais chercher à plaire." *Jeune Afrique* (Tunis) 279 (May 1, 1966): 37.

Sine, Babakar. "Le Problème de la formation d'une critique endogène et introvertie." In *Le Critique africain et son peuple comme producteur de civilisation*, 220-31. Paris: Présence africaine, 1977.

Society of Nigerian Authors. "The Headline Novels of Africa." *West Africa*, August 25, 1962: 941. Headnote says "the Society of Nigerian Authors . . . was founded this year by Cyprian Ekwensi, Chinua Achebe, Onuora Nzekwu, J. P. Clarke [*sic*] and Wole Soyinka."

Sodipo, Ade. Letter. *West Africa*, June 5, 1954: 513.

Soyinka, Wole. "And After the Narcissist?" *African Forum* 1, no. 4 (1966): 53-64.

―――. "The Critic and Society: Barthes, Leftocracy and Other Mythologies." In *Black Literature and Literary Theory*, 27-57. Ed. Henry Louis Gates, Jr. New York: Methuen, 1984.

―――. "From a Common Back Cloth: A Reassessment of the African Literary Image." *American Scholar* 32 (1963): 387-96.

_____. *Myth, Literature, and the African World*. Cambridge: Cambridge University Press, 1976.

_____. "Nigeria: Culture in Transition." In *Esso World Theatre*, 4. Ed. Esso Education Foundation. New York: Esso Education Foundation, 1964.

Stuart, Donald. "African Literature III: The Modern Writer in His Context." *Journal of Commonwealth Literature* 4 (1967): 113-29.

Tanna, Laura. "African Literature and Its Western Critics." *Abbia* 27-28 (1974): 53-63.

"Tchicaya U Tam'si: Entre le rire et le chant." Interview. *Afrique* 57 (1966): 43-44.

Thomas, Dylan. "Blithe Spirits." Review of *The Palm-Wine Drinkard* by Amos Tutuola. *Observer*, July 6, 1952: 7.

Tidjani-Serpos, Noureini. "Aspects de la critique africaine: méthodologie et perspectives." *Présence francophone* 17 (1978): 97-107.

_____. "La Critique africaine: les critères de recevabilité." In *Le critique africain et son peuple comme producteur de civilisation*, 232-46. Paris: Présence africaine, 1977.

Timothy-Asobele, Jide. "African Masterpiece: What Criteria?" *Nigeria Magazine* 141 (1982): 48-57.

Topor Wolor. "The Role of the African Literary Critic as an Instrument of Innovation." In *Le Critique africain et son peuple comme producteur de civilisation*, 105-20. Paris: Présence africaine, 1977.

Touré, Bachir. "Défense et illustration d'un théâtre africain." *La Vie africaine* 9 (1960): 26-28.

_____. "Les Ensembles de la Côte d'Ivoire et du Mali au Théâtre des Nations." *La Vie africaine* 7 (1960): 12-14.

Towa, Marcien. Review of *Cette Afrique-là* by Jean Ikelle-Matiba. *Abbia* 3 (1963): 184-86.

"Transition Conference Questionnaire." *Transition* 5 (1962): 11-12.

Traoré, Bakary. *The Black African Theatre and Its Social Functions*. Trans. Dapo Adelugba. Ibadan: Ibadan University Press, 1972. First published as *Le Théâtre négro-africain et ses fonctions sociales*. Paris: Présence africaine, 1958.

_____. Préface to Cheik Ndao, *L'Exil d'Albouri suivi de La Decision*. Paris: P. J. Oswald, 1967.

Tucker, Martin. "The Headline Novels of Africa." *West Africa*, July 28, 1962: 829.

Ugirashebuja, Octave. "Senghor poète." *Documents pour l'action* 3, no. 18 (1963): 333-43.

Usman, Yusifu. "Cultural Colonialism." Letter. *West Africa*, October 5, 1963: 1128.

_____. "Muslim Writers." Letter. *West Africa*, November 2, 1963: 1243.

Viderot, Toussaint. "Avant-Propos." In his *Pour toi, Nègre, mon frère . . . "Un homme comme les autres,"* 7-14. Monte Carlo: Regain, 1960.

Vignondé, Jean-Norbert. "Quelle critique pour la littérature africaine?" *Notre librarie* 78 (1985): 9-19.

Vilakazi, B. W. "Some Aspects of Zulu Literature." *African Studies* 1 (1942): 270-74.

Vincent, Theo. "Black Aesthetics and the Criticism of African Literature." *West African Journal of Modern Languages* 2 (1976): 19-25.

_____. Review of *Icheke and Other Poems* by Glory O. Nwanodi. *Black Orpheus* 18 (1965): 58-59.

Wade, Amadou Moustapha. "Autour d'une poésie nationale." *Présence africaine* n.s. 11 (December 1956-January 1957): 84-87.

Wake, C. H. "African Literary Criticism." *Comparative Literature Studies* 1 (1964): 197-205.

Wali, Obiajunwa. "The Dead End of African Literature?" *Transition* 10 (1963): 13-15.

Williams, Adebayo. "The Crisis of Confidence in the Criticism of African Literature." *Présence africaine* 123 (1982): 79-102.

Williams, Adisa. "Men of Two Worlds!" Review of *Arrow of God* by Chinua Achebe. *Spear* (Lagos) (May 1964): 43.

Wright, Edgar. "African Literature I: Problems of Criticism." *Journal of Commonwealth Literature* 2 (1966): 103-12.

_____. "Critical Procedures and the Evaluation of African Literature." In *The Critical Evaluation of African Literature*, 1-22. Ed. Edgar Wright. London: Heinemann, 1973.

Zaourou, Zadi, and Christophe Dailly. "Langue et critique littéraire en Afrique noire," 441-80. In *Le Critique et son peuple comme producteur de civilisation*. Paris: Présence africaine, 1977.

Index

About the Author

RAND BISHOP is an Associate Professor of English at the State University of New York at Oswego. He has contributed articles to *Journal of the New African Literature and the Arts*, *Africana Library Journal*, *Présence africaine*, and *Ba Shiru*.